ACTIVE VISION

D1581700

OXFORD PSYCHOLOGY SERIES

Editors

Mark D'Esposito   Daniel Schacter
Jon Driver   Anne Treisman
Trevor Robbins   Lawrence Weiskrantz

ACTIVE VISION: THE PSYCHOLOGY OF LOOKING AND SEEING

JOHN M. FINDLAY,

*Centre for Vision and Visual Cognition,
Department of Psychology, University of Durham*

and

IAIN D. GILCHRIST,

*Department of Experimental Psychology,
University of Bristol*

OXFORD
UNIVERSITY PRESS

OXFORD
UNIVERSITY PRESS

Great Clarendon Street, Oxford OX2 6DP

Oxford University Press is a department of the University of Oxford.
It furthers the University's objective of excellence in research, scholarship,
and education by publishing worldwide in

Oxford New York

Auckland Bangkok Buenos Aires Cape Town Chennai
Dar es Salaam Delhi Hong Kong Istanbul Karachi Kolkata
Kuala Lumpur Madrid Melbourne Mexico City Mumbai Nairobi
São Paulo Shanghai Taipei Tokyo Toronto

Oxford is a registered trade mark of Oxford University Press
in the UK and in certain other countries

Published in the United States
by Oxford University Press Inc., New York

A catalogue record for this title is available from the British Library

Library of Congress Cataloging in Publication Data

(Data available)

ISBN 0–19–852480–3 (Hbk)
      0–19–852479–X (Pbk)

10 9 8 7 6 5 4 3 2 1

Typeset in 10/12 Minion
by Integra Software Services Pvt. Ltd, Pondicherry, India
www.integra-india.com
Printed in Great Britain
on acid-free paper by T.J. International Ltd., Padstow

To Clare and Josie

CONTENTS

PREFACE

What were the motivations for this book on Active Vision? We can identify many—perhaps too many, since they are not entirely compatible.

First, we had a didactic aim. We both enjoy teaching about our chosen research area and felt a need to summarise our views on vision in a form that would support our teaching. Second, we had an academic aim. Years of experience habituates the practice of digesting and reviewing academic literature. We wished to provide a thorough review of the many facets of the active vision process. Finally, we had a polemic aim. We both believe that much work in visual science has over-emphasised the approach referred to as passive vision in our first chapter and in particular has been too ready to assign importance to covert, rather than overt, attention. We wished to redress the balance.

The Active Vision approach presents a dynamic view of the process of seeing, with a particular emphasis on visual attention. However we contend that *the regular sampling of the environment with eye movements is the normal process of visual attention.* An enormous research effort has been made in recent years directed at understanding covert attention; attending mentally to one location while looking at another. We believe that this balance is wrong and overemphasises a significant, but subsidiary, process in vision to the neglect of a far more important set of processes. As we hope to show in the course of the book, *covert attention acts to supplement overt movements of the eyes, not to substitute for them.*

Our main focus is to provide an account at a functional level. We devote several sections to the neurophysiological substrates underpinning the processes of active vision, but we cannot claim to do much more than provide pointers to the fascinating rapid developments that are occurring in our understanding of the way the brain works. We also provide some pointers to the substantial amount of relevant applied work but again we do not attempt to encompass such topics.

Above all we have attempted to write a book that is readable. In order to do this we have kept the overall length of the book down and as a consequence have been forced to exclude completely discussions of some relevant topics and have skimmed over others. As a result this book is not an exhaustive review of the area and neither did we want it to be—we have instead tried to keep our reader's exhaustion in mind.

Since vision is such an overwhelmingly important part of the human mental make-up, we hope our book may be of use to the many students and teachers attempting to grapple with its mysteries. We anticipate that our book will be of interest to the minority of vision scientists who have already accepted our premise and who have contributed to the wealth of work discussed in the book. This group may find our polemic approach rather quaint. Indeed, even in the three years gestation of the book, progress in the area of active vision has been considerable and the area has become increasingly mainstream. Nevertheless we believe that there is still a large body of individuals interested in how we see, who either ignore or deny the importance of eye sampling. We hope that some of these individuals may nonetheless be tempted to consider our arguments that such ignorance is folly.

We are grateful to the University of Bristol who granted a Benjamin Meaker Fellowship to JF which enabled him to spend a period as Visiting Professor at Bristol and to start work on the enterprise. We have been very appreciative of the support and encouragement of many individuals during the course of the preparation of the book. The staff of Oxford University Press, Vanessa Whitting, Martin Baum and Laura Johnstone assisted in many ways. In addition, the following generously offered comments on chapters or sections: Heiner Deubel, Martin Fischer, Bruce Hood, Christof Körner, Simon Liversedge, Casimir Ludwig, Eugene McSorley, Keith Rayner, Thomas Schenk, Nick Scott-Samuel, Dorine Vergilino-Perez, Françoise Vitu, Robin Walker and Sarah White. As ever, the authors take full responsibility for the text and the inevitable errors and omissions that lie within it. We would be grateful to have our attention drawn to these should readers find them.

John Findlay (j.m.findlay@durham.ac.uk)
Iain Gilchrist (i.d.gilchrist@bristol.ac.uk)

CHAPTER 1

PASSIVE VISION AND ACTIVE VISION

1.1 Introduction

A Martian ethologist observing humans using their visual systems would almost certainly include in their report back: 'they move these small globes around a lot and that's how they see'.

The starting point for this book is an acceptance of the premise of that ethologist. We believe that movements of the eyeballs are a fundamental feature of vision. This viewpoint is not widely current. Many texts on vision do not even mention that the eye can move. In this chapter, we try to outline the reasons why most work on vision pays so little attention to the mobility of the eyes and set out how we feel this balance should be redressed.

1.2 Passive vision

The understanding of vision must stand as one of the great success stories of contemporary science. This project has involved the contribution of a number of key disciplines. It would be impossible to see how such progress could have been made without contributions from psychophysics, mathematics, physiology and computer science. A thumbnail caricature might look as follows.

Science thrives on precise and reproducible results and psychophysics has provided a key methodology for obtaining such results in the area of human vision. Many of its methods are based on determining thresholds. One favoured way to study perception at the threshold is to limit display duration. This, by preventing eye movements, also ensures that a precisely specified stimulation is presented on the retina. Vision is studied 'in a flash' with very brief displays. Mathematics provides ways to formally describe the retinal stimulation. For example, a description widely used in visual studies is based on Fourier analysis. With Fourier analysis any image can be re-described by a series of sine wave patterns. Alongside this, physiologists have investigated single cells, initially in anaesthetised animals, whose properties and patterns of connectivity can also be described precisely. For its part, Computer Science incorporates these insights into attempts to produce machine architectures that could simulate human visual processes. These take as their starting point a static image and attempt to process it with a series of mathematically tractable algorithms. Processing occurs in parallel across the image, and these algorithms chart the progress from a grey-scale retinal input to an internal representation in the head.

We feel sure our readers will recognise this account which we shall term *passive vision*. It is the approach that David Marr explicitly advocated (Marr, 1982) and many others subscribe to. It has led to a thriving research field that has been dominant in visual science in recent years. The passive approach is plausible for two reasons. First, it is undeniable that parallel processing mechanisms deliver a wealth of information in an immediate way to our awareness. This is confirmed by numerous experiments that use very brief exposures and, although these tachistoscopic methods are not without problems, similar information can be obtained from other approaches (see Chapters 5–7). Providing gaze is directed appropriately, a brief exposure will allow recognition of one or two individual simple objects or words and will frequently permit the identification of a face. Such a brief glimpse also permits the extraction of a certain amount of 'gist' information from a natural scene (Chapter 7). We believe that the plausibility of the passive vision approach also comes about because of a second, much less sustainable, reason. We have the subjective impression of an immediate, full detail, pictorial view of the world. We are prone to forget that this impression is, in a very real sense, an illusion. However, this detail is not available in any abstract mental representation (see Section 7.2.6 for some relevant experimental evidence). Rather it is *potentially* available in the environment and can be obtained at any location by directing our eyes there. The illusion is created through our incredible ability to direct our eyes effortlessly to any desired location.

The passive vision approach has been successful, but nonetheless we believe it is inadequate in a variety of ways. We suggest that the most serious of these is the assumption that the main purpose of vision is to form a mental representation. The assumption, in its crudest form, appears to consider that the internal mental representation of the world is a 'processed' representation of the retinal image. The idea of a mental picture in the head would surely be denied at an explicit level by all vision scientists, but we feel that its legacy lurks in many dark corners. Another major weakness of the passive vision approach is that it generally appears to regard the inhomogeneity of the retina and visual projections as rather incidental—often a nuisance because it complicates the mathematics—rather than, as we shall maintain, probably the most fundamental feature of the architecture of the visual system.

Certain perplexing problems emerge as a direct consequence of using a passive vision approach. These have often appeared to be the most difficult ones to envisage a solution. One immediate issue concerns the vast amount of neural machinery that would be required to process the visual information from all retinal locations. In addition, more processing machinery would be required to deal with two further questions. The first problem concerns how the supposed internal representation produced by passive vision might be maintained when the eyes are moved. This issue, *trans-saccadic integration*, becomes more acute as the amount of information assigned to the mental representation is increased. A process 'compensating' for the movement of the eyes is frequently invoked, at least in textbooks of vision. Integration of information across saccadic eye movements undoubtedly occurs, as we shall discuss in Chapters 5, 7 and 9. However it is not 'compensatory', and is on a much more limited scale than passive vision would require. The second problem is known as the *binding problem* (Feldman, 1985; Treisman, 1996). Visual processing mechanisms are generally recognised to be analytic, delivering information about the local presence of a particular visual feature, such as a red colour or a horizontal orientation. The binding problem is the problem of integrating these features in a veridical way, so that when a red horizontal line and a blue vertical line are presented together, the perception is of this combination rather than blue horizontal and red vertical. Solutions offered to the binding problem from passive vision workers have generally involved the concept of visual attention. As we discuss in the next section, active vision requires a major change in the way visual attention is conceived.

1.3 Visual attention

We shall be very concerned in this book with the processes of visual attention. Traditionally, when the term is used in relation to perception, attention implies selectivity. Attention is the preferential processing of some items to the detriment of others. Traditionally also, selection of a *location* where attention is directed is important, although this is not the only way in which selectivity can occur. Attentional selection of a region of visual space can be made in two distinct ways. We say that something 'catches our eye' when we orient and look at it. We can, however, also look at one thing and be attending to another. *Overt attention* is the term we will use to describe attending by means of looking and *covert attention* will be used to describe attending without looking, often colloquially termed looking out of the corner of the eye.

The past two decades have seen an intensive investigation into the properties of covert attention (for summaries, see Pashler, 1998; Styles, 1997; Wright, 1998). We shall make frequent reference to many important findings in the following pages. Taking an overall perspective, however, we are concerned that much of this work has failed to escape the pitfalls that we have noted in our discussion of passive vision. The uniform mental image view lurking within passive vision is often accepted uncritically and covert attention is seen as a 'mental spotlight' that can be directed to any location on this hypothesised internal image. Little consideration is given to the rapid decline of visual capacities away from the fovea (nonhomogeneous visual field representation and lateral masking as described in Chapter 2). We have no wish to deny that much experimental work studying covert visual attention has been ingenious, thorough and illuminating. Our criticism is rather directed to the assumption, often held implicitly, that covert attention forms the main means of attentional selection and that the findings of passive vision, together with an account of covert attention, might integrate to give a complete and coherent picture of visual perception.

Many workers emphasize the cognitive processes of covert attention to the exclusion or downgrading of peripheral motor overt attention. A clear demonstration of this thinking is seen in a recent text. Styles (1997) states 'Of course, visual attention is intimately related to where we are looking and to eye movements. Perhaps there is nothing much to explain here; we just attend to what we are looking at.' We disagree profoundly with this viewpoint which illustrates succinctly the disdain often found amongst cognitive psychologists and others for the study of anything other than 'pure' mental activity. What we shall try to do in this book is delineate a different perspective, in which overt attention plays the major role in attention selectivity. When attention is redirected overtly by moving the gaze, rather than covertly, the attended location obtains the immediate benefit of high-resolution foveal vision. In general, the eyes can be moved quickly and efficiently. Why would it make sense to use covert attention instead? We shall consider possible answers to this question in Chapter 3. In Chapters 5 and 6 we shall discuss the phenomenon of peripheral preview and show how covert attention acts in an efficient way to supplement overt eye scanning.

The arguments presented in this section and the preceding one lead to an interpretation of vision which differs considerably from the conventional one. We argue that the parallel processes of passive vision can achieve relatively little unless supplemented by the serial process of eye scanning. The regular rhythm of saccadic movements at a rate of 3–4 gaze redirections per second is an integral and crucial part of the process of visual perception. The study of the way these saccadic movements are generated and integrated forms the topic of active vision.

1.4 Active vision

To recapitulate the arguments of the previous sections, in this book we shall emphasize the contributions made by gaze shifts to visual perception and cognition. We reject as highly inadequate the view that vision is simply a process of passive image interpretation. Rejection of a dominant paradigm in visual science for many years cannot be made lightly but we feel that various strands of thinking now justify such a rejection.

What are the critical questions of active vision? A primary question concerns how visual sampling is achieved. All evidence points to the fact that the answer relates to the fixation-move-fixation rhythm. This pattern is found in the vision of humans, most other vertebrates and some invertebrates, although intriguing variants also occur (Land, 1995; Land and Nilsson, 2002). We are then led to the following set of inter-related questions

a) how is the decision made when to terminate one fixation and move the gaze?

b) how is the decision made where to direct the gaze in order to take the next sample?

c) what information is taken in during a fixation?

d) how is information from one fixation integrated with that from previous and subsequent fixations?

These are the questions that this book sets out to address

How might active vision be investigated? Since we are concerned with active redirections of gaze, an obvious starting point would appear to be to record patterns of gaze redirection. This is technically challenging but a variety of devices have been designed over the years which have adequately met this challenge. We shall not discuss technical details in this book, but a good recent account is provided by Collewijn (1998). Records of eye scanning such as those shown in Figs. 7.1 and 7.2 are often reproduced.

One of the major emphases of the new approach concerns the inhomogeneity of the visual system. We have pointed out that much thinking in passive vision implicitly downplays the role of the fovea. We make the counterargument that the radial organisation of the visual system based on the fovea is far from co-incidental but is rather its most fundamental feature. A simple but telling argument considers a hypothetical brain, which provided the same high resolution as found in human foveal vision at all locations in the visual field. It has been calculated that such a hypothetical brain would be some hundreds of thousands times larger than our current brain and so would weigh perhaps ten tons. A mobile eye constructed on the principles of the vertebrate eye is not a co-incidence or a luxury but is very probably the only way in which a visual system can combine high resolution with the ability to monitor the whole visual field.

Mobility of the eye is most obviously achieved by the six extraocular muscles and, in general, study of 'eye movements' has referred to the study of movements made by these muscles. It is important to realise that the extraocular muscles provide only one way in which human eye mobility occurs. Orienting movements larger than about 20 degrees are normally achieved by a combination of head and eye movements and for very large re-orientations, trunk and whole body movements also take place. We discuss in Chapter 8 an individual whose eye muscles are non-functional. She has good vision and achieves this by moving her head in order to redirect her eyes. Her head movements show many similar features to the eye movements in an unimpaired individual and in particular show a clear sequence of fixations and movements like saccades.

The development of the need for a new approach can be traced through various papers in the 1990s. Nakayama (1992) pointed to the gap between studies of low level vision and those of high level vision, arguing that increased understanding of low level vision could not expect to bridge the gap. O'Regan (1992) argued that the 'real mysteries of visual perception' were not elucidated by the traditional approach and instead argued for an approach similar to that we propose. A polemic article entitled 'A critique of pure vision' (Churchland *et al.*, 1994) argued that the 'picture in the head' metaphor for vision was still much too pervasive among vision scientists. Another important impetus came from workers in computer vision who became dissatisfied with the lack of progress made by the parallel processing and sought to include a serial contribution (e.g. Ballard, 1991). It is from this quarter that the term 'Active Vision' originated (Aloimonos *et al.*, 1988). The suggestion that activities such as the sampling movements of the eyes 'provide an essential link between processes underlying elemental perceptual events and those involved in symbol manipulation and the organisation of complex behaviors' was made in an important article by Ballard *et al.* (1997) to be discussed in Chapter 7 (see also Hayhoe, 2000).

1.5 Active vision and vision for action

In fact, for many years, the passive vision approach has been complemented by work in which vision controls and supports action. One early trenchant critic of passive vision was Gibson (1966, 1979), whose position has become well known. Gibson appreciated the limitations of the passive approach and also appreciated, in a far-sighted way, that a major function of vision was to direct action. However, his concentration on optic flow, and neglect of the details of how the eyes work, led to an account that was limited and sometimes simply incorrect. In particular, recent work has made important advances by emphasising the importance of a fovea within the general area of vision for action. (Regan and Beverley, 1982; Rushton *et al.*, 1998; Wann 1996; Wann and Land, 2000).

Gibson also appreciated that eye movements were used to sample the visual world, apparently believing that these were in turn directed by the visual array as shown in the following extract

What causes the eyes to move in one direction rather than another, and to stop at one part of the array instead of another? The answer can only be that interesting structures in the array, and interesting bits of structure, particularly motions, *draw* the foveas towards them. (Gibson, 1966)

Gibson's stance on this issue anticipates some of the ideas in this book. However his exclusive emphasis on the environment, perhaps arising from his unwillingness to countenance any cognitive contribution to perception, appears somewhat dogmatic. We argue that the sampling procedure is the very place where cognitive contributions to perception occur. The eye samples what is interesting but what is interesting can change from moment to moment, guided by the observer's thought processes and action plans.

We agree with Gibson's view that vision evolved to support behaviour but do not accept the necessity for the link to be always as direct as the vision-action sequences which are usually associated with his approach. We discuss (Section 2.2) the important proposal (Milner and Goodale, 1995) that vision for recognition and vision for action are two separable functions of vision. While we believe this proposal has considerable merit, we do not find that it is easy to assign the sampling movements of the eyes exclusively to either the recognition side or the action side of the picture. Thus, for example, both dorsal and ventral streams converge on the frontal eye fields, a major centre for saccade generation (Schall and Hanes, 1998). Saccades are an action system in that they are a visually controlled motor response. However they are not just this, since their operation controls the input visual sampling also. Their involvement with vision takes the form of a continuously cycling loop, so that vision and cognition can integrate in an intimate way. This interaction was indeed proposed many years ago by Neisser (1976) who introduced the idea of the 'perceptual cycle' as a way of reconciling the Gibsonian and mainstream approaches to perception.

1.6 Outline of the book

In Chapter 2 we discuss in more detail the necessary background to the active vision approach. As discussed above, properties of both the visual system and the oculomotor system are important here.

One theme that is important throughout the book is *attention*; Chapter 3 discusses this topic in depth and looks in detail at the relationship between covert and overt attention and the part both processes play in visual selection.

Chapter 4 contains a summary of work dealing with gaze *orienting* to simple, clearly defined targets. This task has minimal cognitive involvement and thus investigations are directed to questions about the basic mechanisms of orienting. Nevertheless, some important principles emerge from these studies concerning, for example, preparatory processes, visual spatial integration, etc. Moreover, studies in this area can be related in a convincing way to the brain neurophysiology of eye movements and orienting movements. Brain mechanisms are not our primary consideration in the book but in various places we show how closely the ideas of active vision find neurophysiological parallels and sketch some of the recent advances made in this rapidly developing area. The final section of this chapter considers a longer term perspective, showing how the orienting process develops in infancy and is kept in tune by various self-correcting mechanisms.

One area of perceptual psychology where the active vision perspective has long been the dominant paradigm is the area of *reading*, discussed in Chapter 5. When reading text, sampling takes place very largely in a predetermined sequence from left to right along each successive line and the reader has a clear cut goal of extracting information from the print. These constraints have enabled scientific progress to be made in relation to all four of the key questions of active vision. A particularly influential breakthrough came with the development of the *gaze-contingent* methodology in which the material viewed could be manipulated in relation to where the gaze was directed. Reading provides a situation in which high-level cognitive activity is present. There is little doubt that the reader's cognitive processes affect the visual sampling in a direct way but a lively debate is still in progress about the extent and nature of these influences.

In the past decade, a number of workers have appreciated that the task of *visual search* can also provide a constrained methodology suitable for attacking the questions of active vision. In a visual search task, an observer is looking for a specified target which, as with reading, involves the observer's cognitive mechanisms but in a limited and constrained way. Visual search is discussed in Chapter 6. Another reason for the development of visual search as an important area concerns the insight, associated with the work of Anne Treisman (Treisman and Gelade, 1980), that perceptually serial and perceptually parallel processes interact in visual search. Although we take issue with the specific way that Treisman and many subsequent workers have developed these ideas, we fully acknowledge their fundamental importance.

Arguments have already been advanced about the difficulty of interpreting visual exploratory behaviour in the more general case of scene or picture scanning. Statistical generalisations can be made such as that which provides the title of a classic paper by Mackworth and Morandi (1967): 'The gaze selects informative detail within pictures.' Chapter 7 reviews this type of work as well as looking at some exciting recent developments where active vision is studied in freely moving observers.

An important theme in current cognitive neuroscience is that great insights can be obtained by studying disorders of function. Chapter 8 considers a number of pathologies that provide insights into the nature of active vision. This chapter does not attempt to provide a complete encyclopaedia for the neuropsychology of active vision but instead highlights a number of disorders that provide particular constraints on the form that an active vision theory should take.

The final chapter (Chapter 9) discusses experimental work but also works towards a theoretical synthesis based around important new findings showing how information is integrated across eye movements.

We have emphasized throughout the book our belief that overt gaze orienting is an essential feature of vision. We give particular critical focus to the idea that every overt shift of attention is preceded by a covert mental shift. Does this view escape the infinite regress associated with the concept of an homunculus? The attempt, which permeates the book, to understand when and why the gaze is redirected is in essence an attempt to understand the processes behind an activity that is recognisably voluntary. Active vision studies are studies of how the brain makes up its mind.

CHAPTER 2

BACKGROUND T'
ACTIVE VISION

2.1 Introduction

In this chapter we shall discuss features of the visual and oculomotor systems that are particularly important for understanding active vision. The accounts of both systems will be highly selective and specific to our perspective. Many detailed reference works are available (Carpenter, 1988; Cronly-Dillon, 1991; Wurtz and Goldberg, 1989; are good sources).

We argued in Chapter 1 that the passive vision approach contains many pitfalls. While the existence of a fovea may be acknowledged at some point in such accounts, its importance is very often downplayed. Many discussions of visual perception make the implicit assumption that the starting point is a homogeneous 'retinal' image. We suggest this approach is misguided for at least three reasons. First, and most obvious, it neglects a basic feature of visual physiology and psychophysics, which is that the visual projections are organised so that the projections away from the central regions are given uniformly decreasing weighting. Second, it frequently leads to the assumption that the properties of foveal vision, for example faithful spatial projections, are found throughout the visual field. Third, accounts of visual perception starting from this basis frequently require supplementation with an attentional process such as a 'mental spotlight'. As we discuss in Chapter 3, we believe that this approach to visual attention is misguided.

Active vision takes as its starting point the inhomogeneity of the retina, seeing the fovea not simply as a region of high acuity, but as the location at which visual activity is centred. Moreover, vision away from the fovea must also be treated differently. Traditionally, vision away from the fovea is regarded as a degraded version of foveal vision, but serving the same purpose. In the active vision account, some visual representation is formed away from the fovea (although this representation turns out to be much less substantial than might be expected) but the major role of peripheral vision is to provide the appropriate information for subsequent orienting movements and foveal recognition.

The inhomogeneity of the visual projections

2.2.1 Introduction

In this section we shall largely be discussing the properties of vision away from the line of sight. For a single eye, the convention for specifying a location in peripheral vision is simple and straightforward. The *angle of eccentricity*, as shown in Fig. 2.1, measures the angle between the *visual axis* where the fovea is directed, and the peripheral location under consideration. Its complete specification involves both the angular distance from the fovea and the direction in the visual field, measured with reference to the axes up-down and left-right (or nasal-temporal). The term *perimetry* is used to describe the systematic measurement of peripheral vision throughout the visual field. A typical perimetric plot, as shown in Fig. 2.2, would show some visual property plotted with reference to the visual field. The projections are organised so that properties change gradually and systematically from the central fovea into the periphery, rather than with sudden transitions. This means that designation of subregions within the peripheral visual field, and even the designation of the foveal region itself, has no basis other than descriptive convenience. However it is often customary to delineate the *foveal* region, extending out to an angle of eccentricity of 1°, the *parafoveal* region from 1° to 5°, and the *peripheral* region encompassing the remainder of the visual field.

For most purposes in active vision, we can justify a treatment that is monocular. Vision evolved primarily as a distal sense. If the eyes are both directed to a point in a frontoparallel plane at 40 cm (a typical viewing distance for a VDU screen), other objects in this plane will have an eccentricity only about 1 per cent different between the two eyes. Of course when an activity involves viewing objects at different distances, considerations of retinal disparity come into play (Section 2.5.2).

Many visual functions show gradually declining ability as the stimuli are placed more eccentrically (Section 2.2.2). However, there are important exceptions.

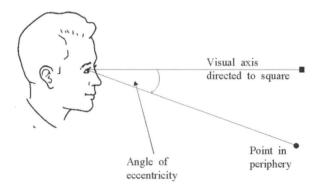

Figure 2.1 Demonstration of the angle of eccentricity.

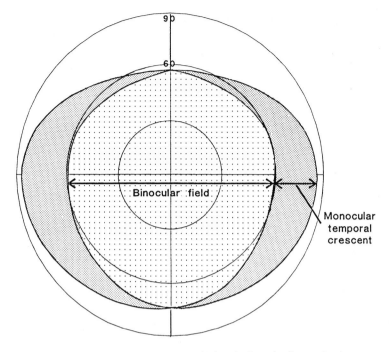

Figure 2.2 An example of a perimetric chart, in which a plot is made of some visual property at locations throughout the visual field. The centre of the plot corresponds to the foveal axis and the vertical and horizontal scales are the visual axes up/down and nasal/temporal respectively. This particular plot (from Henson, 1993) shows the extent of the visual field that is seen with each eye, and also the area of the binocular field, seen with both eyes.

Monitoring for change in the visual environment is a function of peripheral vision that has obvious evolutionary significance. Hence it is not surprising to find that some variables connected with temporal change, such as flicker and movement sensitivity, do not follow the general rule of declining abilities but actually demonstrate improved peripheral performance (Baker and Braddick, 1985).

2.2.2 Physiology of the visual projections

Anatomical descriptions of ocular structure have always provided an important launch point for visual science. Study of the retina with suitable microscopic techniques has yielded several basic facts about the specialised foveal region. First, the retinal surface is generally flat, but has a shallow pit (Fig. 2.3) of diameter about 1500 μm coinciding with the area of acute vision. The thinning of the retinal layers occurs because, although the photoreceptors (cones) are present in their highest density within this region, the other visual cells of the retina (bipolar, horizontal, amacrine and ganglion cells) are displaced towards

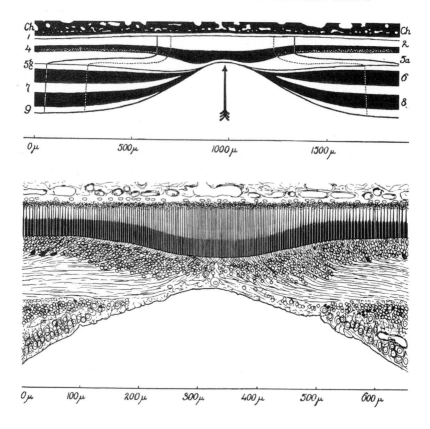

Figure 2.3 Cross-section of the human retina through the foveal area (from Polyak, 1957). Measurements on the retina are given in microns: 1 degree of visual angle corresponds approximately to 300 microns.

the periphery away from the pit. This leaves a thinner retinal layer, presumably improving the optical quality of the image on the photoreceptors. The diameter of this pit corresponds to a visual angle of 5°, according to Polyak (1957), and is thus somewhat greater than the usually accepted functional definition of the size of the fovea. The term *foveola* has been used to delineate the region in the very centre of the pit, although, as with the fovea itself, the boundary is arbitrary. In fact, cone density continues to increase to the very centre of the foveola, where the intercone spacing is about 2.5 μm, decreasing to a value of 5 μm at 1° eccentricity (Hirsch and Curcio, 1989). Visual acuity appears to show a similar result, being best in the very centre of the fovea. In approximate correspondence with this depression, there is a region of retina that contains only cones. The rod-free region has a diameter of somewhat less than one degree (Hirsch and Curcio, 1989). A final related demonstration from the anatomists is that a region of yellow pigmentation is often observed over the fovea. This yellow spot is termed the *macula* or *macula lutea, macular vision* being an alternative term for foveal vision.

The photoreceptors initiate the neural processing of the visual signal, which then proceeds through the retina to the ganglion cells and along the optic nerve to the visual centres of the brain. Local spatial interactions play a highly important role in the processes of adaptation and receptive field formation. However, a key feature of the visual projections is their topographic or retinotopic mapping, whereby neighbourhood relationships are maintained and the map of the retinal surface is reproduced in the ganglion cell and subsequent levels. Directional relationships within the map are maintained faithfully but a transformation occurs whereby more central regions are given an increasing proportion of the representation as the signal proceeds. From the retinal ganglion cell layer, the optic nerve sends the visual signal to the visual cortex, through the lateral geniculate nucleus of the thalamus. In primates, this is the principal projection pathway but a number of subsidiary pathways split off at the stage of the optic tract (following the partial crossover of fibres at the optic chiasm). The most substantial of these projections goes to the *superior colliculus*, a midbrain region of particular concern in active vision.

Figure 2.4 shows very schematically a remapping in which the central regions are disproportionately emphasized but the topology is maintained. It is widely accepted that the visual remapping has this general character. The magnification appears to come about because of transformations both in the cone $\rightarrow$ ganglion cell projections and also in the ganglion cell $\rightarrow$ striate cortex projections (Azzopardi and Cowey, 1993; Drasdo, 1991).

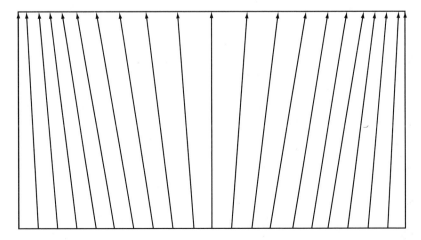

Figure 2.4 Schematic remapping in which topological relationships are maintained but increased magnification is given to the central region.

The *magnification factor* is the term used to describe the quantitative properties of the remapping and is defined as the distance on the cortical surface that corresponds to one degree of visual angle (Wilson *et al.*, 1990). For the purposes of this book, the absolute value of the magnification factor is of less significance than the manner in which the factor changes with eccentricity (E). The expression

$$M = M_f /(1 + E/E_s) \qquad (2.1)$$

gives a reasonably accurate representation of experimental findings concerning the magnification factor. M_f is a constant (ca. 1 cm/deg) showing the value at the fovea. E_S gives the scaling factor and shows the eccentricity where magnification has fallen to half its foveal value. Estimates between 0.3° and 0.9° have been obtained (Wilson *et al.*, 1990), and it has been suggested that different values may apply to magnocellular and parvocellular systems (Section 2.3.1). An alternative description of the projection between retina and cortex has been proposed by Schwartz (1980), who notes that the projection can be well approximated by the following mathematically elegant transformation

$$u(r,\phi) = \log r$$
$$v(r,\phi) = \phi \qquad (2.2)$$

Here r and Φ define a point in peripheral vision using radial co-ordinates while u and v describe the corresponding point in the cortical map using Cartesian co-ordinates.

2.2.3 Psychophysical performance in peripheral vision

Wertheim (1894) carried out a careful set of studies in which he plotted the ability to resolve a grating target presented at various positions in the visual periphery. His findings (Fig. 2.5) show that, for the range of values up to about 20 degrees in the near periphery, a surprisingly tight linear relationship between the size of the just resolvable grating and the angle of visual eccentricity. Similar results have been obtained by subsequent workers. It is possible, to a quite good approximation, to describe the decline in acuity by the following function

$$V_E = V_f /(1 + E/E_s) \qquad (2.3)$$

where V_E is the acuity at eccentricity E, V_f is the acuity at the fovea and E_S is a scaling constant, which may be interpreted as the point at which the acuity has declined to one-half of its value at the fovea. For grating acuity, the constant is approximately 2.5° (Wilson *et al.*, 1990). As a rough approximation for some purposes, the constant component can be ignored and, as demonstrated by Anstis (1974), this leads to the simple but important approximate property of peripheral vision shown in Fig. 2.6.

Figure 2.7 also shows how acuity declines in the periphery, using a somewhat different procedure. In this example, the discrimination tested was the

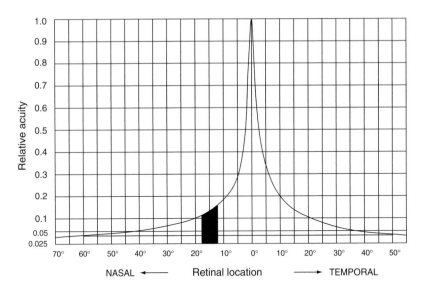

Figure 2.5 Measurement of grating acuity at various locations in the visual field. The black area shows the blind spot. Redrawn from Wertheim (1894).

identification of single letters, presented individually at different retinal locations. Two points are at once apparent. First, in a similar manner to the grating discrimination shown in Fig. 2.5, the discrimination ability declines gradually as the stimuli are placed more eccentrically. There is an extensive region over which partial, but imperfect, discrimination is possible. Second, discrimination is profoundly affected by the presence of 'irrelevant' surrounding contours. This is the phenomenon of *lateral masking*, discussed further below.

One obvious consequence of the decline in acuity is that certain discriminations become impossible when the stimuli are presented outside a certain central region. This region has been variously named the *stationary field* (Sanders, 1963), *conspicuity area* (Engel, 1971), *functional field of view* (Ikeda and Takeuchi, 1975), *useful field of view* (Bouma, 1978) or *visual lobe* (Courtney and Chan, 1986). Sanders (1963) also introduced the terms *eye field* and *head field* to denote the regions of the visual field where discriminations could be made by using eye movements alone and in association with head movements respectively (Section 4.1).

The conspicuity region is influenced by the specific task situation. Conspicuity areas shrink when the subject has a second foveal task, simultaneous with the peripheral task (Ikeda and Takeuchi, 1975), but are extended in a direction to which the subject is encouraged to direct covert attention (Engel, 1971). Conspicuity areas become particularly significant in tasks of visual search (Section 6.3.2).

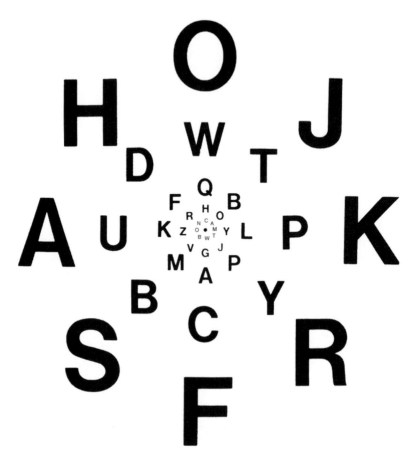

Figure 2.6 A consequence of the variation in visual acuity with retinal eccentricity. When the centre of the display is fixated, each letter is at ten times its threshold legibility. This relationship applies, at least to a first approximation, regardless of viewing distance. From Anstis (1974).

2.2.4 Comparison of psychophysical and physiological measures

To what extent can the decline in visual abilities away from the fovea be *directly* attributable to the differential magnification in the visual pathways discussed in Section 2.2.1? Virsu and Rovamo (1979) suggested that different retinal patterns, which produce the *same* activation pattern on the visual cortex, will be equally discriminable. This implies that discriminability differences are all attributable to the differential magnification. As Virsu and Rovamo showed, this argument seems justifiable on the basis of the data for the case of certain discriminations, where the form of the decline in ability with eccentricity closely matches that of the cortical magnification factor. However in other cases, it is apparent that some further factor needs to be taken into account.

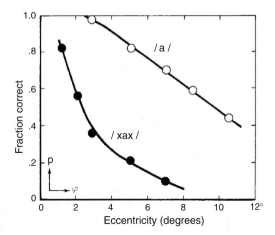

Figure 2.7 Lateral masking. Bouma (1978) required individuals to identify single alphabetic letters at various locations in the visual periphery. For the /a/ plot, the letter was presented in isolation. For the /xax/ plot, the letter was presented with flanking letter x's on either side. Even though the flanking letters were the same on every occasion, their presence profoundly affected the ability to identify the target letter.

There is an obvious similarity between eqs. 2.1 and 2.3, but the scaling factor is substantially different in the two cases. However, for another basic visual task, vernier alignment acuity, psychophysical experiments show that the value of E_s is much less than in the case of grating acuity, implying that vernier acuity is subject to a much greater relative degradation in the visual periphery. In this case, the scaling factor is close to that for the cortical magnification. Wilson et al., (1990) suggest that vernier acuity shows cortical magnification limits whereas grating acuity is limited by the spacing of adjacent cones of the retina.

An important difference between the two forms of acuity is that vernier acuity requires judgement of a localisation difference, whereas detection of a grating can be done solely on the basis of a contrast difference between neighbouring regions. A recent study (Toet and Levi, 1992) of the phenomenon of lateral masking (Fig. 2.7) (study of the lateral masking effect) shows that the interference operates over an increasingly wide range, as stimuli are made more peripheral. Toet and Levi also noted considerable differences among individuals in the extent of lateral masking.

2.3 Parallel visual pathways

2.3.1 Magnocellular and parvocellular systems

Topographic mapping from the retina to the cortex was one fact underpinning the passive vision approach we have criticised in Chapter 1. For quite some time, the view held that the visual pathway transmitted a signal from the retinal image in a monolithic way. One of the most important advances in visual science in recent years has been the appreciation of the existence of multiple types of nerve cell in the visual pathways. As early as 1966, Enroth-Cugell and Robson had demonstrated the presence of X- and Y-cells in cat retina but some time elapsed before the acceptance that a similar division occurred in the primate pathways.

The past two decades have seen the clarification of the distinction between the *magnocellular* (M) and the *parvocellular* (P) categories of cells in primate visual pathways. This nomenclature is based on a clear separation at the level of the lateral geniculate nucleus where the two cell types separate into distinct layers. However the separation of the cell types is also found in the retina, through to the cortex (Schiller and Logothetis, 1990). It is further suggested that the two cell types remain largely separated as two separate processing streams within the cortex (see next section) although there is considerable evidence of convergence from both streams in some cortical areas (Ferrera *et al.*, 1992; Maunsell *et al.*, 1990).

M and P cells are present in both central and peripheral retina, although the relative proportions differ. This has somewhat complicated the establishment of their properties, since the characteristics vary within each population, particularly between cells corresponding to different retinal regions. However, there is now general acceptance that the two cell types differ in a substantial number of ways, set out in Table 2.1. While the distinction between M and P cells is very widely accepted, the significance of the distinction has remained somewhat elusive. M cells have high contrast gain and fast response and thus

Table 2.1 Differential properties of cells in the magnocellular and parvocellular systems. For many of the properties (e.g. receptive field size), the property changes systematically with retinal eccentricity but at any particular eccentricity, the listed differentiation is found. Based on Kaplan *et al.* (1990) and Lennie (1993).

	Parvocellular system	Magnocellular system
Estimated number of cells (millions)	1.2	0.15
Percentage of ganglion cell total	80	10
Distribution on retina	Densest in fovea	Densest in fovea? (but more distributed)
Conduction velocity of axons	~6 m/sec	~15 m/sec
Response to stimulus onset	Tonic (sustained)	Phasic (transient)
Motion sensitivity	Lower	Higher
Receptive field size	Smaller	Larger (also periphery effects)
Spatial frequency sensitivity	Higher	Lower
Linear summation	Linear	Many non-linear
Contrast sensitivity	Lower	Higher (and saturates)
Contrast gain	Lower	Higher (8–10 times as high)
Colour sensitivity	Shown by many cells	None

are well suited for signalling the existence of a sudden change and it is thus very likely that they play a role in the dynamic processes of active vision. P cells, with more linear properties and small receptive field, seem well suited for signalling details of visual forms.

2.3.2 Visual processing in the cortex

Physiological studies of the cortex have shown the dominance and importance of the visual modality. Over much of the posterior half of the cortex, involving parts classified as occipital, parietal and temporal, cells are visually responsive and some degree of retinotopic mapping is retained. A large number (30+) of separate retinotopic maps, or visual areas, have been identified. Cells in each map possess different response properties and the analogy (Zeki, 1993), which considers the visual brain as an *atlas*, has some validity although it is certainly not the case that familiar visual properties such as colour and motion are exclusively differentiated into different areas.

There are well-known and visually attractive diagrams such as those of Felleman and Van Essen (1991), which lay out the cortical areas and their interconnectivity patterns. For many purposes, this level of detail is over-whelming and considerable impact has been made by a simplificatory scheme first proposed by Ungerleider and Mishkin (1982). While acknowledging the multiplicity of interconnecting pathways between cortical visual areas, they suggested that two principal routes relaying the incoming information from visual cortex could be distinguished (Fig. 2.8). A *dorsal stream* runs from occipital to parietal cortex and a *ventral stream* runs from occipital to

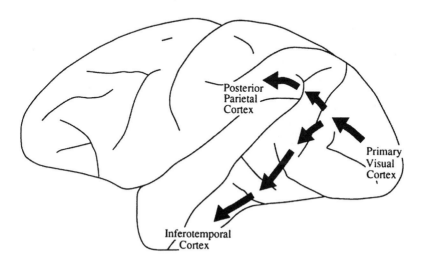

Figure 2.8 The dorsal and ventral streams. Two groupings of pathways that leave the primary visual cortex and can be traced through to parietal and temporal cortices respectively (from Ungerleider and Mishkin, 1982, as redrawn by Milner and Goodale, 1995).

temporal cortex. They suggested, on the basis of work that examined the differential effects of damage to the respective streams, that the ventral stream carried information for visual recognition, and the dorsal stream carried information relating to visuospatial awareness. Livingstone and Hubel (1987), in an influential paper, suggested that the M and P pathways, described above, map onto the cortical routes. This suggestion, however, has proved controversial (Merigan and Maunsell, 1993).

More recent work has modified and refined the original suggestion. Melvyn Goodale and David Milner have introduced a subtle amendment to the original distinction (Goodale and Milner, 1992; Milner and Goodale, 1995). In their modified scheme, the ventral stream supports Vision for Recognition in a similar way to the earlier account. However the dorsal stream, termed Vision for Action, provides for a series of direct vision-action links rather than any more reflective use of vision. In support of their revised position, they describe a patient, DF, who is able to carry out visuo-spatial tasks involving oriented objects (posting blocks through a slot) but has no awareness of the details of the process involved and cannot identify object orientations verbally. The relationship between vision and awareness is a complex topic of considerable current interest, and further discussion is given in Chapter 8. Recent physiological work has provided support for the position by showing that dorsal pathways project to motor areas of the frontal cortex, and their properties support visually guided actions in a rather direct way (Sakata *et al.*, 1997). The cells in the dorsal $\rightarrow$ motor route show a gradual transformation from a visual sensory signal to a motor output signal. We shall encounter a similar gradual transformation in connection with orienting saccades in Chapter 4.

How should the action/recognition distinction be linked to our passive/active vision distinction? The idea that vision operates in the support of action is a clear and welcome advance on the passive vision view. Making a more detailed link is not straightforward, first because the action/recognition distinction largely concentrates on the level of overall visual tasks rather than the subcomponents of these tasks, which is where active vision makes its contribution. There is evidence that areas of the dorsal pathway in the parietal lobe are very concerned with saccadic eye movements (Section 2.5.4). It might thus appear that orienting is simply another 'action' which vision can support. We suggest though that many visual activities involve intimate integration of action and recognition. The example of tea making, where action involves a number of utensils and substances, will receive some discussion in Chapter 7. In our analysis, we shall wish to argue that the orienting (looking) processes characteristics of active vision are indeed visual actions but also often intimately linked to recognition processes.

Another form of parallel processing occurs because the physiological pathways leaving the retina in fact project to several different brain regions. The geniculo-cortical route discussed above is, in primates, the largest and most extensively studied of the visual pathways but visual information is also directed via several other pathways to brain centres such as the superior colliculus, sites in the pretectum, and elsewhere (Milner and Goodale, 1995). A traditional view of these pathways is that they are associated with 'reflex eye-movements'. Although much evidence supports this view, it turns out, rather surprisingly, that the fastest eye responses use cortical pathways (Miles, 1995, 1998).

2.4 The oculomotor system

The essence of active vision is continual sampling through gaze redirection. Although this can be achieved without the use of eye muscles, there is no doubt that the process is achieved most efficiently by using these muscles and that for many human activities, eye movements form the principal means of supporting active vision. In this section we discuss the different ways in which the eyes can be moved.

2.4.1 The muscles of the eye

Each eye is held in place by six extraocular muscles, grouped into opposing pairs (Fig. 2.9). Study of their arrangement and properties has long been of interest and of clinical concern to oculists and optometrists whose terminology is commonly used, although one may regret the passing of an even older terminology which included the term 'amatoris' for the lateral rectus muscle because of its employment in the furtive glances of flirting. Horizontal movements of the eye are achieved almost exclusively by the action of two

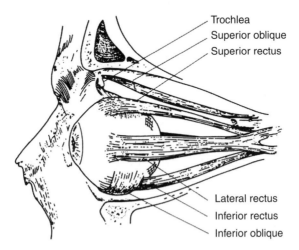

Figure 2.9 The six oculomotor muscles (from Howard, 1982). From the viewing position adopted, the lateral rectus is the closest muscle to the viewer but its corresponding antagonist; the medial rectus is occluded by the eyeball and so not shown.

muscles. These are the *lateral rectus* and the *medial rectus*, responsible for *abduction*, directing the eye outwards, and *adduction*, directing the eye inwards, respectively. Vertical movements are largely achieved by using the *superior rectus*, promoting upward *elevation* movements of the eyeball, and the *inferior rectus*, promoting downward *depressive* movements. The remaining pair of muscles, the *oblique* muscles do however make a partial contribution.

Rotations of the eye are customarily described with reference to the *primary position* of gaze, in which the eye is centrally placed in the socket (see Carpenter, 1988 for a more precise definition). *Secondary* positions refer to gaze directions achievable with a single vertical or horizontal rotation from the primary position and *tertiary* positions to all other gaze directions, that is all oblique directions. Note that these positions refer to the direction of the gaze axis only and for any gaze direction, the eye could, in principle, be in a number of different states, because of the freedom to rotate around the gaze axis (*torsional* movement). An early experimental finding was *Listing's Law*, which states that for each gaze direction, the eye has a unique position in the orbit irrespective of what combination of movements are used to achieve the gaze direction (strictly speaking, this is *Donders' Law*. Listing's Law also includes a specification of the particular position adopted). Listing's Law is a non-trivial result and has excited considerable recent interest since it appears to implicate a sophisticated neural and oculomotor mechanism (see e.g. Crawford and Vilis, 1995).

A loose interpretation of Listing's Law says that although the eye might, in principle, rotate arbitrarily in a torsional manner about its principal axis (assumed here to be the gaze axis), such arbitrary rotations effectively do not occur. A simple practical consequence is that for very many purposes, this degree of freedom can be ignored and eye movements specified adequately in terms of the horizontal and vertical components of rotations, or alternatively in terms of the *amplitude* and *direction* of rotation. However, it is also clear that under some circumstances significant torsional rotations of the eyes do occur. When the head rotates, some partially compensatory *countertorsion* is found (Howard, 1982) and when binocular vision is considered, *cyclotorsion* movements, oppositely directed in the two eyes, are also important (Howard and Rogers, 1995).

2.4.2 Classification of eye movements

Vision is important in a wide variety of situations, from watchmaking to slalom skiing. The evolutionary demand of such tasks, or their forerunners, has resulted in a complex set of oculomotor control processes. These can be separated into a set of distinct categories. A landmark article by Walls (1962), proposed an evolutionary history for the different types of eye movement in an article that was both erudite and entertaining.

Walls proposed that, paradoxically, the extraocular muscles did not evolve to move the eyes so much as to keep them still with respect to the visual environment as the organism moved. Two fundamental systems promote visual stabilisation in this way, the *vestibulo-ocular* and *optokinetic* reflexes (VOR and OKR). In the case of the former, the stabilising signal is derived from the vestibular organs of the inner ear; in the case of the latter, from an extensive pattern of coherent optic flow on the retina. These systems have become elaborated to provide a wonderfully effective way for vision to operate from a stable viewing platform (for details see Carpenter, 1988, 1991; Miles, 1995). Investigation of the stabilising reflexes often makes use of continuing steady stimulation, either by subjecting the observer to continuous body rotation (rotating chair) or to continuous whole field rotation (rotating drum). This results in a characteristic *nystagmus* movement of the eyes. The eyes move in a sawtooth pattern with a *slow phase* in which the eyes are kept stably aligned with the visual surroundings followed by a *fast phase* rapid movement in the opposite direction. These repeat to produce the nystagmus pattern. The sharp movements of the fast phase minimise the time that vision stability is disrupted and, importantly for the current theme, were the probable evolutionary precursors of the saccadic mechanism by which rapid movements of the eye could occur more generally.

VOR and OKR are essentially involuntary and automatic. This contrasts with the remaining eye movement types, all of which might be considered to show rudimentary volition. The *saccadic, pursuit* and *vergence* systems can all be described in terms of target selection, which in turn is likely to be tied to the motivational state of the perceiver and to higher cognitive processes. The saccadic system rotates the eye so that a selected target can be brought on to the fovea. The pursuit system, often termed smooth pursuit, allows a selected target that is in motion to be followed smoothly with the eyes. The vergence system maintains both eyes on a target that moves in depth, or makes an appropriate adjustment of the directions of the two eyes to a new target at a different depth. The saccadic system uses fast, stereotyped, jump-like movements, and typically rotates the eyes for a brief period at speeds up to several hundred degrees per second. These movements are clearly differentiated from pursuit movements that are continued movements of the eyes, generally at speeds well under $100°\ sec^{-1}$. Both saccadic and pursuit movements are essentially *conjugate* with the two eyes rotating equally. Vergence movements are classically (but see Section 2.5.2) described as continuous movements in which the eyes move in a *disjunctive* manner (in opposite directions) with maximum speeds under $20°\ sec^{-1}$.

Both pursuit and vergence systems can operate in a closed loop manner to maintain the eye or eyes aligned onto a moving target. However in both cases, there is an initial component that operates in an open loop manner and facilitates fast target acquisition (Bussetini *et al.*, 1996; Semmlow *et al.*, 1994) and a corresponding fast suppression of the visual stabilisation systems (Lisberger, 1990).

For stationary observers viewing stationary scenes, no stimulation to drive VOR, optokinetic responses or pursuit is present. Thus the expectation is that the eye movement pattern will consist of saccades only, separated by periods where the eye is stationary, together with vergence movements to the extent that parts of the scene are at different viewing distances. For many purposes, only the saccadic movements are significant and these situations form the principal subject of much of the remainder of the book. The term *fixation* is given to the stationary periods between saccades (the term is used both as a generic description of the act and in the noun form *a fixation* that describes each instance). For most practical purposes, it can be assumed that the eye is stationary during fixations but close examination of fixation shows it to be a dynamic state in which the eye makes continuous miniature movements (Ditchburn, 1973). A typical record of such movements is shown in Fig. 2.10 and shows slow irregular *drift* movements of a few degrees per second, together with more rapid irregular movements termed *tremor*. Occasionally, small, jump-like, movements occur which have been termed *microsaccades*. It should be noted that Fig. 2.10 was obtained by asking an observer to maintain their eyes continuously viewing the same target location for an extended period.

These movements have the effect of jiggling the retina with respect to the retinal image. The relative motion can be eliminated with a *stabilised retinal image* technique in which, for every movement of the eye, an equal but opposing movement of the display being viewed occurs. Such image stabilisation leads to a dramatic 'fading' and entire loss of vision (Ditchburn and Ginsborg, 1952; Riggs and Ratliff, 1952). This result initially led to the idea that the details of the miniature eye movements might be of fundamental importance for vision and a period of intense study ensued (see Ditchburn, 1973). The original use of 'involuntary' for these fixation eye movements was shown to

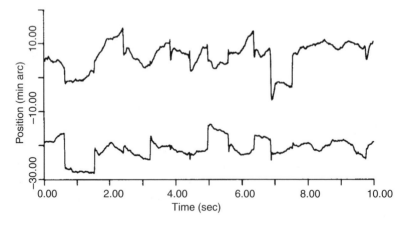

Figure 2.10 Record of fixational eye movements (the terms 'physiological nystagmus' and 'miniature eye-movements' are equivalent), showing drift, tremor and microsaccades. The upper and lower traces show the vertical and the horizontal components of the movement. The traces have been displaced vertically, for clarity. From De Bie (1986).

be inappropriate by the demonstration of some higher-level input into the fixation mechanism. The incidence of microsaccades could be changed with instructions (Steinman *et al.*, 1967), and directed drift movement was found to occur in anticipation of a subsequent target following a saccade (Kowler and Steinman, 1979). Interest in the topic waned with the appreciation that, particularly in head free situations, quite substantial retinal image movement was usual (Steinman *et al.*, 1982). Nevertheless, no thoroughly worked out neurophysiological account of visual loss under stabilisation has emerged, and the phenomenon offers a challenge to some thinking in the passive vision tradition.

2.5 Saccadic eye movements

Saccadic eye movements are a ubiquitous feature of vision. Credit for the recognition that the eye moves in a series of jerky jumps should be given to the group of nineteenth century French ophthalmologists amongst whom Javal (1878, 1879) was a prominent figure. The term saccade can be traced to Javal's work and its incorporation into the English language credited to another influential early investigator, Raymond Dodge, one of many Americans who profited from a spell of study in the German laboratories (Dodge, 1900; Dodge and Cline, 1901; Erdmann and Dodge, 1898). A fascinating historical account of the early work on eye movements may be found in Tatler and Wade (2002).

In most visual activities (see Chapters 5–7) we move our eyes by making saccades 3–4 times each second. Simple calculation shows that we must make many tens of thousands of saccades each day and many billions over the course of a lifetime. They can be made voluntarily (for exceptions, see Section 5.8.2, Section 8.3 and Section 8.5) but for the most part operate well below the level of conscious awareness. In everyday activity, most saccades are only a few degrees in size (Bahill *et al.*, 1975a; Land *et al.*, 1999). However, particularly during active tasks, a small number of very large saccades also occur and a recent estimate of the average saccade size during an everyday task (tea-making) is 18–20° (Land *et al.*, 1999)

2.5.1 Characteristics of saccades

Saccadic eye movements are *stereotyped* and they are *ballistic*. The *trajectory* of the saccade refers to the exact details of the way that the eye rotates. Figure 2.11 shows typical trajectories for horizontal saccades of various sizes. The eye is initially stationary. At a quite well defined point, it begins to accelerate, reaches a maximum velocity, and then decelerates rapidly to bring the eye to rest in its new position. The angular rotation is referred to as the *amplitude* of the saccade. The stereotypy of saccades is shown by the fact that every time a saccade of the same amplitude occurs, the same trajectory is followed closely. The *duration* and *maximum velocity* of saccades are measures readily obtained

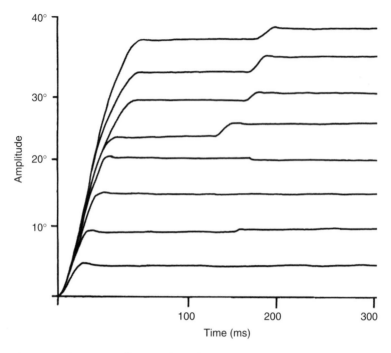

Figure 2.11 Time course of horizontal saccadic eye movements of various sizes (from Robinson, 1964).

from the trajectory. Plots such as that of Fig. 2.12 show how these parameters vary little for saccades of a particular amplitude, but depend systematically on the saccade amplitude. The term *main sequence* has been adopted for such plots following an imaginative analogy with an astrophysical relationship (Bahill *et al.*, 1975*b*). For saccade duration, the main sequence is well described (Carpenter, 1988) by the expression

$$T_S = 2.2A_S + 21 \tag{2.4}$$

where T_S is the saccade duration in ms, and A_S is the saccade amplitude in degrees.

Some qualifications must be made to the basic picture. The oculomotor system is a biological system and such systems are invariably characterised by greater variability than mechanical ones. Saccades can occur which are slower (occasionally also faster) than the main sequence. Although the oculomotor system does not appear to be subject to fatigue through repeated use, slower saccades than predicted by the main sequence are sometimes found in states of drowsiness and also occur as a result of some drugs such as benzodiazpenes (Glue, 1991). An attempt to slow saccade trajectories by a biofeedback training procedure showed some success (Findlay and Crawford, 1986). Slow saccades can also occur as a result of brain damage (Zee *et al.*, 1976). The termination

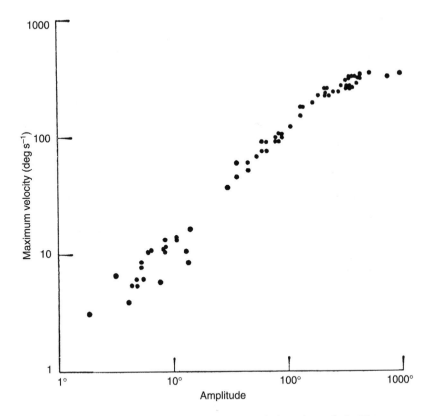

Figure 2.12 The relationship between saccadic maximum velocity and saccade size. The amplitude scale stretches from microsaccades to large voluntary saccades. Plot from Zuber, Stark and Cook (1965). The term 'main sequence' was later introduced to describe this relationship (Bahill *et al.*, 1975*b*).

of the trajectory may be marked by *dynamic overshoot*, a brief overshoot of the final position followed by a velocity reversal. The eyeball trajectory itself may show such overshoot: it is also a feature of records from some types of eyetracker (Deubel and Bridgeman, 1995). Finally the eye may not always return to a halt at the end of the saccade but instead show a continuing slow drift movement. Such post-saccadic drift, particularly in eccentric gaze positions, is characteristic of certain forms of brain damage (Leigh and Zee, 1983). It can also be induced in normal observers (Kapoula *et al.*, 1989), demonstrating that post-saccadic gaze stability is maintained by an active adaptational process (Section 4.6).

During horizontal saccades, the visual axis normally moves purely in the horizontal plane. However the trajectories for oblique and vertical saccades are rarely simple rotations about an axis, but more complex so that a plot of the successive optic axis positions through the movement will show a moderate degree of curvature. This curvature is systematic (Viviani *et al.*, 1977: Fig. 2.13). One situation in which curvature might be expected is when an oblique trajectory combines a horizontal component and a vertical component of different amplitudes. If such a movement came about through a simple additive combination of the movements made for each component, then it would be expected that the shorter amplitude component would have shorter duration (because of the main sequence). The curvature found with oblique saccades does not show this pattern; the shorter component shows *stretching* to match it to the other component (Van Gisbergen *et al.*, 1985).

A ballistic movement cannot be modified by new information once it is initiated. Saccadic eye movements have this character. This is shown from studies of two-step tracking (Section 4.4.2), which shows that visual information arriving less than about 70 ms prior to the start of a saccade cannot modify the movement. If the saccade goal is modified immediately prior to this deadline, curved saccade trajectories may be obtained which show clear target-seeking properties (Van Gisbergen *et al.*, 1987). Such curved goal-seeking saccades have been observed when brain damage causes saccade slowing (Zee *et al.*, 1976). They are of some significance because they demonstrate that an internalised goal seeking process operates as part of the saccade generation mechanism. Nevertheless, such goal seeking trajectories are almost entirely absent for *small* saccades (Findlay and Harris, 1984), suggesting that the goal is predetermined at the outset.

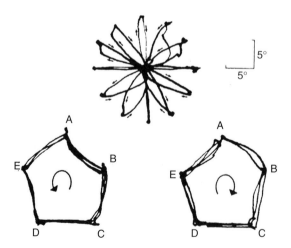

Figure 2.13 Plots of the trajectories of saccadic eye movements showing that each movement is associated with a systematic curvature. The top traces show a set of saccades made from a central point to and from a series of locations on a clock face. The bottom traces show scanning around the points A–E in a counterclockwise (left trace) and a clockwise (right trace) direction. From Viviani *et al.* (1977).

2.5.2 Combining saccadic movements with pursuit and vergence

It was stated (Section 2.4.2) that the saccadic, pursuit and vergence systems were regarded as separate systems. This claim will now be analysed in more detail. Figure 2.14 shows a plot of eye position as an observer tracks an object moving in a smooth course with reversal of direction at the end of a fixed period. This shows a clear separation of following movements and faster velocity saccades. If a target that an observer is asked to follow commences a regular but unpredictable movement, the eye commences pursuit after a short delay (the pursuit latency). Shortly afterwards, a saccade in the direction of the target movement usually occurs and the term *catch-up* saccade is used for saccades occurring during smooth pursuit. This situation and similar ones were the subject of a set of classical experiments (Rashbass, 1961; Westheimer, 1954) that supported the separation of a pursuit system, driven by target movement, from a saccadic system, driven by target position (retinal error). Subsequent work has shown this to be a useful generalisation but there is some cross talk between the systems. Thus the pursuit system shows some response to whether the eyes are lagging or leading the target (Wyatt and Pola, 1981) and the saccadic system shows the ability to program saccades to the anticipated future position of a moving target, taking into account subsequent target movement (Newsome *et al.*, 1985).

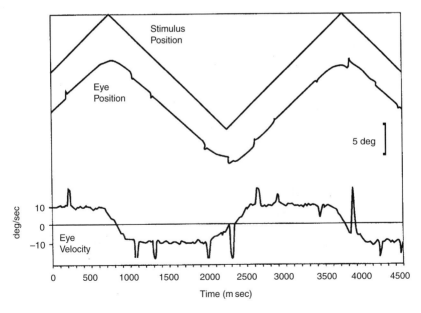

Figure 2.14 Eye movements of an individual tracking a spot moving smoothly in a horizontal left → right → left → right regular sequence. The eye position trace shows periods of smooth movement, interrupted by occasional small saccades. The saccades show up clearly as brief peaks on the lower trace of eye velocity. The record also shows the phenomenon of anticipatory changes in pursuit direction prior to direction reversal of the target. From Boman and Hotson (1992).

Early studies of the vergence system measured the response to unpredictable target steps or movements in depth (Rashbass and Westheimer, 1961). The view that emerged from these studies was that the vergence system moved the eyes slowly, with retinal target disparity being the principal input. A critical situation is that of *asymmetric vergence* where a target steps to a new position, differing from its previous one in both distance and direction. Following records reported by Yarbus (1967) it was long believed that the response to this situation was a rapid conjugate movement of the eyes to the appropriate target direction, followed by a much slower disjunctive vergence movement which gradually

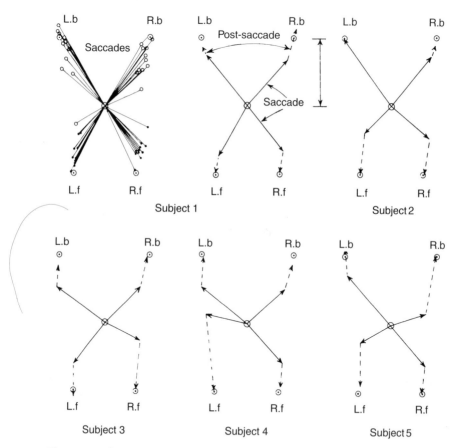

Figure 2.15 Schematic illustration of the fast and slow components of fixation changes in depth (asymmetric vergence). The plots show the movement in the horizontal plane of the point of intersection of the visual axes of both eyes. The subject initially fixated the display centre and a target appeared unpredictably in one of four positions, left behind (L.b), left front (L.f), etc. The top left panel shows a set of individual records, the others show averaged data from five subjects. The solid lines point to the eye position immediately after the saccade and the dashed lines to the position 1 second later. After Enright (1986).

brought the two eyes into alignment in the appropriate target depth plane. It has subsequently emerged that a much more integrated pattern is often found.

Enright (1984, 1986) recorded saccades in the asymmetric vergence situation. He showed that saccade movements under these conditions were unequal in the two eyes with the disconjugacy acting to bring the eyes together onto the target (Fig. 2.15). This finding was confirmed by Erkelens *et al.* (1989). These results are disturbing for the classical picture of separate saccadic and vergence subsystems and require a major modification of its basic postulates. Two possibilities have been suggested. In the first, a distinction between a conjugate saccadic system and a disjunctive vergence system is maintained but the vergence system is boosted so as to speed up during saccades. In the second, the idea that saccades are conjugate movements is abandoned and the alternative proposed that saccades in each eye are programmed separately. These positions are fiercely debated (Mays, 1998; Zhou and King, 1998) and since both can predict the behavioural findings, resolution will depend on a full understanding of the brain processing pathways for both conjugate and disjunctive movements. A further well-established phenomenon is that, during the course of a saccade, a period of transient divergence is found since the abducing eye moves more rapidly than the adducing eye (Zee *et al.*, 1992).

2.5.3 Saccadic suppression

Saccades have always been somewhat troublesome for the passive theory of vision. As we emphasized in Chapter 1, this theory assumes that the aim of vision is to create a stable mental representation of the visual world. How then can we move our eyes and maintain a stable 'world-picture' in the face of the changes, which are evidently taking place on the retina? The regularity with which this question is addressed in texts of vision, to the exclusion of other questions concerning the role of saccades in vision, is indicative of the pervasive nature of the passive vision view.

A partial answer to the question comes from the finding that visual thresholds are elevated during the course of saccadic movements. An informal demonstration of this can be experienced by obtaining a retinal after-image and moving the eyes around with the eyes closed. Latour (1962) used a visual probe to measure the ability to detect brief faint light flashes. His results (Fig. 2.16) showed a decrease in threshold that commenced some time before the start of the actual movement. This threshold decrease is a central phenomenon, shown by the suppression of visual phosphenes (Riggs *et al.*, 1974). However its magnitude is relatively small. It has been recognised that other contributions come from the way the visual system handles full field retinal motion. As well as the obvious blurring that results, a masking mechanism comes into play (Matin, 1974). It has also been suggested that a similar masking mechanism is important in preventing information from one fixation interfering with that from the subsequent one (Breitmeyer, 1980). Detection of visual motion occurring during the course of saccades is particularly poor

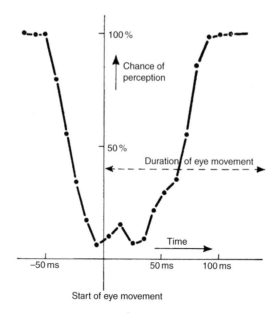

Figure 2.16 Time course of the suppression of visual threshold for lights flashed during a saccadic eye movement (from Latour, 1962).

(Bridgeman, 1983). The term *saccadic suppression* is used to describe the loss of vision resulting from these processes.

A series of recent studies by Burr and colleagues (Burr and Morrone, 1996; Burr *et al.*, 1994; Ross *et al.*, 2000) has supported the idea that saccadic suppression is primarily occurring in the magnocellular system and very little suppression (as opposed to smear blurring) occurs when discriminations can be carried out exclusively with the parvocellular system (e.g. high spatial frequency gratings).

2.5.4 Physiological pathways for saccadic eye movements

Using a similar approach to that of tracing visual input pathways into the brain, it has been possible for neurophysiologists to identify a set of brain areas concerned with oculomotor output. We shall concentrate here on the cortical areas involved in saccadic orienting movements (see Section 4.3.1 and Section 4.4.5 for further details of the immediate pre-motor mechanisms). Such areas are characterised by two properties. First, stimulation of each area will produce orienting movements of the eyes and second, electrical recording shows that cells in the area discharge prior to the production of a saccadic eye movement (Schall, 1991). Further confirmation comes from two other approaches. Careful study of the way in which the saccadic system is affected in patients with damage to cortical areas of the brain (Pierrot-Deseilligny *et al.*, 1991) has been used (see Chapter 8) together with lesion studies on animals. Recently, direct investigations of cortical activity have become possible using PET and fMRI techniques (Corbetta, 1998).

The emergent picture shows clearly that there are multiple parallel routes involved in the generation of saccades. Figure 2.17 shows a diagram of the main areas and their interconnectivity. The areas of cortex that are most intimately linked to saccadic eye movements are the area LIP of posterior parietal cortex and the frontal eye field region of the pre-motor frontal cortex (FEF). Saccades can be elicited by electrical stimulation in each of these areas. Studies using the lesion technique have shown that no single pathway is essential. However, the combined loss of both the superior colliculus (SC) and FEF renders an animal unable to make saccades (Schiller *et al.*, 1980), attributable to the fact that these centres form parallel output pathways. There are direct projections from FEF and SC to the brainstem saccade generators although the direct FEF pathway seems to be of subsidiary importance (Hanes and Wurtz, 2001). Loss of ability to make saccades occurs also

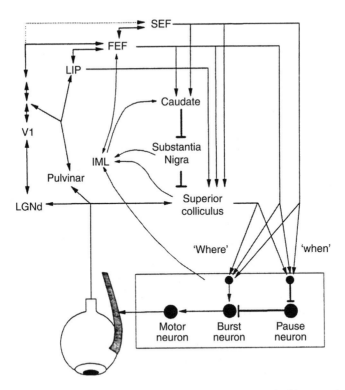

Figure 2.17 Schematic diagram of the oculomotor output pathways involved in generating saccadic eye movements. LGNd – dorsal part of the lateral geniculate nucleus, V1, LIP, FEF, SEF are the cortical areas Visual 1, lateral intraparietal area, frontal eye field and supplementary eye field respectively. IML is the internal medullary lamina of the thalamus. From Schall (1995).

with lesions to both SC and occipital cortex (V1), presumably because no visual input pathway is available (Mohler and Wurtz, 1977). It is probable that the saccade related regions in the parietal and occipital lobes send their signal through the SC, since stimulation of these regions, in contrast to stimulation of FEF, no longer elicits saccades following SC ablation (Schiller, 1998). A further important pathway links FEF and SC via the caudate and the pars reticulata of the substantia nigra (Hikosaka and Wurtz, 1983; Hikosaka *et al.*, 2000).

Recent work has attempted to go beyond the simple identification of brain regions involved in saccade generation, to detailed discussion of the computational mechanisms. The most well elaborated instance concerns the superior colliculus (Section 4.3.2). This region, and also the cortical regions (FEF, LIP) which project to it, contain motor maps, such that, for example, the orienting saccade generated by electrical stimulation is dependent on the exact locus of stimulation. Within several such maps, lateral inhibition has been shown to operate as a selection process to enhance processing in one direction at the expense of neighbouring directions (inferior temporal cortex: Chelazzi *et al.*, 1993; frontal eye fields: Schall and Hanes, 1993; superior colliculus: Glimcher and Sparks, 1992). The areas can then be considered to operate as salience maps in which the selection of a saccade target is achieved. This concept is developed further in connection with visual search in Chapter 6.

2.6 Summary

This chapter has attempted to digest information about the visual and the oculomotor systems that is of particular importance for active vision. We adhere strongly to the principle that active vision is a sub-area of neuroscience and thus its study must be grounded in neurobiological principles. Of course we appreciate that many of the topics that feature in texts about vision (colour, depth, motion, spatial frequency, cortical areas) have been almost entirely ignored. Likewise, only the saccadic part of the oculomotor armamentarium has received any detailed consideration. The approach of the chapter has been 'outside-in', in the sense that the visual and oculomotor system have been treated principally as fixed entities which operate to interface with the environment. We have thus adopted the time-honoured approach of ignoring plasticity, learning and development (some redress occurs in Section 4.7), recognising that, for many purposes, the assumption of biological hardwiring is a productive one. We have also not yet made much reference to an active perceiver, having dealt only with the processes operative within such a perceiver. In the next chapter we begin the link between neurobiological and cognitive accounts through consideration of the topic of attention.

CHAPTER 3

VISUAL SELECTION, COVERT ATTENTION AND EYE MOVEMENTS

Our visual environment is crowded with multiple objects, however at any one time we tend to be aware only of a limited part of this array of information (James, 1890). William James noted that the object that we are paying attention to appears to receive more processing and is more richly represented in perception. In addition, paying attention to an object is clearly linked to being able to act on that object—for example, reaching out to pick it up. These then are the central phenomena of visual attention: selection of only part of the visual array and the link between selection and action (see Allport, 1993). The central question in this research area is how to best characterise the mechanisms of visual attention that support these phenomena.

3.1 Covert and overt attention

What happens when we pay attention to some part of the visual environment? With some effort we can fix our eyes straight ahead while at the same time paying attention to some part of the periphery of vision (Helmholtz, 1866). This ability, to pay attention to part of the visual array without moving the eyes, or *covert attention*, has become a cornerstone observation of research on visual attention.

With no effort at all we can move our eyes to align the fovea with an object in the visual array. This ability, to saccade and foveate part of the visual array, or *overt attention*, appeared for many years to be a question that attracted far less interest.

At the heart of our discussion of work on attention is a belief that this emphasis on covert attention is wrong. We argue that spatial selection is best achieved by fixating an item so that it can be processed by the fovea; the processing advantage gained by fixating in this way is substantially greater than the covert attentional advantage. We believe that understanding visual selection primarily has to be about understanding *overt* attention. It is only with this new perspective that we can begin to understand what might be happening when we pay attention. An important issue here is the relationship between covert attention and overt attention or movements of the eyes and we discuss this issue in detail below (Section 3.3 and Section 3.7).

Visual attention appears to have a spatial character; attention after all is most often paid to a location. So in discussing attention we will start with a discussion of spatial attention and more specifically covert spatial attention.

3.2 Covert spatial attention

In a now classic series of experiments, Michael Posner (Posner, 1978, 1980; Posner et al., 1978; Posner et al., 1980) demonstrated that reaction times to visual targets were faster for spatial locations that had been previously cued. Typical experimental displays and results are shown in Fig. 3.1. Subjects were instructed to maintain fixation on a central fixation point. After some interval, an arrow *cue* appeared at fixation indicating the possible location of a subsequent *target*. On the majority of trials the arrow correctly indicated the location of the target: so called *valid trials*. However, on a minority of trials the target appeared in the opposite direction to the cue: so called *invalid trials*. In addition to these two conditions, on some trials no arrow appeared; because these trials gave no prior indication of where the target might appear they were called *neutral trials*. By comparing reaction time across these conditions Posner and colleagues were able to investigate the *costs* and *benefits* of the spatial cues. When compared to the neutral condition, the valid condition led to faster reaction times. In addition, when the cue was invalid, reaction times were slower compared to the neutral condition. These results showed that, even when the eyes did not move, prior information about the possible location of a target led to a benefit, and incorrect information led to a cost.

Such costs and benefits could also be observed when the cue consisted of a peripheral visual event such as a flash. Again, there was a benefit if the peripheral event was in the same spatial location as the target and a cost if the peripheral event was in the opposite location.

These two types of cueing effect share many similarities. However there are a number of reasons to suspect that these two types of cues are, at least in part, functionally different. First, the time course of the cueing effects was different. (e.g. Müller and Rabbitt, 1989). The peripheral cue gave the largest advantage when it occurred around 100 ms before the target and the central cue gave a maximum benefit around 300 ms before the target. Second, when the cue was uninformative—indicating the position of the target on only 50 per cent of the trials—the costs and benefit were still present for a peripheral cue but were absent for a central cue. Posner and others suggested that peripheral cueing was *automatic* and that central cueing was *voluntary*. These two types of cue also map onto the distinction between *exogenous* attention, as demonstrated by the peripheral cue, and *endogenous* attention, as demonstrated by the central arrow cue.

In subsequent experiments Posner and Cohen (1984) demonstrated that for much longer intervals between the cue and the target, there was actually a cost

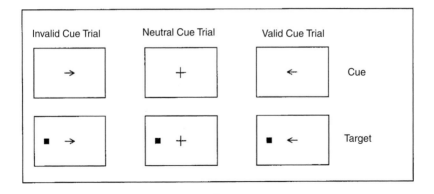

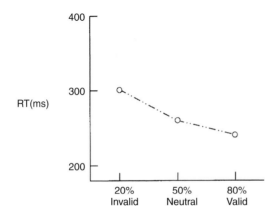

Figure 3.1 The Posner cueing paradigm. The upper panel shows the display sequence for the three trial types. The target is preceded by a cue that indicates the probable location of the target, this cue can be invalid, valid or no cue can be present (so called neutral cue). The cue is followed by a target that the participant is required to respond to as quickly and accurately as possible. The lower panel shows a graph of typical results from this type of experiments. Participants are both faster than the neutral condition for valid trials and slower than the neutral condition for invalid trials.

associated with the cue indicating the target location. They argued that this reflected a process which actively inhibited attention returning to previously visited location. They called this process *inhibition of return* (IOR). As discussed in Section 6.6, IOR may provide an important mechanism to structure scanpaths and prevent rechecking in visual search (see Klein, 2000 for a thorough review of IOR).

A number of models have been proposed to account for these and related attentional enhancement effects, as we shall see in the following sections. One dominant approach is to conceptualise an internal spotlight that has a spatially restricted extent and enhances processing in part of the display; this will be discussed in detail in Section 3.2.1. An extension of this type of model is a zoom lens account in which the spotlight can have a variable spatial extent and so can be distributed over a large part of the display or focused on a small section; this type of account is discussed in Section 3.2.2. Alternatively, as we shall see later on in this chapter, one account of the facilitation effects is that attention is allocated to specific objects rather than parts of space (see Section 3.6.1).

None of these models makes any reference to the fact that the eyes are mobile. An alternative model, proposed by Rizzolatti *et al.* (1987), is the *premotor* model (Section 3.3.3), suggesting that covert attention arises out of the mechanisms of eye movement preparation, although with the actual movement withheld. We propose that such an approach can account for the results as effectively as that of the other approaches and can also, as we discuss in Section 3.7, allow incorporation of the phenomenon of covert attention into our account of active vision.

3.2.1 Spotlights

Posner and colleagues explained their results by suggesting that the costs and benefits resulted from the action of a spatial attentional mechanism that could best be conceptualised as a *spotlight* which was spatially localised and 'moved' across the visual display to facilitate processing in a restricted part of the visual scene. The benefits in the cueing experiments arose when the attentional spotlight had moved to the location where the target appeared and the costs were a result of attention being located at the incorrect location so that attention had to be reallocated in the display to the target.

Within this framework the action and behaviour of the attentional spotlight was characterised by a number of operations. When a location was being attended to, the spotlight was *engaged* at that location. In order to pay attention to a new location, the spotlight had to be *disengaged* from the current location, *moved* across the display and *engaged* at the new location. This cycle of disengage-move-engage characterised the action of the attentional system; each process was assumed to take time and it was these processes which lead to the reaction time costs and benefits in the cueing tasks. So when the cue appeared, attention would disengage from the central fixation point and move to the cued location; if the cue was valid, then detection of the target would occur. However, if the cue was invalid then attention would have to disengage from the cued location and move across the display to the target location; these additional processes took time and led to the costs of invalid cues.

The framework was supported by studies of patients who apparently had a disorder in one of these functions. Patients with damage to the parietal lobe appeared to have a deficit in disengaging attention (Posner *et al.*, 1984): damage to the midbrain, as a result of supranuclear palsy, appeared to result in a deficit in the ability to move the covert attentional spotlight (Posner *et al.*, 1985), and damage to the thalamus resulted in deficits consistent with an inability to engage the spotlight of attention (Rafal and Posner, 1987). Work on visual search (see Chapter 6) initially also supported this spotlight metaphor for attention and it was integrated into one of the dominant models of search, Treisman's Feature Integration theory (Section 6.2.1).

The spotlight metaphor for attention bears many detailed similarities to the properties of the saccadic system. First, like the fovea, the spotlight gives preferential processing to a small area of the visual input. Second, movements of attention, like saccades, take time to initiate and carry out. And third, like saccades, covert attention appears to be slowed down by activity at the fixation point (Mackeben and Nakayama, 1993). Why should covert attention have such similar properties to the saccadic system? Different reasons might be suggested. First, the spotlight model of covert attention might have been inspired by the properties of overt attention; indeed such a similarity may be a great part of its intuitive appeal. Second, the two may share such similar properties because they share some common underlying neural mechanism; this second idea is developed in Section 3.3.3.

3.2.2 Zoom lens accounts of attention

One alternative to the spotlight model of covert attention was proposed by Eriksen and St James (1986). They suggested that rather than having a fixed spatial extent, attention could be allocated over a variable area. This *zoom lens* account of covert attention fitted well with a range of empirical findings (e.g. Egeth, 1977; LaBerge, 1983). If attentional resources are limited and finite then one consequence of increasing the size of the spotlight should be a reduction of the amount of attention allocated to any given location. In support of this, Castiello and Umiltà (1990) used a Posner cueing paradigm and showed that the size of the area cued influenced the extent of a cueing advantage found.

Intuitively, it might be expected that visual attention would allow selection of different visual scales, given the enormous range of scales that objects of interest in the visual environment can take. We will discuss instances elsewhere in the book where it appears that overt attention can also be allocated to spatial regions of different sizes. As discussed in Section 6.8, Zelinsky *et al.* (1997) monitored eye movements during a search task and found that the eye movements were directed to the geometric centres of progressively smaller groups of objects rather than being accurate fixations to individual objects in a display. This *zooming in* of the saccades to progressively smaller units of the display is reminiscent of the zoom lens model. In the search situation the focus is initially broad and so saccades are directed to the centre of groups of items. With subsequent narrowing of the search region, smaller groups are selected until only the target is fixated. The global effect (Section 4.4.3) in which initial saccades to pairs of items are often directed to the centre of mass of the two items also shows the importance of processing at a broad spatial scale. However, McPeek *et al.* (1999) have shown that focused attention may be a requirement for saccade programming. Therefore, it may be that the pattern of saccades observed by Zelinsky *et al.* (1997), and the global effect, reflect the focusing of attention on the centre of mass of a number of elements rather than the action of a more dispersed attentional spotlight.

3.2.3 Late vs. early selection models of attention

One fundamental issue within studies of covert attention is at what stage in information processing attentional selection occurs. Posner's spotlight model of covert spatial attention, like most models of attention, implicitly incorporated the idea of two stages of information processing (e.g. Broadbent, 1958). The first pre-attentional stage is computed in parallel, prior to selection taking place. The second stage involves the more in-depth processing of only a restricted part of the input. This later post-attentional stage has a limited capacity and so only a few items, or a small part of space, can be processed at one time. It is this dichotomy, which pervades research on attention, that results in the questions of how much processing is performed in the first parallel stage, and, conversely, what processes require attention. And models of attention have been classified on this basis. Models are characterised as either *early selection* accounts—attention is required to extract all but the simplest of visual information—or *late selection* accounts—complex object properties are computed from the stimuli before the attentional selection. A similar contrast appears in the models of visual search discussed in Chapter 6. One of the underlying principles that drives this debate on the location of selection is the extent to which one of the functions of attention is to compensate for the limited capacity of the nervous system. Put simply, the argument is that there is insufficient neural capacity to process in-depth all the properties of every item in the visual input. To compensate for this shortcoming, attention is required to select the limited number of items, or part of the display on which in-depth processing will occur. Such a position is more consistent with the early selection models. In the case of vision, it is important to note that a degree of selection occurs simply as a result of the structural distinction between he fovea and the periphery (Section 2.2).

In contrast to the early selection viewpoint, Allport (1993) argued that selection has no single locus and can occur throughout the visual system, at different stages of processing. Within this framework, attention gates the output from multiple visual areas that can drive a response, only allowing a limited part of the information to activate motor areas. This allows outputs from multiple visual areas to drive a single action and ensures that action sequences are produced in a co-ordinated manner. Work on the neuropsychology of attention has provided additional support for multiple anatomical and functional sites for selection, and inspired a number of models (e.g. Humphreys and Riddoch, 1993; Desimone and Duncan, 1995). These multiple sites for selection may reflect functional differences in visual input. Under some circumstances selection will be object-based (see Section 3.6.1) and, as we have seen, selection can be spatially based. In addition, the multiple sites for selection may reflect the involvement of different action systems. For example, the motor systems required to act in reaching space are different from those required to act in the space beyond reaching space (Cowey *et al.*, 1994; Halligan and Marshall, 1991).

3.2.4 The visual benefits of covert spatial attention

There is clearly a huge wealth of evidence that it is possible to allocate attention covertly. However, one of the central questions is what function does covert attention alone serve? Covert attention appears not to be a useful means to accommodate the limited capacity of the system as selection appears to occur throughout the system (Section 3.2.3). A further possible argument that covert attention can scan displays more rapidly than the eyes will be considered (and rejected) in Section 3.4.

One additional, and often neglected, problem facing a model of covert attention is that the magnitude of the effects tends to be relatively small. For example, spatial cueing often leads to a reaction time advantage no greater than 40 ms. A number of studies have attempted to measure which perceptual properties of the stimulus are facilitated and to what extent. The allocation of covert spatial attention lowers orientation thresholds far more than contrast thresholds, and bi-directional vernier thresholds are far more affected than unidirectional thresholds (Lee *et al.*, 1997). In a similar manner, Carrasco *et al.* (2000) found variable levels of facilitation dependent on the nature of the judgement (see also Downing, 1988; Müller and Findlay, 1987). Across all of these studies, the facilitation is relatively small compared to the huge differences in detection thresholds across the visual field (Anstis, 1974). This difference between overt and covert benefits is made even more extreme when the greater effect of lateral masking in the periphery is taken into account (Bouma, 1970). In addition any covert attentional benefits may result in part from differential setting of decision criteria (Downing 1988; Müller and Findlay, 1987).

The magnitude of the benefit associated with covert attending and the apparent lack of some independent function for covert attention suggest that covert attention only makes sense when considered as part of an integrated attentional system that includes both covert and overt attention. To return to the question at the beginning of this section: what function might covert attention *alone* serve? Our answer would be 'very little'. Instead we would strongly argue that covert attention is an integral part of the active vision cycle of fixating items that are of interest. *The fixation act is the process of paying attention* and is supported by covert processes that result in peripheral preview for the next fixation location (see Section 5.3.3, Section 7.2.3 and Section 9.4). In this way covert and overt selection are intrinsically linked. Unfortunately, although the acuity benefits accrued by fixating an item far outweigh the advantage gained by selective attention, such overt attentional explanations for visual selection are often disregarded. However, this approach with its focus on the central role of overt orienting has been embodied in a few models of attention including the Sequential Attentional Model (Section 3.3.2) and the pre-motor theory of attention (Section 3.3.3), which are discussed in detail below.

3.3 The relationship between covert and overt attention

Covert attention leads to processing advantages for localised parts of the visual field without any overt movement of the eyes. As a concept it provides an important organising principle to understand a large body of research findings. One of the central questions of this chapter and others that follow is, what is the role of covert attention when eye movements are not prevented? A critically important point must be to establish the relationship between these two forms of orienting. The relationship between these two processes has been the topic of extensive research and debate. Three clear positions can be identified. The first is that the two processes are independent and co-occur only because they happen to be driven by similar visual input (e.g. Klein, 1980). The second is that the two are closely coupled, with saccades being directed by the location of covert attention. Here covert attention takes the lead and hence can be allocated without a saccade being prepared but not vice versa (e.g. Henderson, 1992). In the third position, developed by Rizzolatti and colleagues (Section 3.3.3), the two phenomena arise out of the action of a single motor system: covert attention is achieved by preparing to generate a saccade. Here, covert attention comes closer to being a by-product of the overt scanning system.

3.3.1 Klein's independence account

Klein (1980; Klein and Pontefract, 1994) argued that two clear predictions could be made if there was a close link between saccade programming and attention. First, that if a subject attends to a location, then saccades to that location should be facilitated. Second, if a subject is preparing a saccade to a location, visual performance at that location should be facilitated. For endogenous cues, Klein (1980) found no evidence for either effect. Klein argued that, although an exogenous cue may attract both the programming of a saccade and an attentional shift concurrently, this correlation is no evidence for a causal link. For endogenous cues, covert attention can be allocated without the programming or preparation to make a saccade. Klein's result has been controversial since a number of subsequent studies have found evidence for coupling effects under various cueing conditions (Deubel and Schneider, 1996; Hoffman and Subramanian, 1995; Kowler et al., 1995; Shepherd et al., 1986). One important factor in determining whether such effects can be detected may be task difficulty. Dual task interference may only be measurable when the task is more difficult (see McPeek et al., 1999).

Klein does not deny that under normal circumstances the processes of generating a saccade and shifting covert attention will occur together or that the two systems are related. His claim is simply that the two responses are not the differential manifestations of the same system. Endogenous covert orienting is accomplished independently of eye movement programming. Remington (1980) also argued for a loose relationship between an attentional and saccade system, suggesting that the saccadic system and the attentional system are both drawn concurrently to peripheral events, but by different mechanisms.

3.3.2 The sequential attentional model

Henderson (1992) developed a *sequential attentional* model in which there is a closer relationship between covert and overt attention. The model is based on four basic assumptions. First, at the beginning of each fixation, attention is allocated to the stimuli at the centre of fixation. Second, attention is allocated to a new stimulus when the fixated stimulus is understood (or identified). Third, the reallocation of attention is coincident with the commencement of saccade programming to the new location that becomes the target for the next saccade. Fourth, the allocation of attention to the new location gates higher level processing at the new location. Within this model eye movements are necessarily led by an attentional shift. Support for such a conjecture comes from work by Shepherd *et al.* (1986) who found that subjects were unable to attend to one location when they were required to programme a saccade in another direction (see also Deubel and Schneider, 1996).

There is considerable evidence that more than one saccade can be programmed concurrently (Section 4.4.4). However, the model is based on a strictly sequential allocation of attention and then the saccade (although this condition is relaxed in the E-Z Reader model that developed from it—see Section 5.7.3). The model Henderson has been developing allows for the parallel programming of saccades by allowing attention to move at a faster rate than saccades and so to be allocated sequentially to two locations before the programming of a saccade to the first location is complete. We shall argue below that the evidence is at best weak that covert attention can move faster than overt attention in the manner that would be required for covert attention to be allocated sequentially in this manner. Henderson (1992) considers the possibility of parallel processing as an alternative to sequential attentional allocation. He rejects the idea that parallel processing might occur across the fixation location and the to-be-fixated location because a benefit is not found for the intermediate locations. In addition he rejects the possibility of the concurrent parallel processing of the fixated location and the spatially independent parallel processing of the to-be-fixated location, in part because this undermines the idea that attention can only be allocated to one location at a time (Eriksen and Yeh, 1985; Posner *et al.*, 1980).

The model also contains a fixation cut-off property; fixation will only be maintained up to a fixed time. After the fixation cut-off point is reached, a saccade is generated regardless of whether a candidate location for the next fixation has been generated by covert attention. Such a property is consistent with results from visual search. In difficult search conditions saccades are often initiated before a peripheral discrimination has been made even though such a discrimination is possible when the eye movement is delayed by training (Brown *et al.*, 1997).

3.3.3 The pre-motor theory of attention

Rizzolatti and colleagues (Rizzolatti *et al.*, 1987; Rizzolatti *et al.*, 1994; Sheliga *et al.*, 1997) have argued for the strongest link between saccades and shifts of covert attention. In the *pre-motor theory of attention*, covert attention effects are a result of activity within the motor systems responsible for the generation of a saccade. Spatial facilitation of the type reported by Posner and colleagues occurs as a consequence of the motor system preparing to generate a saccade. Within this framework, attention is a by-product of the action of motor systems, and attentional effects can be associated with different motor systems or spatial co-ordinates (e.g. in visual neglect, see Chapter 8).

There are two distinct experimental phenomena that provide strong support for a pre-motor theory, in which covert spatial attentional phenomena are a result of processing within the motor systems responsible for overt orienting. These will be considered in turn below.

The first of these is an experimental observation that arises out of experiments using the Posner cueing paradigm as discussed in Section 3.2. A number of groups (e.g. Downing and Pinker, 1985; Reuter-Lorenz and Fendrich, 1992; Rizzolatti *et al.*, 1987) have demonstrated that the reaction time cost in the invalid condition was greatest when the invalid cue was in a different quadrant to the target. This would suggest that there was an additional cost of attention 'moving' across the horizontal or vertical meridian to the target; this effect has been referred to as the *meridian crossing effect*. It is difficult at first to see how this effect could be explained. However, if attentional facilitation is a component of motor preparation, as suggested by the pre-motor theory, then the cost of shifting attention will be a function of the extent of motor reprogramming required to attend to the new location. When reprogramming is required to a different quadrant as opposed to the same one, reprogramming of both direction and amplitude is required; this is not the case for shifts within a quadrant. The meridian crossing effect is well documented for endogenous cueing although it does not appear to occur for exogenous orienting whether the orienting is covert (Reuter-Lorenz and Fendrich, 1992; Umiltà *et al.*, 1991) or overt (Crawford and Müller 1992). Rizzolatti *et al.* (1994) argue that this difference is due to differences in the nature of the motor programme generated in the two cases. In contrast, Klein and Pontefract (1994) argue that the difference is in the nature of the cognitive representation that serves the two types of attentional orienting.

The second piece of evidence that provides support for the pre-motor theory comes from studies of saccade trajectories. Rizzolatti *et al.* (1987) asked subjects to make a vertical downward saccade to a box in response to a cue that could appear in a horizontal row of boxes above fixation (Fig. 3.2). They measured the horizontal deviation in the saccade trajectory and showed that saccades were curved away from the horizontal location of the cue (see also Sheliga *et al.*, 1995). The allocation of covert attention thus has a direct spatial effect on the motor response. Such a direct interaction between the location of covert attentional allocation and a saccade trajectory provides strong support

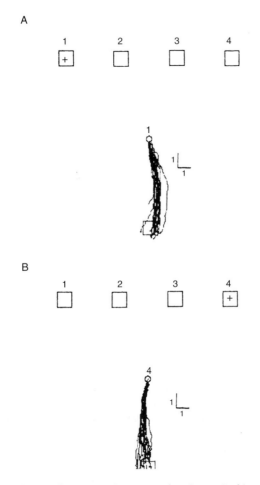

Figure 3.2 The influence of covert attention on saccade trajectory. In this experimental task the participant's covert attention was allocated to the location of the cross that could be located in one of the four boxes in the upper portion of the display. The appearance of the cross was the signal for the participant to generate a saccade to the lower box. For the saccades reproduced in panel A the cross (and covert attention) was allocated on the extreme left hand side and the saccades curved to the right. In contrast when attention was allocated to the right hand side saccades curved to the left. (Reproduced from Rizzolatti *et al.*, 1994, Fig. 9.2).

for the idea that the two responses share a common neural substrate and provides additional support for the pre-motor theory of attention (see also Kustov and Robinson, 1996 for similar effects in monkeys).

3.4 Speed of attention

One of the functional properties often suggested for covert attention is its ability to move around items of a display more rapidly that overt attention. If this were the case then covert attention would allow more items to be scanned in a given time than would be possible with overt attention alone, conferring an obvious functional benefit for the use of covert attention. Thus, a critical question is how quickly can covert attention move around a visual display.

With this motivation, a number of studies have attempted to measure the speed of attention. One indirect method to measure the speed of attention is to calculate the speed on the basis of visual search slopes (Chapter 6). Serial search, when the target is absent, often shows search slopes around 40–60 ms/item. If it were assumed that only one item a time is processed with the attentional spotlight, such a figure would be an estimate of the speed of redeployment of covert attention. This estimate is a great deal quicker than the speed of a series of saccades where the maximum scanning rate would be about 200 ms/item. However, alternative accounts (Section 6.4) propose that multiple items can be processed in parallel even during apparently serial search (Duncan and Humphreys, 1989, 1992; Treisman and Gormican, 1988). Thus it may be argued that serial search slopes are generated by parallel mechanisms, either wholly (Müller *et al.*, 1994; Townsend, 1971) or partially (Wolfe *et al.*, 1989; Wolfe, 1994). These points highlight the serious limitations of using search rates to estimate the speed of attention.

A number of other studies have attempted to measure the speed of attention more directly. Saarinen and Julesz (1991) asked subjects to report letters presented sequentially around fixation. Even with an interval between presentation of the letters as short as 33 ms, performance was above chance. They concluded that covert attention could be moved at a rapid rate. Some doubt has been cast on the exact way that chance performance should be calculated for such tasks (Egeth and Yantis, 1997) and it remains unclear the extent to which performance could be accounted for by parallel mechanism. This paradigm also addresses exogenous attention (Section 3.2), which may show different properties to endogenous attention.

One alternative direct method to measure the speed of covert attention is to use rapid serial presentation (RSVP) techniques. In a majority of these experiments, attentional speed is assessed for responding to two stimuli presented at the same location; these studies are reviewed in detail elsewhere (Egeth and Yantis, 1997) and are not central to the current discussion. However some studies have been carried out using an RSVP type task in which items are spatially separated. Duncan and co-workers (Duncan *et al.*, 1994; Ward *et al.*, 1996) measured the time course for shifting attention by asking subjects to perform two temporally and spatially separated tasks (Fig. 3.3). The two tasks interfered with each other up to and beyond an interval of at least 200 ms. These experiments provided a more direct estimate of the speed of attention. And because of their experimental simplicity they are less likely to suffer from the confound of memory capacity (Egeth and Yantis, 1997). The issue of the speed of attention is clearly still a contentious one and a matter for further detailed experimental study. Given that parallel processing of stimuli may occur in a number of these paradigms, the balance of evidence suggests that the longer estimates more correctly reflect the speed of attention. Estimates of around 200 ms are very close to the time course of overt eye movement based scanning. If these direct estimates

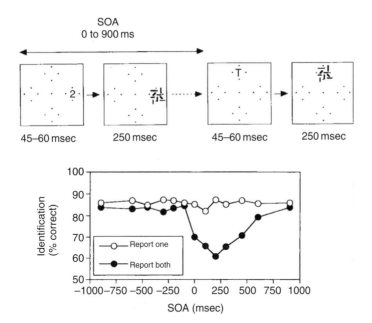

Figure 3.3 The time course of attentional movements. The upper panel illustrates the display sequence for the experiment. A number appears in one of the four locations followed by a mask, this is followed after a variable interval (the SOA) by a letter at a different spatial location. The participant's task is to report both the letter and the number. The graph shows the relationship between the SOA and the percent of items correctly identified. The open circles show the results from a control condition when only a single character has to be reported. The filled circles plot the data when both items have to be reported. It is clearly difficult to attend to (and so report) both items even with a relatively long interval (up to 500 ms at least) between them. This gives a measure of the time it takes attention to 'move' between the two spatial locations. (Adapted from Ward, Duncan, Shapiro 1996, Fig. 2 & 3).

are correct, covert attention simply cannot be a mechanism that allows fast scanning of the visual scene.

Without a good explanation for the purpose of an independent attentional mechanism it seams more probable that covert attention reflects the action of a system closely tied to the overt saccade system, in a manner similar to that proposed by the pre-motor theory of attention.

3.5 Neurophysiology of attention

There have been extensive and detailed studies over the last thirty years, on the neurophysiology of both overt and covert attention. A number of brain

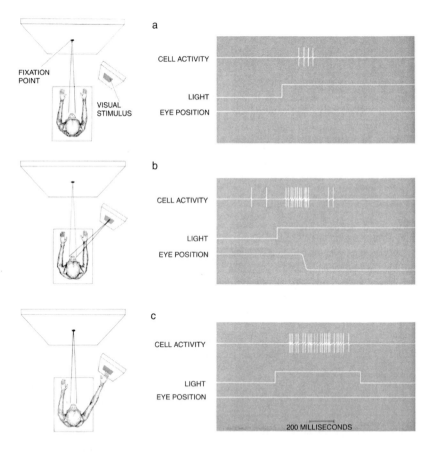

Figure 3.4 The response of cells in the parietal lobe under different attentional conditions. In (a) the monkey maintains fixation and makes no response to the visual stimulus. In (b) a saccade is generated to the same stimulus and this results in cell activity. In (c) the money makes a pointing movement towards the stimulus while maintaining fixation. (Reproduced from Wurtz, Goldberg and Robinson, 1982).

areas have been identified as playing an important role in the control of saccades (Section 4.3). These include the parietal lobe, frontal eye fields and superior colliculus. In each region, covert attentional effects have also been reported.

In a now classic series of studies Wurtz and colleagues (e.g. Goldberg and Wurtz, 1972; Mohler and Wurtz, 1976) recorded from the superficial layers of the superior colliculus in a monkey that had been trained either to make a saccade to a precued light or to attend to the light without making an overt response. Cell activity was linked to the onset of the cue specifically and did not occur when a saccade was generated without sensory stimulation. These cells appeared to be responding as a result of selective attending rather than simply as a result of the subsequently generated eye movement. In contrast, when a manual response was required then the attentional activity from the cells did not occur to the presentation of a cue. This provides strong support for a close coupling between covert attention and saccade generation that both arise from the same basic neural processes.

The response properties of cells in the parietal cortex also show attentional effects but appear to be less dependent on the nature of the response. Wurtz *et al.* (1982) showed that these cells responded equally, regardless of whether the response was a saccade or a manual response to the target without a saccade (Fig. 3.4). At first, this appears to indicate the existence of 'attentional cells' that are not directly linked to the nature of the output. However a manual response is normally associated with a saccade, and so units that allow for the co-ordination of attention across these two may serve an important purpose. Kustov and Robinson (1996) showed that the effects of cueing on cells in the superior colliculus were linked to the presentation of the cue when the response to the target was either a saccadic eye movement or a manual response. This suggests that even when the response does not require a saccade, such spatial cueing results in activity in the SC. When a response is not required or is actively inhibited, attentional allocation may generate concurrent activity in multiple motor systems, particularly if the motor systems act in a co-ordinated manner to control behaviour (see Colby and Goldberg, 1999). Recent evidence from the frontal eye fields provides compelling evidence for a close link between saccades and spatial attention. Moore and Fallah (2001) carried out subthreshold microstimulation in the frontal eye field. Such stimulation was shown to result in improved performance on a covert attention task. Together, these results suggest a close link between spatial attention and saccade generation.

Corbetta and Shulman (1998) review a range of functional anatomical studies in which spatial attention and saccade generation have been studied by means of neuro-imaging (Fig. 3.5). Together, these data indicate that a common set of neural signals in parietal and frontal cortex mediates the covert and overt allocation of attention. The frontoparietal network includes the frontal eye field and supplementary eye field. This anatomical overlap

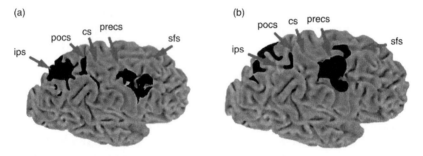

Figure 3.5 Brain activity in the human during covert attention (panel a) and saccadic eye movements (panel b). The areas of activity are shown in black superimposed on a view of the right hemisphere. Results from a number of brain imaging studies are combined, see Corbetta and Shulman (1998) for full details. The following sulci are also indicated: *ips*, intraparietal sulcus; *pocs*, postcentral sulcus; *cs*, central sulcus; *precs*, precentral sulcus and *sfs*, superior frontal sulcus. (Adapted from Fig. 4, Corbetta and Shulman, 1998).

between tasks requiring overt and covert shifts of attention also suggests a close link between these two processes which are more consistent with the pre-motor theory of attention (Section 3.3.3).

3.6 Non-spatial attention

So far this chapter has focussed on spatial selection and we have argued that overt attention to achieve foveation of the target is the primary method by which attention is paid to a specific item and selection of that item occurs. However, selection does not only occur spatially. In this section we discuss non-spatial selection. In the first sub-section we will discuss evidence that selection can occur on the basis of objects. And in the second sub-section we will discuss attention to visual properties.

3.6.1 Attention to objects

The cueing experiments carried out by Posner suggested that attention was allocated to a region of space. Items that were within that part of space received more processing. However, the experiments were equally consistent with a non-spatial, *object based*, allocation of resources, particularly since his design frequently used peripherally located boxes to mark the locations to which attention was to be directed. Duncan (1984) proposed a three-way classification for theories of attention. Object-based theories suggest that processing is limited to a restricted number of objects: objects are the units of selection. Discrimination-based theories propose that a limited number of discriminations can be made. Finally, space-based theories suggest that selection is limited to a fixed part of space. To test these theories, Duncan (1984) asked subjects to perform two simple perceptual tasks concurrently

Figure 3.6 Duncan (1984) showed that participants are less accurate when attending to two properties of different objects than two properties of the same object. Participants were presented with a box stimulus superimposed on a line. Two example displays are shown above. In separate trials they were required to report properties of the line (direction of tilt; dotted or dashed) or the box (size of the gap; shape of the box), or one property from each object (Taken from Duncan, 1984, Fig. 1).

(Fig. 3.6). The stimuli consisted of a box and a line drawn through it. The box varied in size (large or small), and had a gap in it (left or right). The line varied in tilt (clockwise or counterclockwise), and pattern (dotted or dashed). The two tasks that subjects were required to do each involved reporting two attributes, either both relating to one object (line or box) or one relating to each object (line and box). Duncan found that there was a large drop in performance when subjects had to attend to two separate objects, rather than to one alone. This was true even if the two objects occupied the same spatial area (as they were overlapping) and were small (so did not require multiple fixations). The parts of the display, relevant to the task, always occupied the same locations, whether part of 1 or 2 objects; so spatial selection factors were held constant across the two tasks, as was the number of discriminatios required. The results could only be explained in terms of an object-based attention account, in which there is an additional cost for attending to two objects over one. Duncan's (1984) result suggests that the selection procedure is not firmly linked to spatial co-ordinates. And in addition, support is provided for a late-selection account of attention, in which there is extensive preattentive processing, with even spatially overlapping items competing independently for selection (see also Baylis and Driver, 1993; Egly *et al.*, 1994; Vecera and Farah, 1994).

The challenge for attentional theory, including the active vision perspective, is to integrate overt attentional allocation into a model of attention in which objects that are behaviourally relevant are facilitated and receive preferential processing via fixation. The contrast between space-based attention and object-based attention will re-emerge in consideration of how to account for eye movement control during reading (Section 5.7). Some influential models take as a start point that attention is deployed at the level of the word unit while others assume a spatial framework.

3.6.2 Attention to visual properties

If a subject is required to select all the red apples from a basket which contains both red and green apples, the red apples are more likely to be selected. This non-spatial facilitation of all red items forms part of the attentional processes that guide selection and clearly cannot be explained by the selection advantage given by fixation alone. Such processes are particularly important in visual search, which is discussed in detail in Chapter 6.

PET studies by Corbetta and colleagues (1991) showed that attending to colour or form or motion increases activity in largely non-overlapping regions of extra-striate cortex. These activated areas corresponded to the areas which, in non-human primates, are known to contain cells that were tuned to these stimulus dimensions. These areas are anatomically distinct from the superior parietal-frontal network that was proposed to be involved in the allocation of spatial attention (Fig. 3.5). These conclusions complement single cell electrophysiology studies carried out by Moran and Desimone (1985). They recorded in area V4 and found that within the classical receptive field, spatial attention could modulate the extent of responding of the cell. These results may build a bridge between how stimuli specific effects—such as attending to the red items in a display interact with spatial selection mechanisms (see also Section 6.7).

3.7 Active vision and attention

An active vision account of attention places fixation as the primary method by which items are selected. As we have seen, fixation confers a large advantage in terms of acuity when compared to the advantage gained by covertly attending. An active vision approach to selection, in which selection occurs via fixation, is in one sense an extreme early selection model. In a single fixation, some items in a display are not selected simply because the sensory apparatus is not sufficient to process them—in some cases visual selection occurs at the retina! However, which items suffer the cost of the poor visual abilities of the periphery can be determined by a range of factors including higher level visual constraints and task demands.

Overt selection becomes more complex when we consider the process by which the next item becomes selected in a series of fixations. Mechanisms drawing on information in peripheral vision determine the next item to benefit from being fixated. These attentional processes themselves operate with reduced visual input. Understanding how the next location for fixation is selected is one of the core questions that this book addresses. And it is clear that these mechanisms themselves are limited. For example, subjects find it difficult to generate a saccade to a face when it is presented amongst a set of jumbled faces (Brown *et al.*, 1997), but saccades can be guided to an item on the basis of colour and shape (Findlay, 1997; see also Chapter 6).

One benefit that covert scanning could confer is that it could allow faster scanning of the visual environment than is possible with overt scanning eye movements. Our review of measures of the speed of attention in Section 3.4 shows that the direct evidence for fast covert scanning is weak. Indeed it appears more likely that covert scanning rates are close to the scanning rates that are possible with overt eye movements. We return to this issue in Chapter 6, where we again conclude that there is no evidence for fast sequential scanning of items with covert attention during visual search.

A rather different argument relating to speed comes from theorists such as Henderson (1992) who believe that there is a close link between covert and overt attention as discussed in Section 3.3.2. This argument suggests that covert attention 'moves' to the target of a saccade some time prior to the eyes themselves moving. The basis for such an argument comes from findings that show improved visual discrimination abilities at the saccade target, immediately prior to a saccade (Kowler *et al.*, 1995; Deubel and Schneider, 1996). This important result is sometimes used to argue that covert attention is primary with saccades being secondary. We prefer a somewhat different approach, since the (potential) dismissal of saccades as secondary is scarcely consistent with their ubiquitous nature. Rather than commenting on the chicken and egg problem raised if the two types of attention are treated as separate, we argue that the two forms of attention are normally inextricably linked and the phenomenon of preview advantage is an important component of active vision.

We should also mention that other possible functions have been suggested for covert attention, although at present the evidence for these functions appears at best weak. One intuitively appealing use would be to allow deception to occur in social situations: covert attention might allow us to pay attention to one person while, because of our point of fixation, appearing to pay attention to someone else. However it remains to be demonstrated that processing facilitation (Section 3.2.4) can be achieved in such a naturalistic situation.

Our argument for the importance of overt attention and the minor role for covert attention is based on some very basic facts about the structure of the visual system. Why then, has research on covert attention dominated for so long? We think there may be multiple possible contributing factors here. First, research in visual attention had its origins in work on audition (e.g. Cherry, 1953). The classic observation from this field is the cocktail party effect. In a crowd where there are many voices speaking at once we can pay attention to just one voice and ignore the others. When we switch auditory attention in these circumstances the process is clearly an internal one although, even in this case, actively orienting the head towards a sound source confers a benefit. When researchers from an auditory background began to study vision they may have taken the auditory system as a model to begin starting to think about visual attention, with the result that they overemphasized covert processes. Second, work on visual attention formed part of the cognitive revolution in psychology; cognitive psychology in general has tended to neglect the motor aspects of task performance and focused on the internal (and so by definition covert) processes. Third, until recently it has been relatively difficult to measure eye movements and so studying covert attention was the most easily achievable goal. Finally, as we have emphasized previously, implicit belief in the passive vision model has been very strong.

3.8 Summary

Attention allows us to select part of the visual information available for further or more detailed analysis. The fovea provides the primary mechanism for such selection to occur. Items that are not fixated receive greatly reduced processing, particularly in terms of acuity. In addition it is possible to attend to items without moving the eyes. This covert attending also confers some processing advantage but these effects are small in comparison to the advantage associated with fixating the item of interest. Both the behavioural and physiological evidence suggests that this covert orienting is closely related to overt saccadic selection. The spatial selection processes works alongside mechanisms that allow feature-based selection; these mechanisms can guide eye movements to behaviourally relevant items.

CHAPTER 4

VISUAL ORIENTING

4.1 Introduction

Visual orienting involves redirecting the gaze to a new location in the visual field. This process has been intensively studied, particularly in relation to the *target-elicited saccade*, the orienting saccadic eye movement that readily follows the appearance of a new target in the field of vision. One reason for the interest is the close correspondence between processes discovered in human behavioural studies and those shown in studies of primate brain physiology. To emphasize this correspondence, the chapter is sectioned so that the two principal variables in connection with a saccade, the latency and the metric properties, are treated in separate sections (Section 4.2 and Section 4.4) with each section followed by an account of the underlying physiology (Section 4.3 and Section 4.5).

In chapter 2, we emphasized that the foveal region provides a high acuity region for detail vision. For it to be used, it must be directed at the part of the visual world that is of current interest. This is the process of visual orienting. The gaze redirection may, for distant objects, involve movements of the body, head and eyes. The orienting mechanisms for head and eyes are closely coupled (Jeannerod, 1988). For close objects, manipulations may also occur which bring the object into the gaze direction rather than vice versa but these will not be given further consideration here.

A classic study by Sanders (1963) distinguished regions in which different combinations of effectors were used to achieve orienting. For an individual initially facing forward with gaze in the primary position, an *eye field* extends out to eccentricities of about 20°. Within this region, orienting is achieved by moving the eye only. Beyond this region, a *head field* extends out to eccentricities of about 90° where orienting involves both eye and head movements. For objects outside the head field, whole body movements are additionally employed. Sanders suggested that transitions between the different zones resulted in increased task load and performance decrements.

These regions are only loosely delineated, and other factors, both of an individual and a situational nature, may affect the way in which orienting is achieved. For example, individuals wearing spectacles may increase the incidence of head movements, in order to maintain the gaze direction through an appropriate part of the spectacle lens. In Section 8.5, we discuss an individual whose orienting is entirely achieved with head movements.

A large number of studies on visual orienting have restricted consideration to orienting with the eyes alone. Orienting in this case is achieved using saccadic eye movements, and the study of the target-elicited saccade forms one of the major concerns of this chapter. Such saccades occur when a new target makes a sudden appearance in the parafoveal or peripheral regions of the visual field. Although clearly a voluntary response, saccadic orienting in this situation has an automatic and natural quality, ensuring that reliable data can readily be acquired.

Two other important paradigms can be mentioned at this point as both have been widely used to extend our knowledge of visual orienting. In the *anti-saccade* paradigm, discussed in Section 4.4.5, observers are instructed to respond to the target by moving the eyes in exactly the opposite direction. An anti-saccade requires suppression of the automatic orienting response and the creation of a different set of motor commands. Another paradigm requiring more voluntary activity on the part of the observer is the *memorised saccade* paradigm. Typically, a peripheral target is flashed briefly and the observer required to withhold the immediate orienting response, but to respond at the end of some period of time during which the location of the target must be held in short-term memory. This paradigm is discussed together with other work on saccades to remembered locations, in Section 9.2.4.

4.2 What determines the latency of orienting saccades?

In the target-elicited saccade paradigm, the observer is asked to make a saccadic orienting movement to a target that appears in some location in the peripheral visual field. A delay, termed the *latency* of the saccade, occurs between the appearance of the target and the time that the eyes start to move. This delay is the reaction time of the eye response and represents the cumulative time taken by the brain processes that enable orienting. We shall, in this chapter, show how study of these saccades can give insight into the underlying brain processes but a cautionary note is first in order. The brain is an integrated system and although saccadic orienting is a very automatic process, it is never completely independent of other brain activity. Zingale and Kowler (1987) demonstrated this point neatly by showing that, when a number of saccades were required, the latency of the first orienting saccade increased steadily with the length of the sequence. Likewise, saccade latencies are augmented when observers are required to do concurrent cognitive tasks (Takeda and Findlay, 1993).

4.2.1 Target properties

One might expect that the latency for an orienting saccade would be dependent on the properties of target to which the eye is moving. Several studies have shown this to be the case. For example, saccades to a bright target show

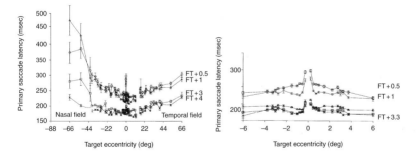

Figure 4.1 Latency of target-elicited saccades plotted as a function of target eccentricity for targets of varying intensity (FT + 1 indicates 1 log unit above foveal threshold etc.). From Kalesnykas and Hallett (1994).

shorter latencies than those to a dim target (Kalesnykas and Hallett, 1994; Reuter-Lorenz *et al.*, 1991). Targets with little low spatial frequency information show prolonged latencies (Findlay *et al.*, 1993). However, the magnitude of these effects is rather small, except when the targets are close to threshold visibility.

The effect of target location is of some interest. In a review of a number of studies, Findlay (1983) concluded that the variation of latency as a function of target eccentricity was a bowl-shaped function. Over a broad range (approx. 1°–15°), latencies changed rather little while latencies increased for very small movements (less than about 1°; Wyman and Steinman, 1973) and for large movements (greater than about 15°). Orienting in the latter case almost invariably involves a corrective saccade (Section 4.4.5). A systematic study by Kalesnykas and Hallett (1994) confirmed this relationship, as shown in Fig. 4.1. (note however Hodgson, 2002)

4.2.2 The gap effect

Target-elicited saccades are often studied in an eye tracking task when an observer is required to follow a visual target which makes an unpredictable step movement. In this case, the target simultaneously disappears at the previously fixated location when it reappears at the new location. Saslow (1967) realised that, under these circumstances, the disappearance of the visual stimulus at the previously fixated location might contribute to the programming of the saccadic orienting movement. He studied this by treating the fixation target disappearance and the target appearance as separable visual events. He carried out an experiment in which the two events were not simultaneous, but were separated in time by a temporal offset. The fixation stimulus could disappear before the appearance of the peripheral target, leaving a *gap* period with no visual stimulation. Alternatively, the fixation stimulus might not disappear until after the appearance of the peripheral target, the *overlap* situation. Saslow found that this manipulation strongly affected the saccade latency.

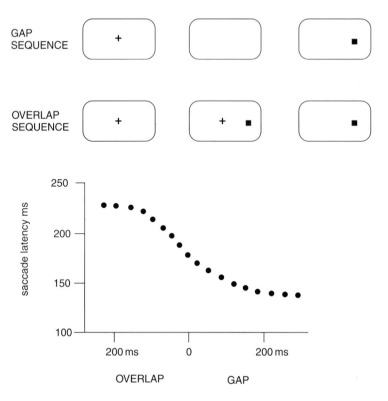

Figure 4.2 The gap effect. Top panels show typical display sequences in gap and overlap conditions respectively. The task is always to initially fixate the centre and make an eye saccade to the target when it appears, either on the left or on the right of the screen. Latencies are measured from the target appearance. The lower panel shows schematically typical results from the paradigm.

As Fig. 4.2 shows, saccade latencies become progressively shorter in the gap situation with increasing temporal offsets (up to gaps of about 200 ms) and conversely become progressively longer as more overlap occurs.

This effect, the *gap effect*, is highly reproducible and occurs irrespective of whether the observer can predict the direction in which the target will appear (Kingstone and Klein, 1993; Walker *et al.*, 1995). This suggests that the offset of the fixation point initiates some general preparatory process in connection with the saccadic movement, with the spatial metric of the saccade assigned at a late stage in the programming of the movement (Section 4.6). Work on the gap effect (Forbes and Klein, 1996; Reuter-Lorenz *et al.*, 1995) has led to the proposal that there are two general preparatory components. The first is a general alerting component found with any warning signal (Tam and Stelmach, 1993, showed that manual reactions benefit from this component).

The second effect is specific to ocular orienting and has been assigned a variety of terms (fixation offset, fixation release, fixation disengagement or ocular disengagement).

4.2.3 The remote distractor effect

Ross and Ross (1980) reported a related converse result in the situation where, rather than disappearance of the fixated material, a new stimulus appears at the point of fixation around the time of target onset. Such a stimulus onset resulted in a latency *increase* if it occurred simultaneously with the target appearance. If the onset occurred substantially before the appearance of the target, its effect reversed and a latency reduction occurred, presumably because it operated as a warning signal. The latency increase is a robust effect. Walker *et al.* (1995, 1997) carried out further studies of events where distractor stimuli occur simultaneously with target onset. They showed that, in a comparable way to the gap facilitation, the increase occurs

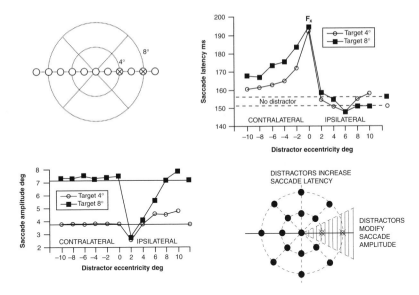

Figure 4.3 The remote distractor effect, studied by Walker *et al.* (1997). Targets appeared at either 4° or 8° on one side of fixation and were, on test trials, accompanied by a simultaneous distractor. In the experiment illustrated in the upper left panel, the distractor could appear in one of the eleven positions indicated by circles. On control trials, no distractor appeared. Distractors at fixation or on the contralateral side produced an increase in saccade latency, shown in the upper right panel. Distractors on the ipsilateral side did not affect the latency of the orienting saccade, but modified its amplitude, shown in the lower left panel. From this and similar experiments, the effect was shown to take the form shown in the lower right panel. Distractors within a narrow sector on either side of the saccade target axis modify saccade amplitudes, whereas distractors in the remainder of the visual field produce an increase in latency.

whether or not the subject has advantage knowledge of the direction in which the eyes will move. The increase in latency results from onsets in any region of the visual field except a sector close to the target (Fig. 4.3). Walker *et al.* introduced the term *remote distractor effect* to describe these findings. Distractors in this critical sector have no effect on the saccade latency but in contrast do affect the endpoint of the saccade, an instance of the global effect (Section 4.4.3). Figure 4.3 shows the highly systematic nature of the remote distractor effect.

The gap effect and remote distractor effect are highly robust and regular, suggesting that visual onsets and offsets have an access route to the saccade generation mechanisms that operates in a very automatic manner. A further result showing this was reported by Theeuwes *et al.* (1998). These workers have shown that if a visual onset occurs at the instant when an observer is about to make a voluntary saccade, there is often an unintended saccade towards this onset, rather than to the intended location.

4.2.4 Express saccades

In 1983, Fischer and Boch reported a remarkable finding. They trained monkeys to make target-elicited saccades in a gap paradigm and measured saccade latencies. They found that the monkeys frequently made saccades with extremely short latencies (80–100 ms). Since, at the time, figures of 200 ms or more were widely described in texts as the 'typical' saccade latency, such short latencies were newsworthy in their own right. A second finding concerned the distribution of saccade latencies over a large number of trials (Fig. 4.4). The short latency saccades very clearly formed a separate

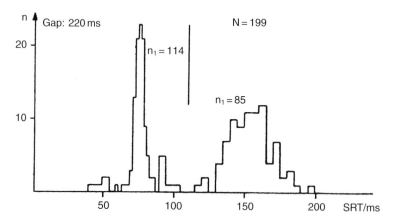

Figure 4.4 The first demonstration of express saccades by Fischer and Boch (1983) in a study with monkeys. The monkey was trained to make an orienting saccade in the gap paradigm. The distribution of saccade latencies shows a separate sub-population of saccades with extremely short reaction times.

sub-population of the total, justifying their identification as a separate *express saccade* category.

In the following year Fischer and Ramsperger (1984) reported that that a similar phenomenon occurred in human subjects, although the latencies of the human express saccades were somewhat greater (100–130 ms) than those produced by the monkeys. Subsequent work has confirmed this finding (Jüttner and Wolf, 1992) although human subjects only rarely show the dramatic bimodality in latency distributions shown in Fig. 4.4 (Reuter-Lorenz *et al.* 1991; Wenban-Smith and Findlay, 1991). A lively debate about their properties and significance of these movements can be found in Fischer and Weber (1993). Express saccades show some unexpected properties; for example, they are less common when the saccade target is close to the fovea (Weber *et al.*, 1992). During free viewing, it is quite common to find fixations whose duration is very short (e.g. Section 4.4.4) and it seems likely that these may be a manifestation of the same phenomenon.

4.2.5 Variability in latencies

Even when testing conditions are controlled as carefully as possible, the latency of saccades varies in an apparently unpredictable way on a trial-by-trial basis. Over a series of trials, a cumulative distribution of latencies can be obtained. The nature of this distribution is of considerable interest. Carpenter (1981; Carpenter and Williams, 1995) has shown that the distributions of reaction times are positively skewed with the distributions of the reciprocal of latency closely approximating a Gaussian distribution.

Such a distribution is capable of being explained by a remarkably simple generative mechanism, shown in Fig. 4.5, which Carpenter has termed the LATER model (linear approach to threshold with ergodic rate). On each trial, a hypothetical variable commences to increase at a linear rate. The saccade is

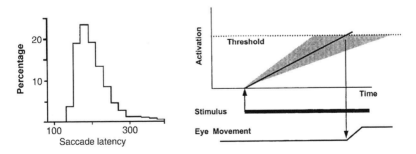

Figure 4.5 The left hand panel shows a typical, positively skewed, distribution of saccade latencies in an orienting task. The right hand panel shows the principle of Carpenter's LATER model, in which the underlying generative process is a linear rise of activation to a fixed threshold level, with the rate of rise being a random variable with Gaussian distribution.

initiated when a certain threshold value is achieved with the time taken to reach the threshold corresponding to the saccade latency. The LATER model postulates that the rate of increase is a random variable with Gaussian distribution. This model is then able to predict a skewed distribution of latencies with the shape observed. Furthermore, differential instructions to aim for speed or for accuracy modifies the distribution of saccade latencies in a way that can be interpreted as a simple change of threshold level (Reddi and Carpenter, 2000). This model has also received support from physiological studies (Section 4.3.3).

4.3 Physiology of saccade initiation

One reason for the intense interest in target-elicited orienting movements is the close correspondence that can be found between the behavioural study of such movements, as described in the previous section, and physiological brain processes.

Primates show patterns of saccadic eye movement control that are similar in very many ways to those of humans. Monkeys can readily be trained in the laboratory to make orienting saccades as well as saccades in more complex tasks such as visual search. Our knowledge of the neurophysiology of the saccadic system has been particularly advanced by studies in several laboratories of the properties of brain cells when awake and alert monkeys carry out trained tasks.

Figure 4.6 shows a set of schematic diagrams of primate brain, illustrating the major regions and pathways important for the generation of saccadic eye movements. The eye muscles themselves are controlled by motor neurons leaving the midbrain and pontine regions via cranial nerves III, IV and VI. The cell bodies of these nerves are found in the corresponding oculomotor nuclei. Adjacent to these nuclei are the important premotor centres of the midbrain reticular formation (MRF) and the paramedian pontine reticular formation (PPRF) shown in Fig. 4.6. The descending input to these centres comes largely (although not exclusively) from the superior colliculus (SC). The SC contains cells responsive to visual stimuli and a partially overlapping set of cells which fire when saccades are made. It is a highly significant visuo-motor centre in connection with saccadic eye movements and receives input from two areas of the cortex (LIP and FEF) important in saccade generation (Section 2.4.4).

4.3.1 Burst and pause cells in the reticular formation

Figure 4.7 shows schematically the neural processes occurring in oculomotor and immediate pre-motor regions of the brain. It provides a very simplified overview of a highly complex piece of neural machinery (for further detail see Fuchs *et al.*, 1985; Moschovakis and Highstein, 1994; Schall, 1991, 1995;

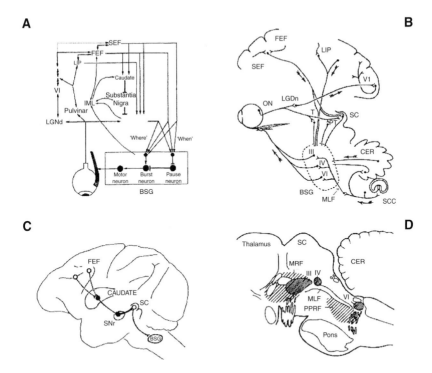

Figure 4.6 Brain centres for saccade generation. (A) Diagram of pathways involved in saccade generation (Fig 2.17) from Schall (1995). (B) Schematic diagram of primate brain showing input visual pathways and output oculomotor pathways, as well as location of the cortical centres involved in saccade generation (modified from Robinson, 1968). (C) Diagram of primate brain showing the oculomotor pathway through the basal ganglia to the brainstem (modified from Hikosaka and Wurtz, 1989). (D) Schematic diagram of the brainstem saccade generator region (from Henn *et al.*, 1982.).

III, IV and VI are the third, fourth and sixth cranial nerve nuclei, the nuclei from which the ocular motor neurons originate, BSG-brainstem saccade generator (elaborated in diagram D), CER-cerebellum, FEF-frontal eye field, IML-internal medullary lamina of the thalamus, LGNd-dorsal part of the lateral geniculate nucleus, LIP-lateral intraparietal area, MLF-median longitudinal fasciculus, MRF-mesencephalic (midbrain) reticular formation, ON-optic nerve, PPRF-paramedian pontine reticular formation, PT-pretectum, SC-superior colliculus, SCC-semicircular canals, SEF-supplementary eye field, SNr-substantia nigra, pars reticulata, T-tectal nuclei, V1-cortical area Visual 1.

Scudder *et al.*, 2002). When the eye is at rest, all oculomotor neurons show tonic activity, firing at a moderate rate that depends on the particular position of eyeball in the orbit. Typical activity in such a neuron during saccade generation is shown in the 'Motor neuron' trace of Fig. 4.7. To generate a saccade, the motor neurons to the appropriate agonist muscles switch

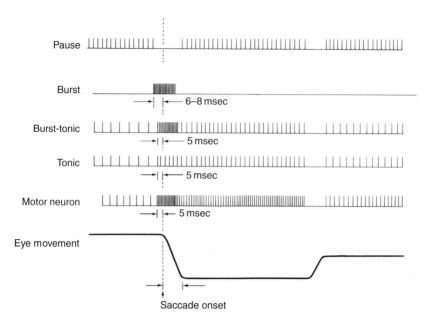

Figure 4.7 Neural activity in various types of brainstem cells accompanying saccadic eye movements (redrawn from Gouras, 1985).

transiently to a very high rate of firing and then settle to a lower, but increased, rate appropriate for the new position. The term *pulse-step* pattern is often used to describe this innervation. The activation to the antagonist muscles consists of a pause in activation at the time of the pulse burst and a lower rate of subsequent activity. The hypothetical motor neuron shown controls the agonist for the first eye movement and shows the pulse-step pattern. For the second, reverse direction, movement, the motor neuron activity shows a pause, indicating that there is no driving signal to the antagonist movement in a saccade.

These patterns of activation are in turn generated by neural circuitry in the adjacent areas of the MRF and PPRF. Within these regions are found two types of cells with very different properties. The *pause* or *omnipause* cells fire at a steady uniform rate at all times except that, when a saccade occurs, their firing stops completely for a brief period. The start of the pause of activity in fact precedes the start of the actual movement by 5–15 ms. The pause occurs irrespective of the size or direction of the saccade and thus the omnipause cells do not code the metric properties of the saccade in any way. Such metric coding occurs in other types of cells, in particular cells which show a brief *burst* of activity synchronised (and, as with the pause cells, briefly preceding) a saccadic movement. The burst cells, however, only fire for a certain direction and size of movement; in other words, this type of cell is coding the metric properties of the movement. Some cells (long lead burst cells) show an increase in discharge rate considerably in advance of the actual movement. The MRF and PPRF are closely coupled regions (via the MLF), with the MRF burst cells relating to the vertical component of an eye movement and those in the PPRF to the horizontal component.

A very important principle demonstrated here is the separation of two streams of control information. Van Gisbergen *et al.* (1981) introduced the following terminology. The pause cells may be said to form a WHEN system because they are concerned with the point in time when a saccade will occur but not where it will move the eye. This is the concern of the burst cell system, which can therefore be termed the WHERE system. One plausible behavioural consequence of the WHEN/WHERE distinction is that preparatory processes for the initiation of a saccade can occur before the destination of the movement is specified (Section 4.2.2).

Pause cells are active at all times except when a saccade occurs and thus may be described as cells active during fixation. It is possible to envisage them as the late stage of a system that is concerned with fixation. Cells in the superior colliculus that code fixation will be discussed in the following section. Cells with similar properties are also found in cortical areas related to eye movements, such as the posterior parietal association cortex (Lynch *et al.*, 1977) and the dorsomedial region of the frontal cortex (Bon and Luchetti, 1992).

4.3.2 Fixation, burst and buildup neurons in the superior colliculus

The superior colliculus (SC) is the major region from which pathways descend to the midbrain and brainstem oculomotor generating centres described in the previous section. Its organisation has been considerably elucidated in recent years and shows some similar characteristics to that of the lower centres. The work of Daniel Guitton, Doug Munoz and Robert Wurtz has been of seminal importance and this section draws considerably on the lucid account given in Wurtz (1996). The presentation here emphasizes the direct pathways downstream from SC. It is becoming increasingly recognised that although these pathways appear adequate to generate saccades, accuracy and adaptability is maintained through parallel SC > brain stem pathways involving the cerebellum (Robinson and Fuchs, 2001).

The SC consists of multiple layers, stacked somewhat like the pages of a book. As elaborated below, the layers contain maps of visual and oculomotor space with each hemifield represented in the contralateral SC. The upper layers, termed the *superficial layers*, receive a direct visual projection from the retina. The lower layers (*intermediate and deep layers*) receive a separate cortical visual projection, as well as being connected to the saccadic generation centres. Studies of the details of these projections in terms of the visual pathways described in Section 2.2.1 shows the following. Activation of the SC superficial layers comes from a homologue of the cat W-system, whereas activation in deep layers comes about mainly through M-cells but with some evidence for a P-contribution (Schiller, 1998). Paradoxically it is believed that the upper and deeper layers do not connect neurally. This visual mapping is anisotropic in a similar way to that of the retino-cortical projection. The central foveal region obtains the largest proportional representation and is mapped at the rostral end of the structure (the *rostral pole*). Upper space is represented medially and lower space laterally. The mappings are eye-centred and are independent of the position of the eye in the orbit although, as in other visual centres, eye position does affect the level of activity (Paré and Munoz, 2001).

The statement that the SC 'maps visual space' refers to the fact that cells, both in the upper and in the intermediate layers, have visual receptive fields whose locations are laid out topographically. The statement that the SC 'maps oculomotor space' refers to the fact that cells in the lower (deeper) layers have the property that electrical stimulation generates a saccadic eye movement with the size and direction of the eye movement dependent on the location of stimulation. Some cells have both visual and oculomotor responsiveness. A highly significant discovery was the fact that visual and oculomotor maps were in register (Schiller and Koerner, 1971; Robinson, 1972). Stimulation of a location in the deeper layers of the colliculus results in a saccade to precisely the region of space which is represented in the visual map at the same collicular location. The SC is thus clearly involved in the visuomotor co-ordination of orienting. Nevertheless, a period of doubt followed the early discovery of the register of the maps because it was unclear how the two maps might interact. Recent progress on the SC has concentrated on the events in the deep layers that precede a saccade, and in particular on the role of the rostral pole region.

The term *fixation centre* can be applied to the rostral pole region of the SC, the location corresponding to the foveal region on the visual map. Neurophysiological studies show that cells in this region show activity whenever the animal fixates and pause during saccadic eye movements (Munoz and Wurtz, 1993a). The region is GABA sensitive (Munoz and Wurtz, 1993b) so that injection of the GABA agonist muscimol into the region increases saccadic activity. An animal with such an injection has difficulty in maintaining fixation. Conversely, injection of the GABA antagonist bicuculline has the opposite effect. Animals produce fewer saccades and saccades with longer latencies than normal. The cells in this region have similar characteristics to those of the omnipause cells of the brainstem. A direct connection has been traced between the region and the brainstem omnipause cells (Paré and Guitton, 1994).

Two important cell types are found in the remaining parts of the deep layers. Both show neural activity preceding saccades but differ in important ways. The *buildup* cells show a pattern of increasing activity that commences

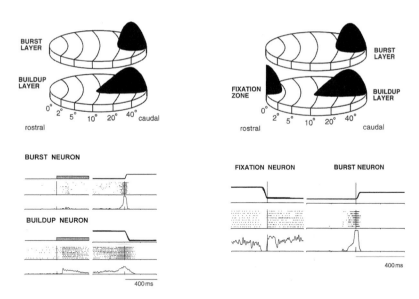

Figure 4.8 Cartoon of activity in the superior colliculus relating to a saccade. The left hand top panel shows two layers of the SC, each topographically mapped. The dark mounds represent neural activity peaks in these two layers. The LH lower panel shows typical activity of neurons in these two layers. The left hand plots show activity in relation to the visual target and the right hand plots show activity in relation to the eye movement. The top plots show the event (visual target or saccade). The middle plots show neural activity in a raster display with each line of the raster corresponding to a successive trial. The bottom plots show averaged neural activity. The right hand panels show additionally the activity of neurons with the fixation zone at the rostral pole of the SC. (Modified from Wurtz, 1996).

well before the actual movement and reaches a peak just before the saccade is triggered. The *burst* cells are similar to their namesakes in the MRF and PPRF, in showing a brief burst of discharge just prior to the movement. In each case, activity is only found preceding movements in the appropriate direction for the oculomotor map, with the burst cells being more tightly tuned in this respect than the buildup cells.

The events in the SC that lead up to a saccade may be portrayed as follows (Fig. 4.8). In the region of the SC corresponding to the location in space to which the eyes will be directed, the buildup cells in the intermediate layers gradually increase their activity. This increase is presumed to occur because of activity in the various descending pathways (Fig. 4.6). At the same time, cells in the fixation region of the rostral pole show a decrease in activity. At some point, the activity balance reaches the point where an abrupt switch is triggered. At this point, rostral pole activity ceases, the burst cells start firing and the activity characteristic of saccades occurs in MRF and PPRF. Whilst the activity in the buildup cells may reflect the very varied nature of the descending stimulation, the subsequent triggering process ensures that, when saccades are produced, they show a very stereotyped pattern. Although latencies will be affected by events both in the fixation region and in the buildup region, Dorris *et al.* (1997) found that, prior to express saccades, saccadic latencies correlated well with prior activity at the buildup location and not with prior activity in the fixation region.

4.3.3 Variability of saccade latencies

An interesting convergence has also occurred between theoretical work and neurophysiological studies concerned with the variability in saccade latencies. The LATER model proposed by Carpenter (Section 4.2.5) appears to be reflected quite well in processes occurring at the single cell level. Studies of cell activity within primate frontal eye field (Hanes and Schall, 1996; Schall and Hanes, 1998) showed that in the period immediately before a saccade, neural activity showed a steady increase. The rate of this increase correlated well with saccade latency, supporting an accumulator model whereby the initiation of the saccade occurring when this becomes sufficiently high. Similar correspondences have been reported at the level of the superior colliculus (Dorris *et al.*, 1997).

4.4 What determines the landing position of orienting saccades?

We are so familiar with the ability to direct our eyes to any target at will that we rarely reflect on the fact that this is a considerable achievement of neural processing although, as described in Chapter 8, the loss of this ability can be devastating. Many studies of target-elicited saccades have investigated the ability in detail (see Hallett, 1986 or Becker, 1989 for a fuller account). For targets within about the central 10 degrees of vision, the most common pattern is for a single saccade to move the gaze directly to the target. Such saccades show the stereotyped saccade trajectories described in Section 2.4 but their amplitudes are variable (the range is typically about 5–10 per cent of the movement amplitude; Kowler and Blaser, 1995). A small secondary, error correcting, saccade may follow the first, primary, saccade. With larger movements, undershoot and secondary saccades become more common. A widely held view is that saccadic undershoot of about 10 per cent is normal, although this has been challenged (Kapoula and Robinson, 1986). For small saccades, the occurrence of secondary corrective movements increases when a task requires scrutiny (Findlay and Kapoula, 1992). An occasional variant on the standard pattern is for the eye to move to the target in a series of small saccades (Crawford, 1991, Section 4.7).

4.4.1 Corrective saccades

Study of the corrective saccades that follow a primary orienting saccade has yielded some interesting insights. If the target for orienting is flashed briefly, so that it is no longer visible when the first saccade is made, corrective saccades are still found but less frequently (Becker, 1972). This suggests that corrective saccades may occur either on the basis of a pre-planned sequence or on the basis of a visual error sampled after the end of the first saccade. The latency of the corrective saccade, i.e. the duration of the fixation following the first saccade, is quite tightly dependent on the size of the gaze error remaining after the first saccade (Becker, 1989).

A typical experiment investigating orienting saccades will present a set of trials with targets at a set of varied different amplitudes. Subjects rapidly become aware of the properties of the set; this is demonstrated by saccades to the lower amplitude targets showing slight undershoot and those to higher amplitude targets slight overshoot (Kapoula, 1985). This is a familiar finding in motor response investigations, known as the *range effect*.

4.4.2 The double step paradigm

In the double step paradigm an observer is asked to follow with their eyes a target which makes two successive movements in a quick sequence. The idea behind the paradigm is to measure the effects of the second stimulus step on the programming of the saccade to the first step. A typical experiment would be designed to prevent, as far as possible, the observer predicting the stimulus properties. Double steps in varying direction and with varying intervals between them would typically occur unpredictably in a set of trials that also contained single target steps. The paradigm has been widely employed (Komoda *et al.*, 1973; Becker and Jürgens, 1979; Findlay and Harris, 1984, Aslin and Shea, 1987) and has been most informative.

Three principal outcomes occur on double step trials. First, the eye following can consist of a separate saccade to each step in turn. This situation will typically occur when the interval between the two steps is long and the response to the first step is complete before the perturbing influence of the second step is felt. At the opposite extreme, the eye may make a single saccade to the final position following the two steps, ignoring the pause at the intermediate position. This outcome is found when the pause between the two steps is very brief. The third possible outcome that is found is where the first saccade goes to neither target position but instead to a location intermediate between the target locations. Such a saccade would generally be followed by a second saccade to the target 2 location. A further option, that the saccade trajectory itself is modified, appears only to occur for large saccades (Section 2.4.1).

Becker and Jürgens (1979) showed that the most important determinant of the type of outcome was a variable measuring the time elapsing between the second step and the initial saccade. They designated this variable D and, as shown in Fig. 4.9, under certain conditions an *amplitude transition function* may be plotted to show the systematic dependence of the first saccade end point on D. For small values of D, the perturbing second step does not affect the saccade. For large values of D, the eye moves to the new position following the second step. Thus the new step fully captures the saccade. Becker and Jürgens found that for an intermediate range of D values, a compromise saccade occurs with endpoints landing between the two positions occupied by the target and showing a smooth transition between the first and second step locations. The point at which this transition starts shows the last point in time at which it is possible influence a saccade about to be launched. For small saccades, this value is about 80 ms, although in the case of larger saccades, Becker and Jürgens reported higher values.

Amplitude transitions of the type shown in Fig. 4.9 are found when the two target positions are at different eccentricities along an axis away from fixation. A different pattern was found when one location was on the right and the

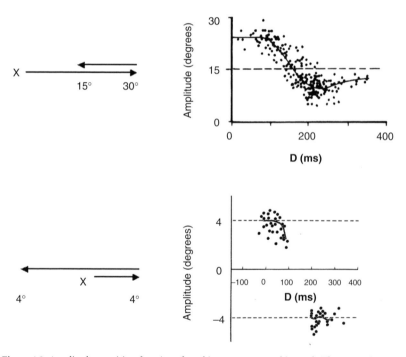

Figure 4.9 Amplitude transition functions found in a two-step tracking task. The successive steps made by the target are shown on the left hand side. In the right hand plots, each dot represents a single saccade. The amplitude of the saccade is plotted against the variable D, the time elapsing between the occurrence of the *second* target step and the initiation of the saccade. Top plot from Becker (1989) and lower plot from Findlay and Harris (1984).

other on the left (only horizontal saccades were considered in the Becker and Jürgens, 1979, study). In this case, as in the one just described, steps occurring with values of D less than about 80 ms had no effect. After this point, all saccades were directed to the second target (contralateral to the first). In the range of D values where the transition function was found in the ipsilateral case, no saccades at all were noted.

On the basis of their findings, Becker and Jürgens (1979) proposed a two stage model of saccade generation. The two stages are shown schematically in Fig. 4.10. The decision stage has the responsibility of deciding when the eyes are to move and in which direction. When the decision is made, a signal is sent to the amplitude computation stage, which is responsible for the magnitude of the movement. The amplitude computation stage works in a completely automatic manner to compute the desired amplitude by sampling the target information. The sampling is not made on an instantaneous basis but integrates whatever information is available within a temporal window. The duration of the amplitude transition function corresponds to the duration of this window. If, during this integration period, the target changes position, the resultant amplitude that

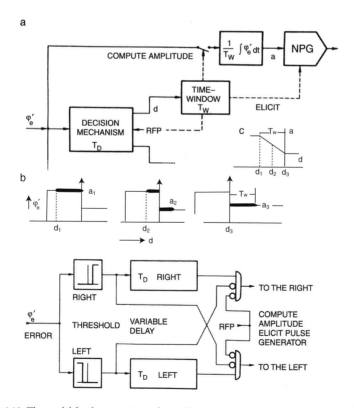

Figure 4.10 The model for the generation of saccades proposed by Becker and Jürgens (1979).

emerges is from a weighted integration of the two target positions. This integration process accounts for the saccades directed to intermediate locations.

The model has affinities with the WHERE/WHEN separation discussed in earlier sections of this chapter. However Becker and Jürgens associated part of the WHEN computation in the decision stage of their model. The model accounts very well for findings from the two-step paradigm and other paradigms in connection with horizontal saccades but runs into some problems when the more general case of saccades in two-dimensional space is considered. Findlay and Harris (1984), and Aslin and Shea (1987) found transition functions for both amplitude and direction in experiments using the double-step paradigm in the two-dimensional case. Findlay and Walker (1999) have argued that the delay in responding to a contralateral step is an instance of the remote distractor effect (Section 4.3.2) rather than representing a specific direction re-programming. They offer an alternative model in which amplitude and direction are not separately programmed but all programming comes about through selection on a 2D spatial map (Section 4.6).

4.4.3 The double target paradigm

Another well studied variant of the target-elicited saccade paradigm has two targets appearing simultaneously. A frequent finding, as noted already in Section 4.2.3, is that, when the stimuli are in reasonably close proximity, the orienting saccade goes to an intermediate location between the targets rather than accurately to either individual target. Following the interpretation of the comparable finding in the two-step paradigm, an explanation may be offered that the saccade amplitude computation is based on stimulation integrated over a wide area of visual space; the term *global effect* reflects this aspect of the finding. The relative properties of the targets such as size and brightness influence the saccade landing position in such a way that the effect is often appropriately described as a *centre-of-gravity* effect (Deubel *et al.*, 1984; Findlay, 1982; Findlay *et al.*, 1993; Ottes *et al.*, 1984). The effect has been demonstrated and studied in monkeys (Schiller, 1998; Chou *et al.*, 1999). These findings show that the effect is one that involves integration of the visual signal in a relatively 'raw' form. Nevertheless, various findings suggest that the effect should be assigned to a relatively late stage in the visuomotor pathways.

He and Kowler (1989) carried out a double target experiment in the form of a search task. Two stimuli were presented that differed in form ($+$ vs. $\times$) and one was designated as the search target. Subjects showed no ability to use peripheral vision sufficiently well to direct their eyes to the search target. Saccades generally landed at intermediate locations but the landing positions were systematically affected by prior knowledge about the most likely location for the search target. He and Kowler argued from this finding that the global effect was dependent on high level strategies. A more appropriate interpretation would appear to be that of Ottes *et al.* (1985) who suggest that the global effect represents a default option for the saccadic system but may be modulated by higher level search or cognitive strategies. The main studies of the global effect have been in connection with visual orienting but claims have been made that the effect plays a role in the choice of saccade landing points in text reading (Vitu, 1991*a* see Chapter 5).

4.4.4 Parallel processing of saccades

In the section on corrective saccades (Section 4.4.1), it was noted that such saccades were occasionally found even when the target was no longer visible after the end of the first saccade. This implies that the second saccade was pre-programmed. Another result suggesting that more than one saccade can be processed at a time is the occurrence of very short fixations (<100 ms) in visual tasks. Becker and Jürgens (1979) noted such short latency second saccades in the double step paradigm discussed above and also proposed that saccades may be prepared in a paired manner. For a pair of saccades to be directed accurately, it is necessary that the second saccade takes account of the eye rotation achieved by the first, raising some important questions which we return to in Chapter 9.

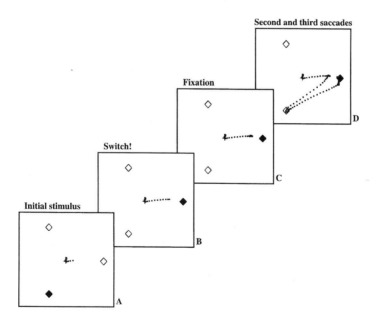

Figure 4.11 Display sequence used by McPeek *et al.* (2000) with superimposed example eye record. The subject is instructed to make a saccadic movement to the target defined as the odd one of the three (actual displays used red and green shapes). On some trials, two of the shapes were switched. The trace shows an example where the switch brings the target to the saccade destination. Nevertheless, the saccade stops short and a further saccade is made to the former target location before a final saccade on to the target at the new location.

Interest in the phenomenon has recently revived with the discovery that short duration fixations occur commonly in scanning and visual search tasks (Findlay *et al.*, 2001; McPeek *et al.*, 2000; Sommer, 1994). This form of programming is also reported for within word refixations in reading (Section 5.6) and may be more common than previously thought. McPeek *et al.* (2000) studied saccades in an oddity search task (Section 6.1). On each trial, a display consisting of three elements occurred, either two red and one green, or two green and one red. The task was to move the eyes to the target with the unique colour. First saccades were frequently misdirected but in many cases, a second saccade to the target occurred following a very brief fixation. McPeek *et al.* combined this task with a saccade-contingent manipulation such that the display changed during the course of the first saccade. The change reversed the colours of the two items away from the direction of the saccade (Fig. 4.11). When the fixation before the second saccade was brief, the second saccade went towards the first location occupied by the target, showing that the target location was registered on the initial fixation. Surprisingly however, such 'memory directed' saccades occurred after normal and even relatively long fixations also. Only when the fixation duration was greater than 250 ms, was the colour switch taken into account. This suggests that pipelined double programming of saccades may be much more common than previously suspected.

4.4.5 Antisaccades

The antisaccade task was first developed by Peter Hallett (Hallett, 1978; Hallett and Adams, 1980). In the task, the participant is required to respond to a visual target by making a saccadic movement to a position in space located at the opposite side to the target. So, for example, if the target is on the right hand side of fixation then the correct response is to make a leftward saccade to the mirror image location. The task is of value for two reasons: first, as a means of investigating the interaction of reflex and voluntary control of saccadic movements; second, as a marker for diverse neurological conditions (Section 8.4). A review of both normal and clinical findings was made by Everling and Fischer (1998). Successful performance in the antisaccade task, requires participants to suppress the natural tendency to make an orienting saccade to the target. In discussions concerned with antisaccades, these reflex-like erroneous orienting movements are frequently termed *prosaccades*.

Participants are normally able to generate antisaccades, however across trials errors do occur in the form of a reflex prosaccade to the target. Interestingly, subjects are often unaware that an erroneous prosaccade has been made (Mokler and Fischer, 1999). The proportion of prosaccade errors decreases with practice, to typically around 20 per cent, although with considerable individual variability, as demonstrated in a large scale study on over 2000 young conscripts by Evokimidis *et al.* (2002). Mean reaction times for antisaccades are somewhat greater than for prosaccades and no antisaccades ever occur with latencies in the express range described in Section 4.2.4 (Fischer and Weber, 1992). Error rates increase and latencies decrease systematically as the target amplitude increases from 1° to 12° (Fischer and Weber, 1996). Krappman (1998) carried out a study of antisaccades in the eight principal directions and showed that the variability in landing positions was high although saccade direction was generally roughly appropriate. Corrective saccades occurred but resulted in only a small improvement in accuracy.

As discussed in Section 8.4, patients with frontal lobe damage experience difficulty in suppressing erroneous prosaccades. This has led to the suggestion (e.g. Walker *et al.*, 1998) that to generate an antisaccade it is necessary for a frontal system to send a signal to the superior colliculus to inhibit the natural reflexive saccade before the antisaccade is programmed. Nevertheless given the increasing evidence for parallel processing of saccades, it seems likely that both prosaccade and antisaccade are prepared in parallel (Section 4.4.4), as proposed by Mokler and Fischer (1999). This would then account for the relatively short latency difference between pro and antisaccades. Zhang and Barash (2000) conclude that the transformation needed to generate the antisaccade is 'visual' rather than 'visuomotor', on the basis of their finding of the early appearance (50 ms after target onset) of increased neural activity in the parietal cortex at the location of the target for the antisaccade.

4.5 Physiology of the WHERE system

In Section 4.4, the role played by the superior colliculus in saccade generation was outlined. Selection of the saccade target was achieved by selecting the point on the oculomotor map at which burst activity took place. An important property of the visual representation in the SC is the fact that although a series of precise maps are present at different layers of the structure, in the layers at which visual and motor systems make contact, the spatial coding occurs in a highly distributed manner. This means that the visual receptive fields are large and overlapping so that any cell maps an extensive region of visual field and the representation of a point target extends over a considerable region of the collicular map. The SC thus uses a distributed population code to represent visual and oculomotor direction, a property first remarked on by McIlwain (1976; see also McIlwain, 1991). Experimental studies such as that of Lee *et al.* (1988), illustrated in Fig. 4.12, have confirmed these findings. Robinson (1972) and others have shown that simultaneous stimulation of two separate locations in the motor map of the SC will produce a saccade which is a vector average, in much the same way as that seen in behavioural experiments (see also Glimcher and Sparks, 1993).

This distributed representation assists in the conversion of a spatial, retinotopically mapped visual signal to an appropriate temporal code for the

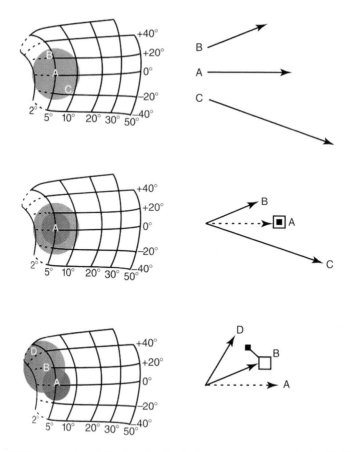

Figure 4.12 Demonstration of distributed coding in the monkey superior colliculus. The left hand column shows schematically the collicular motor map. Stimulation at locations A, B and C respectively leads to saccades with the vectors shown in the top row. The light grey area shows the region of colliculus active before the 5° rightwards saccade obtained by stimulation at A. The lower two rows shows the result of stimulation following an injection of lidocaine centred at point A. The dark grey area estimates the affected region. Stimulation at A (centre) still results in saccades 5° rightwards, because the result of vector averaging from the unaffected regions sums to this vector. However, stimulation at B now results in a saccade displaced towards the direction obtained through stimulation at point D, since the dark shaded region no longer contributes to the vector summation. From Lee *et al.* (1988).

activation of the eye muscles, the details of which process are outside the scope of this volume (see McIlwain, 1976 and Van Gisbergen *et al.*, 1987 for implementation suggestions). When only a single target is considered, distributed representations are as accurate as point-to-point ones. However two co-occurring targets will tend to form a single representation, exactly the feature found in the global effect (Section 4.4.3).

4.5.1 Spatial coding and the saccadic system

An extremely influential article by Robinson (1975) affected much subsequent thinking about the saccadic system. Robinson noted the evidence that saccades were directed towards some internal goal state and proposed that this goal state was a location in a mental representation of space having a head-centred organisation. Support for this came, amongst other reasons, from the demonstrated ability to make a saccade towards the source of a sound (Zambarbieri *et al.*, 1982, Zahn *et al.*, 1978). Sound localisation is dependent principally on the difference in sound characteristics arriving at each ear and is thus initially coded with respect to the head direction.

A further finding which supported Robinson's position was that of Mays and Sparks (1980). Mays and Sparks trained monkeys to saccade to a flashed target in an otherwise dark room. Immediately after the target flash, they electrically stimulated a location in the SC. This has the effect of generating an artificial saccadic movement. The idea was to generate this movement in the latency period of the target elicited saccade and examine whether the manipulation changed the saccade characteristics. The results were unequivocal. The monkey produced the saccade required to reach the target location from the new position of the eyes following the stimulation saccade. In some way, this displacement had been 'taken into account' as the movement was prepared.

The idea of a head centred co-ordinate system has encountered some problems however. Signals in neural centres related to saccadic eye movements seem invariably to use oculocentric, rather than head-centred, co-ordinates (Moschovakis and Highstein, 1994, but see Section 9.3.3). An alternative interpretation of the Mays and Sparks result by Droulez and Berthoz (1990, 1991) emphasizes motor memory. This suggestion involves memory relating to space being encoded in terms of related motor activity so that memory for a visual field location would be encoded in terms of the command signals to direct the eyes at the location. This suggestion has support from the finding of Jay and Sparks (1987) that the auditory representation of space in the superior colliculus shifts with changes in eye position. Thus it is a representation that allows the eyes to be directed to a sound source, rather than having any absolute framework. Recent work, discussed in Chapter 9, shows that the same process occurs also with the visual representation.

4.6 The Findlay and Walker model

Findlay and Walker (1999) proposed that the insights gained into the organisation of the orienting system could be captured by the model shown in Fig. 4.13.

The model is primarily a functional account but is also designed to be compatible with the emerging physiological knowledge of the brain pathways involved in orienting. A principal feature is the separation of the pathways controlling WHEN and WHERE information. This shown by the two vertical streams of the model. The WHERE stream is a set of interconnected activity

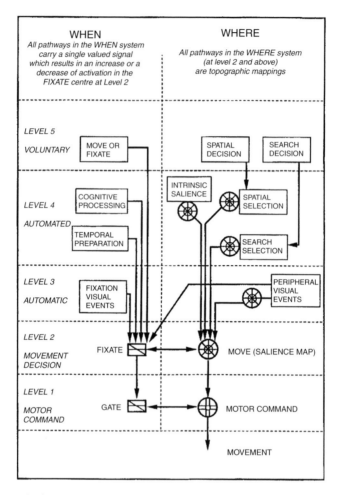

Figure 4.13 The framework for saccadic eye movement generation presented by Findlay and Walker (1999).

maps, resulting in a 'salience map' from which the saccadic target location is selected. The idea of a salience map has figured strongly in theories of visual search (Section 6.4.3). Location coding in the activity maps occurs in a distributed manner. In contrast, the WHEN stream is envisaged as a single individual signal whose activity level varies. The horizontal bands represent processing levels that become progressively less automatic ascending up the hierarchy from bottom to top. Interaction between the two streams occurs at the lower levels in terms of reciprocal competitive inhibition.

Level 1 is specifically designed to capture the interaction in the brain stem between described in Section 4.3.1, with the burst cell system and the pause cell system interacting reciprocally to trigger each saccadic movement. When the balance crosses some critical level, the saccade is irrevocably triggered. This level 1 interaction is in turn influenced by the next level in the hierarchy. At level 2, a push-pull competitive interaction occurs between the *fixate centre* and the *move centre*. The operations at level 2 are similar to those at level 1 but whereas level 1 operates in a highly automatic manner to effect a rapid movement, level 2 works by a slower and more variable build up in one centre and declines in the other. This time consuming process is largely responsible for the exact point in time at which the saccade is generated. Although level 2 shows obvious similarities to the processing in the superior colliculus (Section 4.3.2), Findlay and Walker avoid the exclusive identification with SC processes and suggest that similar competitive interaction may also occur in other brain centres.

Level 3 reflects the fact that transient visual events appear to have automatic and unavoidable influences on the orienting process. Events at the point currently fixated have a substantial and unavoidable effect on the fixation system. Events in the periphery have an automatic effect on the salience map of the move centre, although whether this leads to overt orienting depends on the state of the level 2 fixate/move balance. Events in the periphery also influence the *fixate* system, shown as a cross-linking pathway. Level 4 and level 5 are much more loosely designated and sketch how higher order influences might play a role.

The model accounted for a number of well-established findings in saccadic orienting, specifically the gap effect, express saccades, the remote distractor effect and the global effect. The model was presented in a journal with open peer commentary, most of which was supportive of the approach, often proposing more detailed schemes of implementation. Indeed two such schemes have appeared in subsequent publications (Clark, 1999; Trappenberg *et al.*, 2001). An interesting detail suggestion from physiological workers derives from the proposal originally made by Krauzlis *et al.* (1997) that fixation cells and build-up cells form a continuum. This offers a more integrated account of level 2 processes in which a single activity map projects differentially to level 1; projections in the WHEN pathway being mainly but not exclusively from the region representing the fovea and projections in the WHERE pathway being from the remainder of the map. A final point to note is that the model cannot, as formulated, offer any account of paired programming (Section 4.4.4).

4.7 Development and plasticity

The account given in the previous sections has described a set of smoothly functioning neural processes that are now rather well understood. In this section we review first evidence that these orienting mechanisms are present in some form at a very early stage of life and finally discuss adaptive mechanisms that maintain the accuracy of orienting.

The development of visual orienting has been the subject of much systematic study. Orienting responses to salient peripheral targets are present from birth, at least within the central 30 degrees of the periphery (Maurer and Lewis, 1998). The probability of an orienting response occurring depends upon stimulus variables such as size and contrast. With age, the area of the visual field that provokes orienting expands and the latencies of orienting responses decrease. Aslin and Salapatek (1975) reported that infants in the first two months of life oriented by using a staircase pattern of small saccades rather than a single one, although there is also evidence that more adult-like saccadic responses occur with more realistic stimulus material (Hainline, 1998). Evidence that competition between stimuli at fixation and peripheral targets appears from a very early age comes from the demonstration that the gap effect (Section 4.2.1) is found with young infants (Hood and Atkinson, 1993). A particularly interesting phenomenon termed 'sticky fixation' often occurs at around 1–2 months of age where babies can show great reluctance to move away from a central target (Hood *et al.*, 1998).

One aim in studying visual development is to relate behavioural findings to knowledge about neurological maturation. An influential paper by Bronson (1974) suggested that, below about two months of age, all visual processing was carried out subcortically and that the SC formed the major orienting centre in infants. This position has gradually become less tenable with the appreciation that the retino-collicular pathway is probably not connected to the collicular orienting centres (Section 4.3.2), and demonstrations of infant capacities beyond those previously used by Bronson support his argument (Slater *et al.*, 1982). Johnson (1997) has articulated a position more in line with current understanding of brain orienting processes.

The orienting response achieves a transformation from an input signal, the location of the visual target on the retina, to an output signal, the oculomotor command. Eye saccades are ballistic and stereotyped (Section 2.4) so that the immediate response is deterministic. However over longer time periods, the coupling between input and output can be adjusted. Such adjustment maintains the accuracy of the orienting and allows the system to work effectively in spite of changes in muscle strength, both normal and pathological.

An impressive early demonstration of these adaptive mechanisms occurred in a study by Kommerell *et al.* (1976). These workers studied a patient who had a muscle paresis (weakness) in one eye only. When an eye patch was placed over the normal eye, it was found that, following a period of a few hours, the amplitude of the saccades elicited by a target (presented in either eye) had increased. Switching the patch over to the abnormal eye reversed the process and a gradual decrease in the size of movements occurred. In some way the system was able to adjust to the information that the eye was not reaching its desired target.

Similar adaptation can readily be shown in the laboratory with an ingenious paradigm first introduced by McLoughlin (1967). A target is displayed on a screen to initiate a saccade. The observer's eye position is monitored and, as

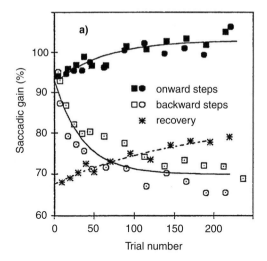

Figure 4.14 Adaptation of saccade gain resulting from displacement of the target during an orienting saccade. The plot shows the steady incremental change in saccade gain (saccade amplitude ÷ target displacement). From Deubel (1991).

soon as the orienting saccade starts, the target is moved to a new location. Saccadic suppression (Section 2.4.3) ensures that such a change is undetectable to the observer. Nevertheless, as shown in Fig. 4.14, if such a manipulation occurs regularly over a series of saccades, adaptation is found. The significance of this finding is taken up again in Chapter 9.

Deubel (1987, 1991, 1995) has demonstrated a number of properties of this adaptation. Generalisation tests involve adapting to changes made to saccades to one specific target location, and testing the effect on target-elicited saccades at a variety of locations. These show that adaptation generalises only to a small set of directions adjacent to that experienced during the adaptation period. In contrast, adaptation of saccades at one particular amplitude demonstrates substantial transfer to saccade of different amplitude in the same direction. Separate adaptation mechanisms can be demonstrated for target-elicited saccades and for volitional saccades.

CHAPTER 5

VISUAL SAMPLING DURING TEXT READING

5.1 Introduction

Literacy is one of the great hallmarks of civilisation. For many people in the modern world, the activity of reading is the most frequent way in which vision is used actively. It is thus no surprise that the reading process forms one of the most heavily investigated topics in the history of psychology. Much scientific work relates to broader scales of analysis than are of interest here but throughout the history of the subject, the detail of the visual sampling process has fascinated many workers. Progress has been made to the point where we have a good understanding of many of the issues concerned with the sampling of information by the eyes during reading. The ability to specify and control the text stimuli has in turn led to the study of reading providing an excellent opportunity to investigate the interaction between lower and higher level processes characteristic of active vision. This chapter reviews the progress in the area.

Studies of eye movements during reading have a long history. The realisation that the eyes do not move smoothly across the text, but rather in a series of jumps, appears to have been first made by Javal (1878) working at the University of Paris (Section 2.4). The development of an effective photographic method for recording eye movement activity led to considerable interest in the topic. The pioneering work on the technique came through the cross-national collaboration of Dodge, an American, who worked in Germany with Erdmann at the University of Halle (described in Huey, 1908). This led to the first wave of interest in the topic during the first forty years of the century. Early work (see Huey, 1908) confirmed and refined the French observations on the basic pattern of eye movements in reading. Subsequent work mainly studied cumulative measures such as average saccade length and average fixation duration. Many studies had an applied emphasis, being particularly concerned with topics such as individual differences in reading speeds, and the effect of different text layouts. A series of reviews by Tinker (1946, 1958, 1965) reflects the flavour of this period.

In the following thirty years, interest in this area, as in all areas of cognitive psychology, waned until the second wave of research took off in the 1970s. Much credit for the revival must be given to two American workers, George

McConkie and Keith Rayner, whose initial collaboration at Cornell University started two very productive research careers with findings that will appear frequently in the following pages. Other centres, particularly the collaboration of Ariane Lévy-Schoen and Kevin O'Regan in Paris also made major contributions. The emphasis now became directed at the moment-to-moment control of the eyes. Once again technological advances played a major role; in this case the digital computer both allowed more sophisticated experimental manipulations and provided the capacity for the analysis of large quantities of data. Interestingly, the possibility must be contemplated that the computer revolution could eventually lead to alternative ways of presenting text in which eye movements are no longer a necessity (Rubin and Turano, 1992).

Consideration of reading, as active vision, generates the questions about active vision addressed elsewhere in this book concerning the details of how the visual world, in this case the text, is sampled. Reading involves an interaction between the perceptual and the cognitive systems. The basic perceptual questions are straightforward. Many studies have shown that, during reading, useful information is only being taken in from a limited region around the fovea. The term *perceptual span* has been used to denote this region and much work has been directed to delineating the perceptual span and factors that affect it. Early work attempted to simulate an eye fixation using the tachistoscope, a device for delivering a very brief stimulus. However, a superior direct technique for studying the perceptual span was developed in 1975 by McConkie and Rayner as described in Section 5.3.1. The perceptual span is related to, but distinct from, the *visual span*, the region around the fovea within which recognition is possible given the acuity limitations (see Chapter 2 and Section 6.4). It turns out that not all the information potentially available is actually used.

The object of reading is to derive meaning from the abstract visual patterns of the text and in some way the visual sampling rate must be matched to the speed of comprehension. A major issue concerns the extent to which the linguistic processes involved in the comprehension of the text can control, or influence, the way the eyes move. A ubiquitous finding is that the pattern of eye sampling is responsive on a moment-to-moment basis to the cognitive demands of the text, this influence mainly appearing in the decision about the point in time when the eyes are moved. A full account of eye movement control in reading thus requires some understanding of how linguistic comprehension takes place. The section on language processing (Section 5.4) provides a description of the rudiments of language processing necessary for this understanding, but the treatment of this vast topic is inevitably very sketchy.

5.2 Basic patterns of visual sampling during reading

During reading, the eye moves along each line of text with a series of saccadic movements, separated by fixation pauses. At the end of each line, a large saccadic eye movement (the return sweep) takes the eye to the beginning of the following line. The great majority of the movements along the line are forward movements but movements in the reverse direction also occur. These can be classified either as within word *refixations* or inter word *regressions*. The latter category appear more deliberate and are clearly related to difficulties in processing the text whereas the former, together with similar forward directed refixations, appears to be an inherent part of the oculomotor strategy, although related to word perceptibility (Vitu, McConkie and Zola, 1998). For fluent readers of English text, the average size of a forward movement is around 7–9 letter spaces in adult readers. The average duration of a fixation is around 200–250 ms and that of each saccade about 30 ms. If regressive movements are ignored, these two figures combine to result in a typical reading rate of about 250 words per minute.

These generalisations have appeared in textbooks since the turn of the century (they were set out clearly by Huey, 1908). It is perhaps somewhat surprising that average figures can be given which are broadly correct irrespective of the characteristics of texts and of conditions of viewing. It is worth considering the implications of our ability to make such a general statement. The size of saccade specified above uses the character space as the unit of measure. Since the size of a text character in terms of visual angle varies considerably with the size of the text and its viewing distance, the saccade size, measured in degrees of visual angle, is equally variable. However, within very broad limits the visual/oculomotor system adjusts effortlessly to scale saccadic movements appropriately to the retinal size of the text being viewed (see Section 2.1.2). A formal demonstration of the truth of this assertion in relation to viewing distance was given by Morrison and Rayner (1981; see also Morrison, 1983).

Variation from the average figure occurs for numerous reasons. Not surprisingly, the content of the text affects reading speed. Reading speed varies with the difficulty of the text and the skill of the reader. This was intensively investigated in the first major phase of research and it was shown that each of the individual oculomotor measures is affected by text difficulty. (Table 5.1). A similar pattern emerges from the study of the way in which reading develops during childhood (Table 5.2).

In addition to these overall changes, there has been considerable interest in the distribution of the measures. Typical patterns are shown in Fig. 5.1. The distribution of fixation times shows a pronounced peak between 200 and 250 ms with a tail of longer fixations and occasional very short fixations which are more common in some individuals than others (Radach *et al.*, 1998).

Saccade length, measured in character spaces, as explained above, shows a bimodal distribution. The great majority of saccades take the eye forward through the text, with quite a sharp peak around 8 letter spaces. Regressive movements are generally quite small, although readers do very occasionally step back a number of lines in the text. The revival of interest in cognitive processes in the 1970s has focused on attempting to explain the factors giving rise to these distributions.

Table 5.1 Average eye movement parameters measured with various types of text (from Rayner and Pollatsek, 1989)

Topic	Fixation Duration (ms)	Saccade Length (character spaces)	Regression per cent	w.p.m.
Light fiction	202	9.2	3	365
Newspaper	209	8.3	6	321
History	222	8.3	4	313
Psychology	206	8.1	11	308
English Literature	220	7.9	10	305
Economics	233	7.0	11	268
Mathematics	254	7.3	18	243
Physics	261	6.9	17	238
Biology	264	6.8	18	233
(Mean)	231	7.8	11	288

Table 5.2 Eye movement parameters of children of average ability at various school grades (from Buswell, 1922 as reproduced in Woodworth and Schlosberg, 1954)

School grade	Fixations per line	Mean fixation duration (ms)	Regressions per line
IB	18.6	660	5.1
IA	15.5	432	4.0
II	10.7	364	2.3
III	8.9	316	1.8
IV	7.3	268	1.4
V	6.9	252	1.3
VI	7.8	236	1.6
VII	6.8	240	1.5
High School I	7.2	244	1.0
High School II	5.8	248	0.7
High School III	5.5	224	0.7
High School IV	6.4	248	0.7
College	5.9	252	0.5

Readers in general use both eyes when reading, and a further topic of some interest relates to binocular co-ordination. To what extent do the two eyes move together in reading? Work by Hendriks (1996) and Heller and Radach (1998) have confirmed that systematic vergence changes occur during fixations in the course of reading. Both studies report convergence movements, consistent with the known transient divergence associated with the execution of saccades (Section 2.4.2). Hendriks reported higher vergence velocity during the reading of prose in comparison to disconnected word lists and suggests that attentional factors may be involved. In the light of suggestions that binocular eye control may be one cause of reading difficulties (Section 5.8.2), these findings are of some interest.

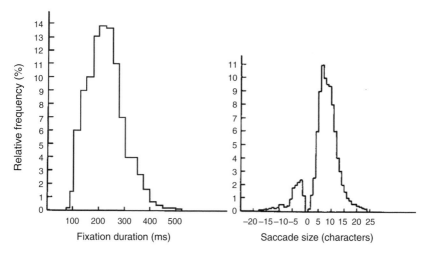

Figure 5.1 Frequency distributions of fixation duration (left hand plot) and saccade size excluding return sweeps (right hand plot) for college age readers (from Rayner and Pollatsek, 1989).

5.3 Perception during fixations in reading

A key question about any process of active vision must be what visual information is contributing to the process. To answer this question, it is necessary to take into account first the decline in acuity for material distant from the fixation point (Section 2.1.1) and second, the brief duration for which material is viewed during a fixation. The invention of the tachistoscope was, in part, an attempt to provide a means of assessing the latter point, and early work (Cattell, 1885) showed that only a limited amount of visual material could be extracted from a briefly flashed presentation. However, there are a number of difficulties in interpreting tachistoscopic data, and a superior way of attacking the question appeared in the 1970s.

5.3.1 Gaze-contingent methodologies

McConkie and Rayner (1975) introduced a technique whereby assessment could be made of the way vision was used during the reading process and indeed during other visual processes. The logic is straightforward. If material from a particular region of the retina is being sampled during reading, then interfering with the visual input to that region will have a deleterious effect on the reading process (as measured by effects on reading rate and/or measures of oculomotor performance). Conversely, if it is possible to interfere with visual input to a particular region without deleterious effect, then a plausible assumption is that material from this region is not generally used. Using this approach, it is possible to probe the way in which information is used during the actual reading process itself. Implementation of this idea demands something of a technical tour de force since it is necessary to maintain a modified region at a fixed position on the retina as the eyes move around the text; the modified region must be made *gaze-contingent*, moving around the text as the eyes move. In a gaze-contingent display, information from an accurate record of gaze position is used to modify the way in which the display on a computer monitor is programmed.

A variety of types of modifications can be made as illustrated in Fig. 5.2. The most common is the *moving window* technique devised by McConkie and Rayner (1975), in which a particular region is designated as a window. As the eyes move, the display is modified so that, for example, all material within the window is seen normally whereas all material outside the window is modified. In the *foveal mask* technique (Rayner and Beretra, 1979), the situation is reversed with material inside the window modified and that outside unaffected. The result is a foveal *scotoma* or local area of blindness. A further variant, the *boundary* technique (Rayner, 1975), causes a change to occur when the eyes cross an imaginary boundary. In the gaze-contingent technique, the text modifications are always carried out during the period when the eye is making a saccadic movement. Subjects are generally unaware of changes that occur during saccades (Section 2.4.3). So under these circumstances there is never any immediate awareness of the manipulation.

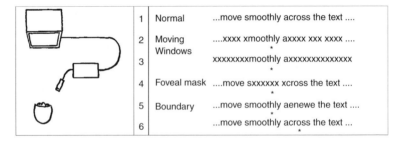

Figure 5.2 The gaze-contingent paradigm. The left hand box shows the essential requirements in a schematised way. A probe measuring the exact position of the eye is interfaced to a VDU in such a way that the material presented on the screen can be made to change in a *gaze-contingent* manner, depending on where the gaze is directed. Several uses of the technique are shown in the right hand box. The top row (1) shows the underlying line of text. In the subsequent rows, the appearance of the text is shown at the point when the eyes fixate the location on the line of text just above the asterisk. The asterisk would not appear on the screen. In the moving window technique, text outside the window is replaced by crosses. The effects of a nine-character window are shown here in two variant forms. In (2) all text characters apart from spaces are changed, in (3) spaces are also replaced. The converse condition of the foveal mask is shown in (4). Material inside the window is replaced. (5) and (6) show the use of the boundary technique. A critical word in the text (here the word 'across') is modified when the gaze crosses an invisible boundary (denoted here by the vertical dotted line). The text is shown when the eye is directed to 'smoothly' (5) and subsequently to 'across' (6).

5.3.2 Measurement of the perceptual span

A great number of experiments have been carried out using the gaze-contingent techniques (for summaries see Rayner, 1995, 1998) and a clear picture has emerged from this research about the way that visual information is sampled during continuous reading. Unsurprisingly, the foveal region turns out to be crucial for reading. If the foveal mask technique is set up to create an artificial scotoma, where text falling on the fovea is mutilated while text in the parafoveal and peripheral regions are unaffected, then reading becomes almost impossible (Rayner and Beretra, 1979). Using a mask that just covered the fovea and corresponded to 7 characters with the text size used, 'reading' rate dropped to 12 words per minute and many errors occurred. One subject misread the sentence 'The pretty bracelet attracted much attention' as 'The priest brought much ammunition.'

Reading is much less affected in the converse moving window situation where only foveal vision is available but nevertheless reading rates are significantly reduced. This shows that information from outside the fovea also contributes significantly to the process of normal reading. The results of a number of studies varying window sizes and the manipulation made to the text outside the window have led to the following conclusions (Rayner, 1995) about the perceptual span during text reading.

The span is asymmetric. Modifications made more than 3–4 characters to the left of the current fixation point (or even closer if they are outside the word currently fixated) have no effect. However modifications made to the right of the word out to about 15 characters can result in significantly slower reading speeds. The asymmetry is functional and its direction reverses for languages such as Hebrew whose reading direction is right to left (Pollatsek *et al.*, 1981). The asymmetry of the span for bilingual readers depends upon the direction in which they are reading. Since the decline in visual acuity away from the fovea is roughly symmetrical (Chapter 2), the asymmetry shows immediately that the perceptual span is determined by attentional, in addition to structural, factors.

Beyond about 7–8 characters to the right of fixation, sometimes referred to as the *word identification span*, useful information is extracted about word boundaries and word initial letters but very little detailed information about letters within words. The size of this span means that it may be possible to identify the upcoming word to the right of the currently fixated word when that word is relatively short, but otherwise only the word currently fixated can be fully identified. It is notable of course that the word identification span is approximately the same as the average saccade size. Attempts have been made to establish at what point during a fixation visual information is taken in. If the word information is available for only the first 50 ms of a fixation and is then replaced by a mask, reading can proceed normally (Rayner *et al*, 1981). Blanchard *et al.* (1984) confirmed this finding but showed that the information was equally effective if it occurred at other points during the course of a fixation. They also found no evidence for left to right covert scanning of the material *within* a fixation, which might have been expected if letters were being processed in a strictly serial left to right sequence, perhaps using covert attention.

Although the figures given above are typical, they are average values and the precise size of the perceptual span depends on many factors. The span relates to information extraction rather than the number of characters per se. In languages such as Japanese or Hebrew, fewer characters are needed to convey the same meaning than in English. In these languages, the figures for the perceptual span are correspondingly reduced. Perceptual span increases with reading skill and thus is lower in children learning to read, and in poor readers (Rayner, 1986; Rayner *et al.*, 1989). An unresolved question that is of some theoretical significance is whether moment-to-moment variations in the difficulty of processing the foveally fixated word will affect the perceptual span on that fixation (Henderson and Ferreira, 1990; Schroyens *et al.*, 1999).

To summarise, adult readers benefit from the extraction of information in the parafovea ahead of the point at which the fovea is directed in the text. Within the word identification span of around 8 characters, detailed information is taken in; beyond this point, out to about 15 characters, some useful general visual information is acquired such as word boundary information.

5.3.3 Preview benefit

It is clear that parafoveal information assists the overall reading process. Information from the parafoveal preview subsequently contributes to the foveal processing, showing that some information is stored trans-saccadically. However, there are a variety of ways in which parafoveal vision might operate to provide this benefit. The stored information might take several forms: the information might be transferred in a totally unprocessed (iconic) form; in some partially processed form; there might be partial activation of the lexical unit for the word, or activation of the semantic networks which relate to the word (semantic priming). A further possibility is that parafoveal information might enable the eyes to be guided towards the optimum position in the upcoming word. As we discuss in Section 5.4.2, there is good evidence that the specific position the gaze lands in a word affects the speed of processing and the extent to which preview can affect landing position is discussed in Section 5.6.

A straightforward way of using the gaze-contingent methodology to assess peripheral preview is to employ the boundary version (Section 5.3.1) of the method as follows. A string of text characters is presented in the periphery or parafovea. The subject is asked to move their eyes to the string and to respond on the basis of its content. During the saccade, the letter string is changed to the target word. Two extreme cases are a baseline where the initial string is unrelated to the post-saccadic word, and a no-change condition where the initial string is itself the post-saccadic word. For letter strings presented in the parafovea or near periphery, the full preview no-change condition results in considerably faster word identification than the control, unrelated, condition. By using initial strings that possess some of the characteristics of the final word, the properties of the string that contribute to word identification can be assessed.

Rayner (1995; Starr and Rayner, 2001) reviews studies on preview facilitation and argues that orthographic similarity is the main contributor. Words with similar spelling (e.g. chart and chest) promote facilitation. The similarity does not need to be at the visual level. Classic papers by McConkie and Zola (1979) and by Rayner, McConkie and Zola (1980) used letter strings printed in alternating upper case and lower case. Exactly the same amount of facilitation was generated when the case alternation was changed during the saccade (e.g. from BrAnD to bRaNd) as when it was not. This suggests that some abstract letter representation is involved. The major part of the facilitation comes from the initial few letters of the word. In normal reading, these are the closest to the fovea when viewed in the upcoming text. No facilitation is observed when the initial string is semantically but not orthographically similar to the subsequent word, i.e. 'song' does not facilitate 'tune' (Rayner *et al.*, 1986). This is in marked contrast to the well-established semantic priming effect observed when such words are viewed sequentially in foveal vision (Section 5.4.1).

As described in the following sections, detailed analysis of the way in which eye movements control visual sampling during text reading shows that this control is intimately linked to the comprehension process. Rayner (1975, 1978) introduced the term *process monitoring* to describe this link, the 'process' referring to the linguistic analysis of the material. The contrast is with, for example, a 'constant pattern' or 'global control' account based around pre-set values for saccade length and fixation duration. In the constant pattern account, the pre-set values could be altered from time to time to adapt to the text difficulty, but moment-to-moment variability would result from random factors. There is general acceptance that some form of process monitoring gives a better account of the data than the constant pattern alternative. A full account of eye control during reading must therefore incorporate an account of the comprehension process, although this need not be to the exclusion of non-linguistic variables such as the visual properties of the text. What then are the characteristics of the comprehension processes that are being monitored? In the next section we give a brief overview of relevant ideas from the field of psycholinguistics (more detailed accounts may be found in Rayner and Pollatsek, 1989; Kennedy *et al.*, 2000).

5.4 Language processing

5.4.1 Lexical access: influences on the speed of word recognition

The word is a unit of language that has both intuitive and theoretical significance. It is evident that each word that an individual is familiar with is represented in his or her memory and can be recognised in isolation as well as in continuous text or discourse. The term *lexical access* describes the process, still not perfectly understood, which occurs when a word's mental representation in memory is activated. The process of recognition is frequently envisaged in quasi-neural terms as the buildup of activation in some hypothetical neural structure to reach a threshold level for recognition. Morton (1969) used this metaphor in an influential paper and introduced the term *logogen* to describe the hypothetical unit in the mental dictionary corresponding to a word. A very influential subsequent paper was that of Rumelhart and McClelland (1982) who demonstrated how such a process might be implemented in a massively interconnected parallel neural network.

In Morton's theoretical account 'recognition' of the word only occurs when the activation of the relevant logogen unit rises above a certain threshold level. It is possible for logogens to be partially activated before they are recognised, this recognition being pre-conscious. Words differ in the ease with which their logogens can be activated. In particular the time required for activation is dependent upon the familiarity of the word, defined in terms of *word frequency*, i.e. the frequency that the word is encountered in everyday use of the language. High frequency words are activated more quickly. Another factor relates to linguistic material recently encountered. When a word unit has been recently activated, it is more readily activated subsequently. This gives rise to the phenomenon of *repetition priming* observed in experiments that measure the speed of word recognition. Another consistent finding from such experiments is that of *semantic priming*. Recognition of a word is also speeded if in the immediate past, a related word has been recognised, thus having encountered the word 'nurse' in a text, the lexical access for a subsequent encounter of the word 'doctor' will be slightly faster. Word units can be activated both from auditory (speech) input and from written (text) input. A further major issue in the psychology of reading is the extent to which the recognition of written words makes use of the word's auditory (phonological) representation (for more detail, see Rayner and Pollatsek, 1989).

A number of other linguistic processes are also engaged during reading. Language has a syntactical structure that must be assigned to the text. A sentence such as 'They are eating apples' is inherently ambiguous because of the two ways that it may be parsed. Likewise in a sentence such as 'Mary gave the book to Jane and she felt pleased', the word 'she' could refer to either of the named females. Such words, termed anaphoric referents, occur frequently in text. Syntactic processing is normally done very automatically but nevertheless the relative ease or difficulty of these automatic processes can be manifest in the pattern of eye sampling, and study of eye movements during text reading provides a sensitive way of investigating these processes. While many studies of these processes have involved eye movements, it is generally the case that the eye movements themselves are of secondary interest, merely being used to index the higher order processes. Recent accounts may be found in Rayner (1998), Underwood (1998), Kennedy *et al.*, (2000).

5.4.2 Optimal viewing position

Another factor affecting the speed of visual word recognition is the initial position within a word that is fixated. A series of experiments studying recognition of isolated individual words has shown that the exact fixation location within a word has a strong effect on recognition speed (O'Regan and Jacobs, 1992; O'Regan *et al.*, 1984). Figure 5.3 shows two sets of results demonstrating this phenomenon. When words are presented in isolation and a recognition response is required, recognition times are fastest at an *optimal viewing position*, located slightly to the left of the centre of the word. They increase dramatically as the fixation position deviates from this optimum position. The effect results from two causes. Refixations become progressively more likely with deviations from the optimal position, but even when the word is only fixated once, fixation duration varies (with an increase of about 20 ms per character offset). Further analyses by McConkie *et al.* (1989) and Vitu *et al.* (1990) showed that, during normal reading, the phenomenon is present but is of reduced magnitude and appears entirely attributable to the increased probability of a refixation. A recent paper reports that there is actually

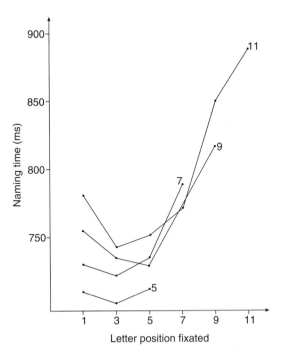

Figure 5.3 Demonstration of how the naming time for a word depends on the location at which the word is first fixated. The four plots show data for words of 5, 7, 9 and 11 characters respectively. Redrawn from O'Regan *et al.* (1984).

a reverse effect for the initial fixation (Vitu, McConkie, Kerr and O'Regan, 2001) with longer duration fixations when the reader fixates the optimal viewing location.

5.5 Control of fixation duration

As illustrated in Fig. 5.1, the durations of eye pauses during reading show considerable variability. Many studies have found that fixation duration is intimately linked to properties of the text on a moment-to-moment basis as well as in the more global sense illustrated in Table 5.1. Indeed the relationship is so well established that eye fixation properties are now regarded as one of the most powerful means of investigating linguistic processing.

A methodological complication must be raised (see also Liversedge and Findlay, 2000). Quite frequently, particularly with longer words, the eye makes more than one fixation on a word. If it is desired to assess the total length of time spent on processing the word, then it makes sense to combine the individual fixation durations to give a measure, *gaze duration*. Just and Carpenter (1980) defined gaze duration as the summed aggregate of the total fixations on a word. A further measure is the *total time* measure, which additionally includes any subsequent refixations back to the word. For workers attempting to relate eye movements to linguistic processing, the gaze duration or total time measures have obvious advantages whereas for workers more oriented to the visual aspects of the situation, control of individual eye movements is more significant.

These measures are affected by properties of the fixated word. The variable of word frequency (Section 5.4.1) has been thoroughly investigated. Inhoff and Rayner (1986) showed that fixations on low frequency words were about 20 ms longer than fixations on high frequency words. However when they used the gaze-contingent method to prevent useful advance parafoveal preview of the word, the fixation time difference disappeared although there remained a difference between the two types of words concerning the likelihood of a refixation (but see Vitu, 1991c). Rayner has convincingly used this type of evidence to argue against theories of oculomotor control in reading based entirely on low-level factors. In a recent study, Rayner *et al.* (1996) showed that differences in oculomotor behaviour for low and high frequency words occur subsequent to the eye landing in the word. Low frequency words received longer initial fixations (by about 20–30 ms) and this increase occurred whether or not the word was refixated. A further difference occurred in the probability of refixation. Word length irrespective of frequency had a strong effect on the probability of a refixation (from about 12 per cent for a 5-letter word to 26 per cent for an 8-letter word). However at each word length, there was a slightly higher probability (about 4 per cent) for low frequency words to be refixated.

Lexical access is established as an important process in language comprehension (Section 5.4.1). Word frequency and predictability has been found to affect both word recognition speeds for isolated words and fixation durations for words that are encountered in continuous text. It is thus clear that the process of lexical access directly affects eye control even though it may initially appear surprising that an abstract mental activity can have immediate effect on what the eye muscles are doing. It also turns out that even higher order abstract mental processes behave similarly. Consider the sentence

Since Jay always jogs a mile seems like a short distance.

It is likely that when you read that sentence, you experienced some confusion. The sentence is a typical example of a 'garden-path' sentence, constructed so that an ambiguous early part (in which the verb 'jogs' can be treated in either a transitive or intransitive way) is followed by a disambiguating phrase. Such sentences are of intense interest in psycholinguistics because they demonstrate a tendency amongst most individuals to use the so-called principle of *minimal attachment*, fitting words into a sentence frame as soon as they become available wherever possible. For the present discussion, the point of interest is the behaviour of the eyes when reading such a sentence. This was first studied by Frazier and Rayner (1982) who found that frequently the disambiguating word (seems) is marked by a much longer fixation than normal, and the eye makes an immediate regression to the earlier part of the sentence. The changed behaviour is clearly not attributable simply to the lexical access of 'seems' but shows that syntactic processes can also exert direct and immediate control of the eye.

In summary, there is impressive evidence that linguistic processes such as lexical access and syntactic disambiguation are able to influence the time the eyes spend in individual fixations as they read through text.

5.6 Control of landing position

An important corpus of data was presented by McConkie *et al.* (1988). These workers collected and analysed data from 43668 eye fixations. The analysis confirmed earlier reports (Dunn-Rankin, 1978; Rayner, 1979) that the eyes do not land on text in a totally arbitrary way but rather show a tendency to land preferentially at certain locations relative to the word boundaries. Rayner (1979) has termed this location the *preferred viewing location* and it is generally somewhat to the left of the optimum viewing position discussed in Section 5.4.2. McConkie *et al.* showed that these landing position preferences were systematically related to the launch position of the eyes at the start of the saccade (Fig. 5.4). These findings indicate systematic dependencies of the landing position on properties of the text regardless of the text content. They have led to proposals, discussed in the next section, that landing position is controlled by low level visual factors such as word boundaries. Nevertheless, a considerable amount of variability remains at all combinations of word length and launch position. An issue which is still controversial concerns whether the remaining factors determining landing position should be accounted for by

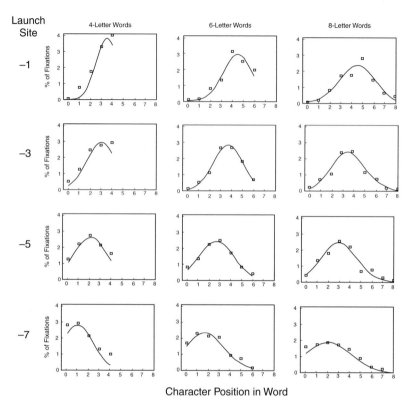

Figure 5.4 Distribution of eye landing positions during text reading from the analysis of 43000 saccades reported by McConkie *et al.* (1988). The three columns show plots of landing positions in 4, 6 and 8 letter words respectively. The rows segregate saccades from various launch positions to the left of the word.

purely random variability, by low-level visual/oculomotor factors not already taken into account, or by control being exerted by more high level linguistic factors relating to the material being processed. Separate analyses of similar large corpuses by Rayner *et al.* (1996) and by Radach and McConkie (1998) have confirmed the basic patterns. Rayner *et al.* showed that exactly the same distribution of landing positions occurred at a particular word length and launch position for saccades into high-frequency words and saccades into low-frequency words.

Reilly and O'Regan (1998) carried out a further analysis of the McConkie *et al.* (1988) corpus. Their assumption was that the data indicated a basic pattern by which the distribution of landing positions fitted a Gaussian error spread about a target landing position (for each value of launch site and word length). They concentrated on the systematic deviations from this Gaussian spread and showed that they could best be attributed to a strategy which involved targeting the longest word in a 20 character window to the right of the current fixation position. Of course a by-product of this strategy is that intermediate short words would be more likely to be skipped.

As mentioned in the previous section, a proportion of the saccades in the corpus (13 per cent for 4 letter words increasing to 31 per cent for 8 letter words) were refixations, which were analysed by McConkie *et al.* (1989). Refixations were particularly common when the eye initially landed near the beginning, or near the end, of a word. Except in the case of very high frequency words, where refixations were very slightly less common, word frequency did not affect the probability of refixation. This suggests that for this category of saccades at least, the speed at which lexical access was occurring had little effect on the landing position. Several recent analyses (Radach and McConkie, 1998; Vergilino and Beauvillain, 2000) have suggested that intraword refixations are programmed in a different manner from other saccades, possibly as part of a grouped programming strategy (Section 4.4.4).

Various attempts have been made to link the control of saccade landing positions in reading to effects known to influence saccade landing positions in orienting tasks (Section 4.4). Thus Vitu (1991*a*) reported evidence for the existence of a centre-of-gravity effect in text reading. She argued that the data did not support a range effect (Vitu, 1991*b*) although we shall see in the following section that some workers have based theories on the range effect. Further support for the suggestion that much of the variability in eye movement patterns may be attributable to non-linguistic factors of oculomotor control came from a study by Vitu *et al.* (1995). They used various tasks in which the linguistic demands were reduced while oculomotor scanning was still required. For example, in the most extreme task (the z-string task), each letter in a text was replaced by a single character (the letter z) and subjects were asked to move along the text as if they were reading it. Both global eye movement characteristics (saccade size, fixation duration) and local characteristics (skipping probability, launch site and word landing effects) were changed very little under the various conditions. Vitu *et al.* use this to argue that the principal determinant of oculomotor behaviour is a predetermined oculomotor strategy with linguistic variables exerting a minor modulating influence. Interestingly, the differences between normal reading and z-string scanning were in the opposite direction from what might have been expected (see also Rayner and Fisher, 1996). During text reading, fixation durations were shorter and the proportion of very small saccades was lower.

5.6.1 Skipping words

Many short words in text do not receive an eye fixation when the text is read. Studies of which factors affect word skipping address, in a direct way, the question of how saccadic landing positions are chosen. Not surprisingly, the variables of launch site and word length identified in the previous section also affect the probability that a word will be skipped. Brysbaert and Vitu (1998) present data. The probability of skipping a two letter word varies from 90 per cent when the launch site is one character prior to the word, to about 50 per cent when the launch site is 8 characters or more before the word. For a five letter word, the corresponding figures are 60 per cent and 10 per cent respectively. While these figures show that the low-level visual characteristics of the upcoming word are important, this might either occur for simple oculo-motor reasons (any tendency for saccades to have a fixed size, or a limited range of sizes, will result in more shorter words being skipped), or because the launch site and word length factors are such that they affect word visibility so that these effects would be expected if skipping depended on whether or not the word had been identified. To disentangle these possibilities, it is necessary to vary high-level factors while keeping low-level factors constant.

For many years, one of the most widely cited pieces of evidence for linguistic effects on landing position was based on the analysis of landing positions relating to short words. O'Regan (1980) carried out an ingenious experiment where sentences were read, some of which contained the definite article 'THE'. Eye movement statistics on these words were compared with those when reading sentences identical up to the point before but diverging afterwards so that THE was replaced by a less common three letter word such as 'WAS'. O'Regan found that saccade amplitudes through the critical region were greater in the former case. The finding has been regularly cited as evidence for high-level linguistic control of eye guidance and often oversimplified in secondary reports to suggest that the eyes always skip short common words. In a subsequent review O'Regan (1992) urged caution and pointed out that the effect was a small one. However, he has recently once again confirmed the skipping effect (Gautier *et al.*, 2000). This study found that saccades into (and across) the French word 'les' are larger than for less common three letter words, and, remarkably, the effect occurred even when the duration of the previous fixation was extremely short.

Other work has also shown that more frequent words are more likely to be skipped (Rayner and Fischer, 1996; Rayner *et al.*, 1996). It is thus clear that linguistic factors have an influence on whether a word will be skipped. Nonetheless, these effects are relatively small. Brysbaert and Vitu (1998) carried out a regression analysis of data on skipping probability using a word length factor and a processing load (word context) factor as independent variables. Both factors accounted for a significant proportion of the variance but the proportion was 44 per cent in the case of word length and only 11 per cent in the case of processing load.

5.6.2 Can linguistic variables influence the landing position within words?

Several other reports that linguistic factors influence landing position have also proved difficult to replicate and are controversial. One issue has concerned eye landing position in words where the crucial information for recognition is localised in part of the word. For example, the word 'vulnerable' can be recognised on the basis of its first five letters, which are shared by no other normal word of the language, whilst in contrast, the first part of the word 'underneath' is shared by several other words but its second half is unique. Hyönä *et al.* (1989) reported that landing positions differed between the two types of words (see also Underwood *et al.*, 1990). Their interpretation was that parafoveal preprocessing permitted the salient part of the word to be identified by the lexical processor, which then enabled eye guidance to this salient region. This position was challenged by Rayner and Morris (1992) who were unable to replicate the findings concerning informative word beginnings and endings (see also Radach and McConkie, 1998).

A further study by Hyönä (1995) using Finnish words might offer a resolution of the discrepant findings. He produced new data to suggest that the effect found in earlier studies comes about entirely because of shorter than average saccades into words with informative beginnings. No effect of the informativeness or otherwise of the word ending was present. Hyönä proposed that the effect might be interpreted as an effect of the visual salience of unusual orthography, suggesting that irregular letter combinations might effectively attract the eyes. Such an effect has also been reported by Beauvillain and colleagues (Beauvillain and Doré, 1998; Beauvillain *et al.*, 1996) using French text and by White and Liversedge (2003) with English sentences.

5.7 Theories of eye control during reading

The previous sections have demonstrated a number of effects that should be accounted for by a successful model of eye control in reading. This section will examine approaches to the theoretical understanding of the process. What should be the ingredients found in a successful model? No complete agreement on this question would be found amongst researchers and indeed, models differ considerably in their philosophy. Some emphasise 'dumb' mechanisms that might easily be implemented by plausible neural processes. For instance: 'direct the eye to the next blank space to the right of the currently fixated point'. Others are more ready to invoke 'smart' mechanisms, in contrast, which would involve some significant computational and linguistic processing in the decision about moving the eyes. For example: 'use peripheral vision to decide on the basis of the first few letters of the next word whether it can be uniquely identified from these letters, if it can, accept this identification and jump the eye into the next word beyond, if it can't, move the eye to the middle of this word'. Of course, neither of these specific suggestions is sustainable on the basis of the data.

5.7.1 Models emphasizing non-cognitive factors

McConkie *et al.* (1988), in considering the data of Fig. 5.4, did not offer an explicit model but suggested that guidance of the eye to its initial fixation in a word was 'largely free from cognitive control'. They noted that their data on saccade landing positions might be accounted for as follows. The next word in the parafovea defined a functional target location, based on its visual properties (such as its visual centre-of-gravity). Saccades were directed to this location but were subject to two sources of variability. The perceptuo-motor variability always found in the saccade targeting system was supplemented by variability due to the saccadic range effect (Section 4.4.1). Landing position was the focus of interest; fixation durations were not modelled, and only entered into the description as a modulating factor whereby the saccadic range effect was reduced for long duration prior fixations. With this limitation, no lexical or other linguistic influences were postulated.

O'Regan (1992) adopted a similar position in his 'strategy-tactics' approach to eye control in reading. He suggested that readers adopt a strategy of, when leaving a word, attempting to saccade to the position just left of centre of the subsequent word (which happens to be close to the optimum viewing location—Section 5.4.1). In a similar way to that proposed by McConkie *et al.*, factors would introduce variability in the actual landing positions and this leads to the tactics. When the eye lands away from the optimal viewing position, a tactical refixation movement is often made to another location in the word that will, in general, be closer to the optimum position.

5.7.2 Models driven by the lexical access process

These two models contrast with models whose starting point is more the cognitive process undertaken during reading. Morrison (1984) introduced a model of eye movement control during reading which has been the basis of several follow-up models. These models regard the process of lexical access as the point where eye control originates. Lexical access is held to control an attentional 'pointer' (see Section 3.3.2/Section 3.6.1), which is directed in turn to each successive word in the text. The eye may be directed to the same location as the pointer, but implementing an eye movement takes longer than implementing a pointer movement and so the eyes will often lag behind. When the eye saccades into word n the pointer is initially aligned with this word. As lexical access of word n is completed, the pointer moves to the next word $n + 1$ and starts the lexical access process for this word. Some time later the eyes will follow the pointer. However it may happen that lexical access of word $n + 1$ is completed before the eyes move, in which case the pointer moves to word $n + 2$. Under these circumstances, the eyes may skip word $n + 1$ and move straight to word $n + 2$. They may also show the compromise movements (Section 4.4.2) and land at an intermediate location between words $n + 1$ and $n + 2$. Under these circumstances it is held likely that an unusually short duration fixation will occur followed by a saccade to position $n + 2$.

Morrison's model can account for the skipping of words and predicts that the skipping probability will increase with the ease of access of the word. However it is unable to account for cases where a word is refixated. Elaborations of a somewhat ad hoc nature have been offered to account for such findings. Henderson and Ferreira (1990) have added an 'oculomotor deadline' while Rayner and Pollatsek have argued that some signal related to the success of the lexical access process is available.

Reichle *et al.* (1998, 1999) elaborated the latter suggestion to generate the latest in the series of attentional pointer models. In their E-Z Reader model (the term ee-zee reader comes from a character in the TV series The Electric Company), the link between attentional movements and eye movements is decoupled. Sequential attentional movements still occur but the signal to move the eyes comes not from the attentional movement, but from a process of 'familiarity assessment' that, while linked to access, is also partly dissociated. Different versions of the E-Z model also incorporate word predictability and differential parafoveal preview. The model has a number of free parameters (5–7 in the different versions) but gives an impressive quantitative fit to data on gaze durations and skipping probabilities. In contrast to the model of Morrison, parafoveal preview can be accounted for in a natural way although recent findings (e.g. Kennedy, 2000) that properties of a parafoveal word influence fixation durations may result in difficulties for the model of Reichle *et al.* and indeed any model in which attention progresses in a strictly serial manner.

5.7.3 Evaluation

Evaluating the different models is not straightforward. Although often presented as incompatible alternatives, the different model types may have more in common than first appears. It may be more useful to regard the approaches as complementary rather than competing. A characteristic of any automatised human activity is that it can be interrupted by other processes. It is generally recognised that this type of 'interrupt' has occurred, for example, when an extensive regression back in the text is found. It might be profitable to think of the system as a hierarchy, recognising that low level factors and high-level factors are involved. Demonstration of the influence of a high level variable need not imply that low-level factors are not important and vice versa.

The 'dumb-process' models are largely concerned with explaining the exact landing position of the eyes. In contrast, the concern of the linguistically based models is largely to describe the sequential process at the level of which words are fixated when. Indeed, a theme that is frequently involved in theories of oculomotor control during reading is the separate control of the programming of fixation durations and saccade landing positions, the two principal variables. At an early point in their studies, Rayner and McConkie (1976) suggested that separate mechanisms controlled the WHEN and WHERE decisions concerning fixation durations and saccade landing positions (cf. Section 4.6). O'Regan's strategy-tactics model did offer an explanation of fixation durations in addition but the findings of Rayner *et al.* (1996) discussed in Section 5.5. showed that the account must be, at best, incomplete.

In the context of active vision, it should finally be noted that the high level theories of Section 5.7.2 in fact make some explicit, and strong, assumptions about early visual processing. These theories invoke a covert attentional pointer which plays a part in selecting the location at which the eye land. This proposal is predicated on the spotlight model of attention (Section 3.2.1) but it is generally assumed that the spotlight can select on a word by word basis, thus working in an object based way (Section 3.6.1). As we showed in chapter 3, there is still considerable uncertainty about what properties can be assigned to covert attention. It may indeed not be possible to move a covert attentional spotlight on a voluntary basis any faster than the eyes themselves can move. The ability to divide attention across two locations in parallel may be important. Starr and Rayner (2001), in a recent review, acknowledge the need for further development of current theories.

5.8 Practical aspects of eye control in reading

5.8.1 Reading and the physical characteristics of the text

An extensive series of studies by Tinker examined the effects of various manipulations of text on text legibility (Paterson and Tinker, 1940; summarised in Tinker, 1965). A variety of factors were investigated—typeface, upper vs. lower case, size of type and width of *leading* (spacing between lines). Reading speed and corresponding oculomotor measures were compared over a range of text sizes. Significant differences occurred but their magnitude was small (generally less than 5 per cent). For example, with the type size variable, a broad optimum occurred around 9–12 point type. Smaller typefaces led to more saccades, greater fixation durations and more regressions, attributed to increased perceptual difficulty. A broad optimum was again found when studying the variable of line width. Shorter than optimum line widths showed increased fixation durations and decreased saccade length. Line widths longer than optimum led to increased difficulties with the return sweep and locating the beginning of the following line. The only typefaces to have substantially decreased legibility were very obviously obtuse ones.

5.8.2 Dyslexia

Dyslexia is a term used for impaired reading ability. This may occur as a result of brain damage in adult life (*acquired dyslexia*) or appear as a problem in learning to read (*developmental dyslexia*). There is little evidence that the two conditions are closely connected. Although a major practical problem, developmental dyslexia has proved difficult to pin down to any precise cause and indeed, even its existence as a discrete syndrome can be questioned (Stanovich, 1994). Early enthusiasm that eye movement methodology might assist in identifying and understanding the problem proved unfounded (Tinker, 1958). Children classified as dyslexic show abnormal eye movement patterns, but the more obvious abnormalities are the consequence rather than the cause of the problem. An exception may be the rare case of significant abnormalities of oculomotor control, which are severe enough to prevent any normal visual sampling (Stein and Fowler, 1982; Zangwill and Blakemore, 1972). Occasional claims have been made that dyslexics show abnormal oculomotor patterns when processing non-linguistic material. Attempts to replicate findings have been generally negative (Brown *et al.*, 1983; Pollatsek *et al.*, 1999) although the possibility remains that a minority of dyslexics have some oculomotor problem (Pollatsek *et al.*, 1999).

There have been a number of suggestions that an abnormality of the magnocellular system (Chapter 2) might be common in reading retarded children. The magnocellular system is heavily involved in eye control and thus an indirect link at least could be made (Eden *et al.*, 1994; Stein and Walsh, 1997). A separate suggestion of a deficit in the fixation system has emerged from the reports of an abnormally high incidence of express saccades (Section 4.2.4) in poor readers (Fischer *et al.* 1993). A recent thorough discussion of the evidence may be found in Everatt (1999). This research may lead to advances in understanding the problem, at least in some individuals, but at present the conservative conclusion appears that reading problems do not come about because of inability to co-ordinate the visual sampling of the material. It is notable in that respect that an individual born without functional eye muscles has been able to achieve a good standard of reading ability by adapting her head movement control system to sample text (Gilchrist *et al.* 1997; Section 8.5.2).

5.9 Overview

The research reviewed has revealed a surprisingly intricate set of control processes that allow readers to sample visual texts. The eye generally appears to rest at each location in the text just as long as is needed for understanding and then to move towards the optimum location for further sampling, frequently skipping over short predictable words in the process. Many of the routines which generate this sampling are routines of eye control which are discussed in other chapters of the book. However there is also no doubt that the mental processes of text comprehension can almost instantaneously affect the motor control of the eyes. Whilst the details of the exact balance between low-level and high-level processes remains to be agreed, our general understanding of the processes of eye control in this has made remarkable progress.

CHAPTER 6

VISUAL SEARCH

Visual search, looking for a specific item or object in a visual scene, is a ubiquitous part of visual behaviour. This is the process that occurs when we are looking for a pen on a cluttered desk, a face in the crowd or our car in a car park. In these examples it is clear that we are moving our eyes as part of the search process. However, a great deal of research and theory within visual search has ignored eye movements altogether. Indeed, the driving explanatory device in search theories has been covert attention. In the current chapter, we review these models of search and discuss recent work on saccades in visual search.

Research on the topic can be divided into several strands. The first is represented by attempts to use visual search as a tool with which to study early visual processes, in particular to identify stimulus characteristics which can be extracted in parallel across an extensive visual display. Visual search is also studied in order to understand the attentional processes that operate in the search task. For reasons that will be elaborated below, both these approaches developed giving little attention to the importance of eye movements in determining search behaviour. This chapter will argue that this is a serious oversight, particularly in relation to the understanding of visual attention. Finally, a third tradition has been concerned in a more eclectic way with real-world tasks involving visual search (e.g. Brogan *et al.* 1993).

6.1 Visual search tasks

In a typical laboratory-based visual search experiment, the displays consist of a number of discrete and separated items. Subjects are asked to search for a pre-defined *target* among a varying number of non-target *distractor* items. Typically the reaction time to indicate the presence or absence of the target is measured. The plot of reaction time against the number of display elements is termed the *search function* (see Fig. 6.1). Two distinct types of function have been identified. Search functions can be flat, with the introduction of additional distractors leading to no increase in overall decision time. This relationship is held to reflect *parallel search*. In contrast, search slopes can increase with display size. Such a relationship is usually referred to as *serial search*.

(a)

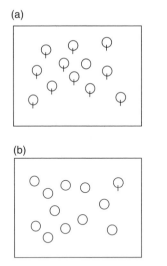

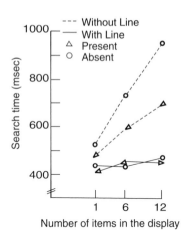

(b)

Figure 6.1 Search functions showing serial and parallel search. Search tasks can be difficult, and lead to linear increases in search slope with the number of items (e.g. display (a) where the target is a circle without a line), or easy, where search functions are relatively independent of the number of items (e.g. display (b) where the target is a circle with a line). Search functions for these two tasks are plotted on the right hand side. (Reproduced from Treisman, 1988; Fig. 3).

This distinction was first made by Treisman and Gelade (1980) and subsequently a vast number of visual search experiments have been carried out, seeking to characterise the types of displays that produce serial or parallel search functions. The work has led to several influential theories of search. These are described in Section 6.2. Reviewing these theories, we conclude (Section 6.2.4) that none qualifies as an adequate account from the active vision standpoint. In the remainder of the chapter, we develop an approach to visual search from the active vision perspective.

6.2 Theories of visual search

Three theories of visual search behaviour will be reviewed. All three theories are based on results from reaction time studies of search, but are inspired to differing degrees by the neurophysiology of the visual system and by underlying assumptions about the nature of covert attention.

6.2.1 Feature integration theory

Treisman and Gelade (1980) proposed that basic visual features (e.g. colour, orientation, etc.) are initially extracted in parallel across the visual scene. Parallel search functions arise when a search target is defined by a unique basic feature relative to the background. As a consequence, this type of search has often been called *feature search*.

In contrast, if the target in a visual search task is defined by a combination of features, which also occur individually in distractors in a display (i.e. when the target is defined by a conjunction of features), it leads to a serial search function. This type of search is often referred to as *conjunction search*. Treisman and Gelade (1980) argued that, if target detection is only possible following the binding together of visual features, then attention is required. Attention, which they proposed acts like a spotlight, also allows items to be localised in space. Conjunction search requires the attentional spotlight to move serially from location to location for target detection. It is this serial scanning that is assumed to be the extra time consuming process involved in the generation of serial search functions.

The above description summarises *Feature Integration Theory* (FIT) and its framework for early visual processing as set out in Treisman and Gelade (1980). The idea complemented studies of the anatomy and physiology of the visual system, which show that visual processing is modularised, at least to some degree, with different cortical areas containing neurons that are selective for different visual properties of the input (see Chapter 2; Zeki, 1976; Maunsell and Newsome, 1987). For example, neurons in region MT respond preferentially to moving stimuli, while neurones in V4 are tuned for (amongst other things) the detection of wavelength information (see DeYoe and Van Essen, 1988). This division of the processing of information seems at odds with the experience of a visual world that contains objects in which colour, motion, orientation etc. are all bound together. This apparent contradiction is known as the binding problem. FIT provides one explanation of how such feature binding could occur (see Treisman 1996). Within FIT, covert attentional processes provide the mechanism by which basic visual features are combined to form a multidimensional percept.

FIT had considerable impact and gave rise to a large quantity of experimental work. Much of this was supportive: indeed the approach was hailed as a further psychophysical route to investigate the properties of early vision. However a number of problems emerged which undermined some of the assumptions embedded in the FIT model. First, that serial search functions reflect the action of a serial internal mechanism. Second, that conjunction search always leads to serial search functions and third, that targets with a unique feature lead to parallel search. All three assumptions have been challenged since the inception of the model. At the heart of much of this criticism lies a breakdown of the simple link between serial search and conjunctions on the one hand and parallel search and features on the other.

In some cases it appeared that quite complex information could be extracted in parallel across the visual display (Enns and Rensink, 1991; Gilchrist *et al.*, 1997). Nakayama and Silverman (1986) found that feature conjunctions where stereodepth was a feature led to flat search functions, although it was often overlooked that these searches took much longer than simple feature searches (see McSorley and Findlay, 2001). It became clear that search slopes vary continuously from parallel to steeply serial (Duncan and Humphreys, 1989; Wolfe, 1998). Theoreticians also noted that serial search functions could, in principle, be generated by a parallel system (Eckstein, 1998; Humphreys and Müller, 1993; Townsend, 1972).

FIT was subsequently developed in a number of ways to accommodate new experimental data (Treisman and Souther, 1985; Treisman, 1988; 1993). However, the idea of an internal spotlight moving over a spatial representation was retained as a characterising feature of the model.

6.2.2 Guided search

FIT proposed that serial search functions arose when a process of attentional scanning was used to work through the display in an item-by-item manner. The rate at which the hypothesised scanning process operated could be estimated from the slope of the search function. The lower slope in the target-present case was attributed to the *self-terminating* nature of the search with, on average, the target being located after half the number of items in the display were scanned, whereas in the target-absent case it was necessary to scan the whole display before the response. The attentional pointer was thus assumed to work through the items systematically, but in no prespecified order. Typical data (such as those of the serial searches in Fig. 6.1) could be accounted for if an attentional pointer scanned at a rate of about 50 ms/item. Such a rate is faster than any possible overt scanning with the eyes but was, at the time, consistent with other estimates of the speed of covert attentional scanning (Section 3.4).

Guided search (Wolfe, 1994; Wolfe *et al.*, 1989) shares a number of properties with FIT. Both models are two stage theories: they postulate a set of parallel feature maps that are available to covert attention only via a map of locations and they both rely on a serial spot-light mechanism for the allocation of attention. However, Wolfe *et al.* (1989) demonstrated that simple colour-form conjunction search can occur in parallel, if the feature differences are large enough. To account for these data, Wolfe *et al.* suggested that the attentional pointer is guided in a systematic way. Specifically, the information from the feature maps is fed to the location map and used to guide the attentional spotlight to candidate target locations. This occurs because activation is passed from the feature maps to the location map. Guided search, like FIT, relies on an internal attentional spotlight to scan the display and allow for target detection.

6.2.3 A late-selection model of visual search

Duncan and Humphreys (1989) developed an alternative visual search theory. The broad framework they presented resembles the structure developed in Duncan (1980, 1984). Search occurs, first, via a parallel stage of processing that produces a multiple-spatial-scale structured representation and, second, via a serial stage that allows conscious processing of the items in the visual field. In visual search this second stage involves the matching of the input descriptions to an internal stored template of the target.

Duncan and Humphreys (1989) showed that search efficiency is determined by two interacting factors. The first is the similarity between the targets and non-targets: search becomes less efficient as targets and non-targets become more similar. The second factor is the similarity between non-targets: as the distractors become more heterogeneous (i.e. more dissimilar from one another), search becomes less efficient.

Duncan and Humphreys (1989) reject the distinction made in FIT that search is either serial or parallel, and suggest instead that search efficiency varies continuously from being efficient and independent of display size, to being inefficient and dependent on the number of items present (see also Humphreys and Müller, 1993; Townsend, 1972). In the parallel stage of processing, descriptions are generated at a number of scales and grouping principles act to organise the visual input into *structural units*. In a display that contains a number of structural units, these items compete for access into visual short-term memory for matching with the target template. This model of visual search is not so obviously tied to an attentional spotlight as FIT or Guided Search. Instead, serial search functions arise out of a sometimes inefficient parallel system.

6.2.4 Overview of the models

Although these theories are distinct in important ways, none qualifies as an adequate theory of active vision. Eye movements are not taken into consideration, nor is the inhomogeneity of the visual projections (Section 2.1). The former omission may be attributed to the substitution of covert attentional processes in many of the theories. However, it is very surprising that so little account has been taken of the fact that early visual processing is dominated by the change of acuity with eccentricity, although the work of Marisa Carrasco, discussed in Section 6.3.2, forms an exception. In the remainder of this chapter we shall show the benefits of treating visual search from the perspective of active vision. Our reasoning has been developed over several years (Findlay and Gilchrist, 1998, 2001) and leads us to conclude that the emphasis on covert attention in theories of visual search has been misguided and misleading. Before embarking on this approach, the next section considers the question of whether eye movements are necessary in search.

6.3 The need for eye movements in visual search

Under some circumstances, it is quite clear that visual search can only be accomplished by moving the eyes. As outlined in Chapter 2, away from the centre of the fovea, visual ability declines in a systematic and continuous manner. As a result, for some searches, the target can only be discriminated if it falls within a limited region of the visual field, centred on the fovea

(Section 6.3.2). If the target is outside this region, then eye movements are required to move the target into this 'visual lobe' and there is a close relation between the time taken to find the target and the number of saccades made in the search (Section 6.4.1). However, the visual search tasks that have been discussed in Section 6.2 have generally used stimuli where the visual lobe is larger than the search display and therefore eye movements are not essential. In the next section, we examine the claim that, under such circumstances, consideration of eye scanning is irrelevant.

6.3.1 Search without eye movements

Klein and Farrell (1989) carried out a series of experiments to investigate the importance of saccades in visual search. Their data are often taken to suggest that visual search behaviour does not depend on saccadic eye movements and, in particular, that the observed serial search slopes are a product of an internal scanning mode rather than the product of overt eye scanning. For this reason we will now look in detail at this paper.

Klein and Farrell (1989) adopted two methods for assessing the importance of saccades in visual search. They used small search displays with a maximum display size of only 10 items and serial search tasks which were relatively easy overall. In Experiment 1 they limited display duration and presented the search display for 180 ms: an interval that was regarded as too short for a saccade to be programmed and executed. Klein and Farrell (1989) found serial search slopes under these conditions, suggesting that serial search functions could not be a result of eye movements alone. Klein and Farrell suggested that in these short presentation conditions, with larger display sizes, subjects adopt, on some trials, an alternative strategy of guessing, as the perceptual representation of the display fades. In their second experiment they presented the display until the response was made, but instructed the subjects not to move their eyes. For parallel search displays there was no effect of restricting eye movements. However, in the case when search was serial, restricting eye movements had a significant effect on performance, leading to an increase in error rates. This increase in error rates, although significant, was not large: the maximum error increase that resulted from preventing saccades was from 9.3 per cent to 18.8 per cent.

These results suggest that restricting eye movements in visual search, even for small display sizes, has a significant effect on accuracy. Search functions without eye movements did resemble the function when eye movements were not restricted. However, as Klein and Farrell themselves argue in relation to the results of Experiment 1, this does not imply that the same mechanisms are used across the two situations. Another study which investigated small size displays was that of Pashler (1987). Pashler argued that with small numbers of items (less than about six), search is carried out in parallel, even though a serial search function may be observed. We suggest that the data from Klein and Farrell's experiment do not demonstrate convincingly that eye movements are insignificant in visual search. In the case of parallel search, the results suggests that eye movements are not necessary. However, in the case of serial search, restricting eye movements does have an impact on performance, even for displays that contain few items and are relatively easy. Other studies in which the serial search task was more demanding (e.g. Scialfa and Joffe, 1998) show a clear cost in performance associated with restricting eye movements.

6.3.2 Visual search and the conspicuity area or visual lobe

As discussed in Section 2.1.2, the region within which a particular discrimination can be made is known as the *conspicuity area* (Engel, 1971), or *visual lobe* (Courtney and Chan, 1986). It is a similar concept to that of visual span in reading (Section 5.1). Not all visual functions decline at the same rate into the periphery, and thus the size of the visual lobe varies considerably with the specific task situation. In Chapter 5, a distinction was made between the visual span, the acuity limited area where a discrimination might be made, and the perceptual span, the smaller region from which information was extracted during the reading task. It would be expected that a similar distinction applied in the case of visual search although there has been relatively little systematic investigation. Rayner and Fisher (1987) asked subjects to search for a target letter in a horizontally displayed set of letters. They used the moving window technique, as discussed in Chapter 5, to assess the extent to which peripheral information was being extracted during search. They identified two spatial regions; the decision region, in which the target had to be in order for a target-present response to be made and a preview region in which partial information is available. They also reported effects of target distractor similarity on the size of these regions. More recently Pomplun *et al.* (2001*b*) have shown how perceptual span in visual search is reduced in conditions with high attentional demands.

The decline in visual abilities away from central vision is gradual, and as a result the visual lobe will not show a sharp transition between the region in which a visual discrimination can be made and the region where it is not possible. Indeed, the data on the visual lobe for letter discrimination of Fig. 2.7 show a transition region extending over many degrees. Nevertheless, nearly all work in visual search implicitly treats all display locations as equivalent, as do the theories discussed in Section 6.2. The inadequacy of this assumption was shown clearly by Carrasco *et al.* (1995) and by Scialfa and Joffe (1998). Carrasco *et al.* used a colour/orientation conjunction search, with a variable number of items between 2 and 36. In different experiments, either free viewing or brief exposures were used. Target eccentricity had a profound influence in both conditions. With free viewing, the time taken to locate the target increased, whereas with brief exposures, the effect was on decision accuracy. They conclude that these effects arose from structural factors (spatial resolution and lateral inhibition) and point out that their data call into question the standard accounts of the search process. In a subsequent study (Carrasco and Frieder, 1997) they show that the eccentricity effect is considerably reduced if displays were used in which the sizes of individual display elements are adjusted in line with the cortical magnification factor to give equal cortical activation.

An alternative way of describing these results is that *proximity* to the visual axis is a highly important determinant of the detectability of a target. We show in the following section that this factor is also of importance when searches are carried out with eye movements.

6.4 Eye movements in visual search

A number of studies through the years have recorded eye movements during visual search. Viviani (1990) provides a review, although his interpretation of search is rather broader than the usage in this chapter. A particularly significant study was that of L G Williams (1966), which anticipated much recent work of the type described in Section 6.2. Williams used displays consisting of rather cluttered, but non-overlapping, geometric shapes whose shape, size and colour were varied. In his displays, subjects could search for an item of prespecified colour much more easily than for pre-specification of size or shape. He showed that the differential pattern of abilities matched a corresponding pattern in the ability to select items of the specified characteristic with eye movements.

6.4.1 Saccades in parallel and serial visual search

The distinction between search that is spatially parallel and that which is serial has been discussed in Section 6.2. If the task is to locate the target with the eyes, then a broadly adequate generalisation is that for searches that are spatially parallel, the target can be located with a single saccade, whereas when searches are serial, more than one saccade is necessary if the display size is large. A number of studies have demonstrated the first assertion, for search that is spatially parallel in reaction time terms (Williams *et al.*, 1997; Zelinsky and Sheinberg, 1997) or search for which the target is defined by a single feature (Findlay 1997; Scialfa and Joffe, 1998). Several studies have also examined the patterns of eye movements in serial search tasks and shown that multiple saccades occur (see also Binello *et al.*, 1995; Williams *et al.*, 1997; Zelinsky and Sheinberg, 1997). Moreover, the number of saccades made correlates highly with search times, accounting for up to 67 per cent of the reaction time (RT) variability in Zelinsky and Sheinberg's study. These results suggest a close link between saccades and overall reaction time performance in visual search. The duration of fixations will be considered in more detail in Section 6.4.4 but it may be noted now that the scanning process is similar to that found in other visual tasks, with fixations generally lasting 200–300 ms.

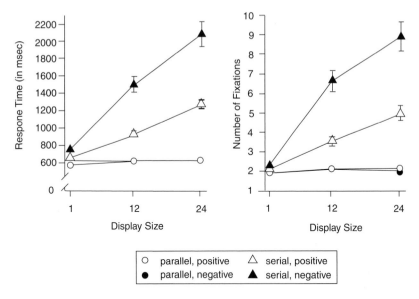

Figure 6.2 Data from the study of Williams *et al.* (1997), in which eye movements were monitored during a visual search task. The left hand graph shows the traditional search function (cf. Fig. 6.1). The right hand graph shows the number of fixations made during the searches. A close correspondence between the two graphs is obvious.

Figure 6.2 shows the relationship in one condition of the study by Williams *et al.* (1997). The task was to search for the target letter **T** amongst a series of **L** distractor letters. As display size is increased from 1 to 24, the average number of fixations increases from 2 to 9. One interpretation of such a finding is that within each fixation, a restricted group of items are monitored. In this case, the number of items would be 3–4; other studies have found a somewhat greater number. This is consistent with the finding (Findlay 1997; Scialfa and Joffe, 1998) that, in feature conjunction searches, the probability of locating the target with the very first saccade suggests that about 6–8 display items can be processed so that if the target is located within this set, the saccade can be directed towards it.

6.4.2 Processing within an eye fixation during visual search

The evidence discussed in the previous section points to the following conclusion. When a search task is carried out with no restriction on eye movements, a number of display elements are effectively monitored during each fixation. If the search target is amongst this set, then the subsequent saccade is directed to the target. In cases where the target pops out (parallel search), the number is very high. In cases normally thought of as serial search, the number is lower, typically between 3 and 10 for feature conjunction searches and probably even lower when the target is more complex (Brown *et al.*, 1997; Findlay, 1995).

The eye movements in this task constitute an overt attentional mechanism. As we discussed in Section 6.2, much thinking about visual search has concentrated instead on covert attentional processes. How should the two types of attention be integrated? This is a fundamental question for active vision and has been addressed by various individuals (Findlay, 1997; Findlay and Gilchrist, 1998; Motter and Belky, 1998a,b). Motter and Belky's study is notable because they trained monkeys to perform search tasks. The monkeys' performance in simple feature and colour/orientation conjunction searches appears in all respect very similar to that of humans.

A variety of possibilities might be proposed for the way in which covert attention operates during an individual fixation. As discussed in Section 6.2, some theories of search have suggested that a covert attentional pointer might scan display items rapidly enough for several items to be scanned within a single fixation, although such a rapid scanning rate has not, in general, been supported by estimates from other approaches (Section 3.4). However, assuming for the moment that such fast covert scanning rates are possible, how might this process be related to the generation of overt eye movements? The most obvious possibility would seem to be for the covert attentional scan to continue until the target was located and then to direct the eyes to it. In this case however, the target would be always located with the first saccade, even though this might take a considerable time. Such a pattern is not found. Saccades frequently land on distractor items before the target is located. A second possibility, echoing suggestions made in the study of reading (Section 5.7.2), is that a serial covert attentional scan operates during each fixation but is terminated by a time deadline. If the target is found before the deadline, the eyes are moved to it but if not, an eye movement occurs when the deadline is reached. On this model, two predictions can be made. First, fixations that precede a saccade directed to the target would be of shorter duration than the rest. Second, saccades which are not directed to the target would be generated as a result of the deadline process and so would not be guided by display characteristics. The evidence shows both predictions to be wrong. Motter and Belky (1998b) found fixations prior to a target-directed saccade to have exactly the same latency as those to distractors and Findlay (1997) found first saccades to targets to have longer, not shorter, latencies than those to distractors. Both studies found that saccades to distractors were more likely to fall on items more similar to the target (in this case, ones possessing a common visual feature).

The alternative to the hypothesised serial processing by covert attention is that several display items are processed in parallel during each eye fixation, a proposal concordant with the suggestion made by Pashler (1987) noted in Section 6.3.1 and one that will be discussed further in the following section. This, as we forewarned in Section 6.2.4, eliminates the role usually assigned to covert attention in the search process, in favour of an active vision account. To reiterate this important conclusion, we are stating that there is *no* evidence that a covert attentional spotlight scans rapidly through the items of a search display.

We propose, as an alternative, that covert attention should be seen as supplementing overt eye movements rather than substituting for them. We believe that an appropriate role for covert attention may be one similar to that which has been described in the study of reading. We noted (Section 5.3.3) that the phenomenon of preview benefit could be said to reflect the movement of covert attention to the saccade target at some point in time before the overt eye movement. While no direct studies of preview benefit have been made in visual search, an indication that a similar process occurs comes from results showing that fixations on distractors may often be unusually brief (Findlay *et al.*, 2001; McPeek *et al.*, 2000). We thus propose that the movements of covert attention are not dissociated from eye movements, but rather operate as an integral part of the active vision process (see Section 3.7).

6.4.3 Guidance of saccades in visual search

The evidence discussed above supports the idea that, during each fixation, two factors affect the way eye guidance operates in visual search. A *similarity* effect results in saccades being directed to items which are similar to the target, and a *proximity* effect leads to saccades being directed to items close to the visual axis. In search containing multi-element displays, saccades are more likely to be directed to items that are near the current fixation (e.g. Motter and Belky, 1998*a,b*). The exact strength of this proximity effect will depend on the display, in terms of both item density and item salience. The observation that parallel search tasks typically require only a single saccade suggests that proximity effects can be almost completely overridden when the target item is salient. In other cases, saccades are directed to targets only if they are close to the fovea (Findlay, 1997; Motter and Belky, 1998*b*; Viviani and Swensson, 1982)

We propose therefore that the display is monitored in parallel, but with increasing weighting for proximity to the fovea. This leads to the concept of a *salience map*. The salience map, an idea introduced into work on human vision by Koch and Ullman (1985), is a representation formed from the retinal image. The information represented in a two-dimensional spatial manner is the single property, salience. The realisation of the map may be envisaged as through the pattern of neural activity in a neural network. The network is two-dimensional with the visual field being mapped spatially in a retinotopic way. The level of neural activity at each point encodes the salience. It is assumed that information feeds into this salience map so that the level of activity corresponds to the level of evidence that the search target is present at any location. As a result, items sharing a feature with the target will generate a higher level of activation than items sharing no target feature. Proximity to fixation also increases an item's salience. Within this framework, the saccade is made to the location of highest activity on the salience map. A final assumption is that the system is not able to encode visual properties perfectly but is subject to random noise fluctuations (cf. Eckstein, 1998). The pattern of erroneous saccades can then be readily accounted for.

The salience map seems to present a useful approach to visual search where eye guidance takes place, and also finds support from work on the neurophysiology of search (Section 6.7). However, guidance by similarity to the search target is only one of a number of factors controlling eye saccades in visual search. It is clear that, in addition, saccades, particularly in large search displays, must ensure that all areas of the display are searched, if possible avoiding repeating searches over parts of the display already looked at. Likewise, saccades should not take the gaze outside the display area. We are beginning to obtain some insight into the strategic factors that mediate these constraints, and these are discussed in Section 6.6. It is also the case that although many instances of eye guidance by similarity have been reported, the extent of such guidance seems variable; thus in a study involving colour/shape conjunction search, Zelinsky (1996) found no evidence for guidance based on shape or colour. Guidance appears to occur under some display conditions and not under others. One possible explanation is that the extent of guidance may depend on the relationship between the difficulty of the foveal discrimination and the ease with which peripheral information can be extracted (see Hooge and Erkelens, 1999). An alternative explanation is that the proximity effect may over-ride the similarity effect (Findlay and Gilchrist, 1998). Whatever the case, guidance appears to be present in some search situations but not all. Recent evidence using gaze-contingent displays (Pomplun *et al.*, 2001*a*) suggests that such guidance mechanisms are flexible and act in parallel across the display.

6.4.4 Saccades in visual search: latencies and fixation durations

Hooge and Erkelens (1996, 1998, 1999) have carried out a series of studies investigating what influences fixation duration in search tasks. Two factors were identified as important. The first is the time taken to analyse the fixated item—the *discrimination task*. The second is the time spent on peripheral analysis of potential locations for the next saccade—*the selection task* (see Hooge and Erkelens 1999). Hooge and Erkelens (1999) show that the fixation duration is mainly dependent on the discrimination task. They suggested that, as the difficulty of the discrimination task determines fixation duration, it will only be under conditions of more difficult discrimination that fixations are long enough to allow the peripheral information to be extracted to allow guidance to occur. This is consistent with the conclusions reached in the study of reading (Section 5.5) and with Henderson's suggestion that the maximum fixation duration is determined by a deadline (Henderson, 1992). In search, guidance will only occur when the peripheral analysis allows useful information to be extracted about possible target locations before the deadline is reached.

Hooge and Erkelens (1998) conducted a visual search task in which subjects had to search for an **O** amongst **C**'s. The **C**'s could be presented at a number of orientations. In one condition, they arranged the **C**'s so that they pointed in the direction in which the target was. Subjects were able to use this foveal information to direct their next saccade. Although present, the benefit that these cues gave was not large; it is clear that although the foveal information can be used to direct the next saccade in search, this information is not used optimally.

6.4.5 Saccades in visual search: landing positions

Our discussion up to now has been concerned with whether the eyes land on the target item or, if not, on which type of distractor. This relatively gross measure of eye guidance may be called saccade *selection accuracy*. A more detailed question concerns whether the eye in fact lands accurately on an item, since it is, of course, quite possible for the saccadic landing position to fall between two items. The issue may be called saccade *targeting accuracy* and is discussed in this section.

Ottes *et al.* (1985), in a very simple search task, asked subjects to saccade to a target of one colour which was presented with a distractor of another colour. A proportion of saccades in these conditions were directed to a location between the two items. This is the so called global effect (Section 4.4.3). Findlay (1997) carried out a simple search task in which the subjects were required to saccade to a red target amongst green distractors or visa versa. On occasional trials, two target items were presented either adjacent to each other or separated by a single distractor. In both cases some saccades were directed to an intermediate position between the two targets (see Fig. 6.3). This occurred even though subjects had been instructed to saccade to one item or the other, should two target items be presented. A final instance of saccades landing on space between display elements, rather than on the elements, is from the study by Zelinsky *et al.* (1997), discussed in greater detail in Section 6.6. They showed that such saccades occurred regularly at the beginning of a scanpath, and that fixations were focussed on to smaller and smaller groups of items as the scanpath progressed. Thus on their account, the intermediate landing positions are selected for strategic reasons, rather than being an automatic outcome of display factors.

Further investigations are needed to disentangle the two possibilities since, under some circumstances, saccade targeting accuracy appears to be high. For the monkey visual searches studied by Motter and Belky (1998*b*), 80 per cent of fixations landed within one degree of a display item and only 20 per cent in blank areas between stimuli, although the proportion of blank area was much higher (65 per cent–98 per cent for different size displays). Gilchrist *et al.* (1999*a*) studied a search task in which eight items were positioned equi-spaced in a ring around fixation. Saccades landed on targets and distractors but much more rarely in between the two. Furthermore, saccades were more likely to be directed to a distractor which was beside the target than to one further away. This effect spread across a large area of the display. The effect contrasts with the global effect in that it

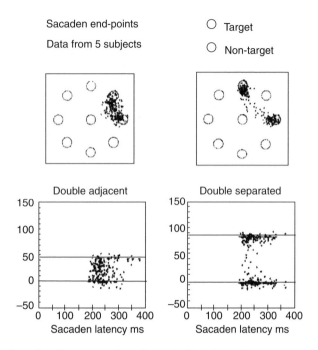

Figure 6.3 The global effect in a visual search task. In this task, participants were required to saccade to the red target (shown in darker grey) among green distractors. The upper panels show the first saccade endpoints overlaid on the display for trials in which two targets were presented concurrently. When the two targets were adjacent, a large proportion of the saccades landed between the two targets (left hand upper panel); this effect appears to be dependent on the latency of the saccades (left-hand lower graph). When the items were separated by a single distractor, this effect was still present but reduced (right-hand panels) (Adapted from Findlay 1997; Fig. 3, 4 & 5).

resulted in an increase in the probability of an item being fixated rather than leading to fixations in intermediate positions between items. By using display items with restricted spatial frequencies, they showed that the effect was dependent on the items sharing the same spatial frequencies.

Gilchrist *et al.* (1999*b*) showed that saccades in search could be targeted to groups of items and that the grouping principles that formed a unit for saccade selection in search were similar to those that determined RT search performance (Gilchrist *et al.*, 1997). Thus, interactions between items play an important role in determining saccade landing position in search in various ways; either by guiding saccades to the target (Gilchrist *et al.*, 1999*a*), generating saccades to the centre of groups or items (Findlay 1997; Ottes *et al.*, 1985; Zelinsky *et al.*, 1997) or by allowing saccades in search to be efficiently guided to display structures made up of the multiple component parts (Gilchrist *et al.*, 1999*a*).

6.5 Ocular capture in visual search

In real-world situations, visual search tasks can involve searching for the most perceptually salient item in the environment, (e.g. searching in a crowd for a friend wearing a bright jumper) or the least perceptually salient items in the environment (e.g. searching for a contact lens). However, as these real-world search tasks can take a protracted period of time, there is also a need for additional monitoring of the environment. Most of the items that require monitoring in these situations consist of new objects that suddenly appear

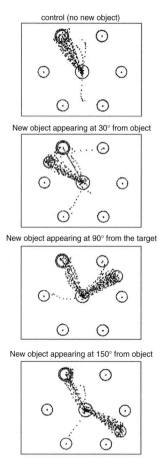

Figure 6.4 Eye movement records associated with the onset of a new object during search. The points of the graphs represent eye position sampled every 4 ms after the onset of the search display. The upper panel shows the condition when no new object appears. The lower panels illustrate conditions where a new object appears at locations at differing distances from the target. Sudden onsets appear to capture the eyes. (Reproduced from Theeuwes *et al.*, 1998; Fig. 2).

(such as a predator). In a laboratory setting, this translates to the ability of new objects that appear during search to capture covert and overt attention. For example, Theeuwes *et al.* (1998) had subjects carry out a search task in which the target was defined by colour. On some trials a new but task-irrelevant object also appeared. Under these circumstances, subjects often made a saccade to the new item (see Fig. 6.4) suggesting that the onset had captured the saccade (see Egeth and Yantis, 1997; Theeuwes 1993 for similar results using RT measures). Fixation duration on the onset object was very short (25–150 ms) and was followed by a fixation on the target. These very short fixations suggest the parallel programming of two saccades; one to the target and one to the onset distractor (Section 4.4.4). Initially, such effects appeared to be restricted to abrupt onsets and luminance increments and did not appear to occur for transient colour changes (Irwin *et al.*, 2000). However, recent work by Ludwig and Gilchrist (2002) suggests that non-abrupt onsets can capture the eyes during search but to a lesser extent than onsets. Their work also showed that the extent of capture was modulated by top-down factors. If the abrupt onset was the same colour as the target, there was more capture than if it were the same colour as the distractors even though the two items were matched for perceptual salience. Capture during search therefore may not simply be a result of a low-level and automatic perceptual monitoring process but appears to reflect the higher level processes related to the task demands.

6.6 Saccades in visual search: scanpaths

In Section 6.4 we discussed how information from the display might be used to guide an individual saccade during visual search in a bottom-up, stimulus driven, way. In this section we consider longer term, top-down, influences that allow searches to be controlled. Considering the case of a difficult search task with a large display, many saccades would be necessary for a complete search. Ideally, these should be controlled so that the search is efficient, covering all regions of the display with no unnecessary repetition of regions. Strategies to achieve this efficiency range from automatic processes that prevent repeat scanning of an item recently scanned, through to deliberate strategic control of the eyes.

An early study by Engel (1977) forms a good starting point. Engel contrasts the extremes of an optimally efficient scanning strategy and a purely random scanning strategy. In the optimal case, regions of the array are selected so that regions previously sampled are avoided and thus no repetition of sampling occurs. Such a strategy, of course, requires precise memory of which regions have been scanned. The random strategy, in contrast, has no memory and chooses the next sample on an entirely random basis. For each strategy, it is possible to calculate a function showing the way the probability of the target being found, p, depends on the number of samples (or on the time taken, t, if it is assumed that samples are made at a fixed rate). It is easy to see that, for the systematic strategy, the function is a steady linear increase, reaching 100 per cent when all the display is sampled. The random strategy can be shown to give a curvilinear function

$$p = 1 - \exp^{(-\alpha t)}$$

where α is a constant. Engel analysed data from a simple search task where the target was a disk of slightly different size in a display of randomly positioned distractor disks of a fixed size. Engel found that the data followed a linear function for about 1.2 seconds, but subsequently appeared to revert to a random process (the maximum time allowed for the search was 4 seconds and this may have been too short for subjects to develop conscious systematic strategies). More recent work by Gilchrist and Harvey (2000) investigated refixation rates in a visual search task. They found that fixations on previously fixated distractors did occur within a scanpath; however, the frequency of these refixations was less than would be predicted from random sampling.

One suggestion for a mechanism to promote efficient search is inhibition of return (Section 3.2), the bias found to slow attentional orienting responses at locations where orienting has recently occurred. Klein (1988) proposed that the role of inhibition of return is to act as a foraging facilitator. More recently (Klein and MacInnes, 1999; Klein, 2000), he has developed the argument and supported it with an experimental investigation. He used a search task that involved a cluttered scene (the search was for 'Waldo', an American cartoon character). At some point during the search, a readily detectable black probe disk was added to the search display, at a controlled location contingent on the eye scan. The subjects were instructed to make an immediate saccade to the disk when this happened. The latency when the target was in a new location was 190 ms, in comparison with 250 ms when the location had been fixated previously (a smaller difference was observed for the immediately prior location). Although this design did not distinguish between spatial inhibition of return and the effects of motor alternation, it provides support to Klein's argument. Furthermore, the time course of inhibition of return (a few seconds) matches well the data from Engel discussed above and the probable time course of most real-life searches.

The finding of a reduced effect for the immediately prior location is in accord with a finding by Motter and Belky (1998b) from their analysis of scanpaths in monkeys during visual search. They studied properties of consecutive saccades. They found a bimodal pattern in the distribution of saccade amplitudes with relatively few movements in the 1°–2° band. There was little relationship between the amplitudes of successive saccades (Fig. 6.5a). Saccades showed a slight tendency to be directed away from the direction of the previous fixation. However, against this trend there was also a sub-population of saccades which were directed quite precisely back to the previously fixated location (Fig. 6.5b).

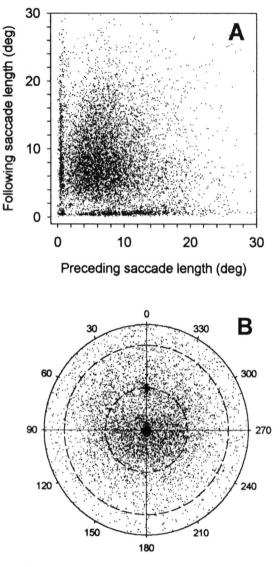

Figure 6.5 Properties of consecutive saccades during a visual search task. The upper panel (A) shows the relationship between the length of a saccade and the length of the subsequent saccade. Large saccades were often followed by small corrective saccades but there was no other strong systematic relationship between saccade sizes. The lower panel shows the direction of the next saccade relative to the direction of the preceeding one. On the radial axis, 0° represents a saccade retracing the direction of the previous saccade, and 180° a saccade in the same vectorial direction as the previous one. The inner of the concentric dotted rings shows saccades with exactly the same amplitude as the previous one and the outer ones where the amplitude is twice that of the previous one. There is a tendency to saccade away from the previously fixated area. The cluster above the centre represents saccades that return to the previously fixated location (Reproduced from Motter and Belky, 1998*b*; Fig. 7).

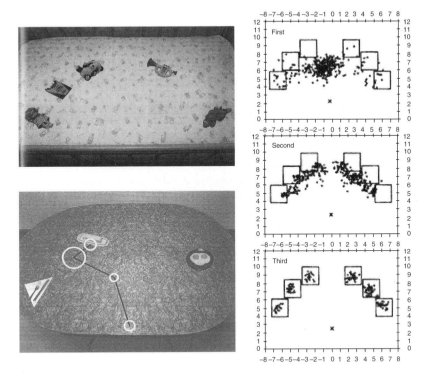

Figure 6.6 Search scanpaths observed by Zelinsky *et al.* (1997) in a task looking for real objects (toys). The upper left panel shows a typical search display and the lower left panel shows a typical scanpath consisting of three saccades from the initial fixation location, always constrained to be centre-bottom. The right hand panel shows cumulative location of the first, second, and third fixations. Subjects appear to use a homing-in strategy and only acquire the target precisely on the third fixation.

Scanpaths in search can also be shaped by more deliberately strategic factors. Hooge and Erkelens (1996) used circular displays and reported that subjects tended to scan in a clockwise or counter-clockwise direction around the display. Under these scanpath conditions, subjects only occasionally skipped an item and only sometimes changed direction. On some occasions the scanpath included a fixation on the target but recognition did not occur. Another interesting pattern was observed by Zelinsky *et al.* (1997) who found that even with a small number of items, subjects made several saccades to locate the target (Fig. 6.6). Analysis of saccade landing positions during the scanpath showed that saccades were initially directed towards the centre of groups of items and progressively focused onto smaller groups, this property is reminiscent of the zoom lens account of covert attention (Section 3.2.2). Zelinsky *et al.* propose that the visual averaging found in the global effect (Section 4.4.3) may contribute to the phenomenon.

6.7 Physiology of visual search

Visual search involves the co-ordination of target identity information; target location information and response generation in the context of a display that contains multiple elements. This section continues the discussion of physiological control of simple eye movements (Section 4.3 and Section 4.5). Here we will focus specifically on visual search.

The search for the neural basis of saccade generation in visual search has focused on a number of structures. As noted above and in Chapter 2, visual information processing in the posterior parts of the brain is, in part at least, segregated, with different visual attributes being processed in independent neural structures. The superior colliculus, on the dorsal aspect of the midbrain, is an important structure in the control of saccades and appears to convert visual information into motor signals for the control of saccades. Neurons in the superficial layers of the superior colliculus are responsive to visual stimulation but do not differentiate between the type of stimulation in the way that cells in the posterior parts of the brain do. A central question then is how information in primary visual areas is processed in order to drive a saccade to the target in a search task. The concept of the salience map (Section 6.4.3) has been prominent in work on the physiology of visual search and it seems likely that several areas that are involved in the control of saccades operate in such a manner.

One candidate region for the control of saccades in search and in turn for the neural substrate of the salience map is that of the frontal eye fields (FEF). The frontal eye fields receive inputs from parietal cortex as well as from prefrontal cortex (see Schall and Hanes, 1998). Although over half the cells in this area are visually responsive, like the cells in the superior colliculus (SC), the cells are not tuned to be responsive to specific stimuli properties. The responsiveness of the cell is spatially mapped and is enhanced if the location is the target for a saccade. This property of the cells and their direct links to both the SC (Goldberg and Segraves, 1987; Segraves and Goldberg, 1987) and brainstem saccade generation circuits (Segraves, 1992) have led to the suggestion that this area may be acting as a salience map. Single cell recording in FEF by Schall and others (Schall *et al.*, 1995) has shown that the response of these cells is suppressed when a distractor falls in the receptive field and is enhanced when the target falls in the receptive field. The cells appear to have a task or target specific selectivity rather than being selective for a specific stimuli attribute. It seems likely that this selectivity of activation is the result of signals originating in more posterior visual areas. Studies that measure the temporal sequencing of the activity associated with a visual stimulus suggest that activity in FEF may build up before the activity of some of the posterior brain areas, for example V2 and V4 (Schmolesky *et al.*, 1998), and as a result saccade selection may occur before signals from these areas are able to contribute to target detection.

Another candidate for the location of the salience map for the control of saccades in visual search is lateral intraparietal cortex (LIP). Kusunoki *et al.* (2000) report a series of experiments in which they record from single units in LIP and show that cells responded to a number of properties of items in multi-element displays. Cells responded to abrupt onset, motion and, importantly, task relevance. However, the cells' responses were not specifically tuned for the generation of saccades but instead appeared to act as a multi purpose visual salience map.

Attentional modulation of cells responding during search is not restricted to the dorsal stream alone. Receptive fields in the temporal stream are particularly large and become larger further into the temporal lobe; cells in inferior temporal cortex (IT) can have receptive fields that cover the whole visual field. Under these circumstances more than one item can fall into the receptive field of a single cell. In a search situation, these multiple items in the receptive field could consist of the target and distractors. A number of studies have shown target-based responding of cells in the temporal stream. Cells in IT tend to have a set of stimuli that will generate the maximum response. This preference appears to be visually determined but it is not the product of a simple visual characteristic such as colour. Chelazzi *et al.* (1998) recorded from cells in IT of macaque monkeys during a visual search task in which a saccade was the required response. In their experiments the search display was preceded by the target for that trial, presented centrally. Activity between the presentation of this cue and the search display indicated a top-down bias in favour of cells for which the target was a preferred stimulus. Within a short interval after the onset of the search display, cell responses were determined by the target stimulus. The cell's response to the search display was equal to the response to the target presented alone, regardless of whether it was the preferred stimulus for that cell or not (see Fig. 6.7). The results were interpreted to reflect a top-down bias in favour of task relevant items mediated by working memory and a model in which items compete for resources when the display is presented.

Chelazzi *et al.* (1998) also carried out a variant of this task in which a manual response was required. They found that the magnitude of the attentional effect when the display was presented was much larger in the saccade version. The reasons for this difference remain unclear. What is clear is that these neurons are not involved in selection for saccades alone. However, the difference in magnitude for different response types (saccade or manual responding) may reflect the different extent to which the target has to be spatially localised.

Luck *et al.* (1997) showed that the responses of neurons in V2 and V4 were similarly influenced by which of two stimuli was the focus of attention. The size of this effect was dependent on the stimuli being presented simultaneously and was restricted to the situation in which both stimuli were presented within the receptive field of the cell (see also Moran and Desimone, 1985).

As discussed above (Section 6.4), visual search is supported by a series of saccades that together form a scanpath. It would appear that the networks of brain areas that construct the salience map select a target for the next saccade in

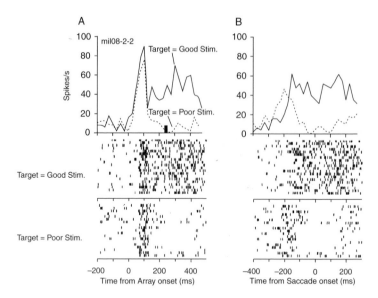

Figure 6.7 Response of an individual IT neuron during saccade target selection. Panel A shows the response time locked to the onset of the array with the vertical bar indicating the average saccade latency to the target. Panel B shows the same data but with responses time locked to the onset of the saccade. Individual raster plots are shown below. (Reproduced from Chelazzi *et al.*, 1998).

a winner-take-all manner. However, a number of studies suggest that two saccades can be programmed concurrently with a very short (<125 ms) intermediate fixation duration (e.g. Findlay *et al.*, 2001; Hooge and Erkelens 1996; McPeek and Keller 2001; McPeek *et al.*, 2000; Theeuwes *et al.* 1999). Recently, McPeek and Keller (2002) made recording in the deep layers of the superior colliculus while the monkey carried out a visual search task. During trials in which two saccades occurred in quick succession, they found evidence for increased firing at the location for the second saccade, before the saccade was generated to the first location. These results suggest that the superior colliculus does not always act in a strict winner-take-all manner. Instead it appears that the salience of two visual goals can be simultaneously maintained. This provides the first basic building block for the neural sequencing of saccades into a scanpath.

In this section we have shown that a number of brain areas are implicated in the process of saccade generation in visual search. This reflects the multiple processes that are involved in successful target detection and localisation.

6.8 Summary

Studies of visual search have been a dominant part of research in vision and visual cognition for the last 30 years. There have been two primary reasons suggested for this emphasis. The first is that visual search provides a diagnostic instrument for identifying features that can be extracted in parallel across the visual display. And the second is that search is a ubiquitous part of visual behaviour and is particularly well suited to the study of the processes of visual attention. Concerning the first reason, given the ambiguity in how to interpret search slopes from RT data (e.g. Wolfe, 1998) it is increasingly unclear how search can be used as a diagnostic tool to differentiate the display characteristics that can be analysed pre-attentively in the visual system.

Turning to the second justification, we also believe that search is an important human behaviour that demands careful study. However, models of visual search have been dominated by the use of covert attention as an explanatory process. When search becomes more difficult, it has been assumed that covert spatially-restricted scanning occurs to serially sample the display to allow for target detection. Even though alternative models have emphasized the importance of parallel processes in serial search and there is decreasing support for the original proposal of serial item-by-item scanning through covert attention, the area continues to be dominated by an exclusive emphasis on covert processes.

We have argued here that this emphasis is misguided. As search becomes more difficult, a number of studies have shown that serial attentional scanning does occur in visual search: this mechanism is overt and consists of a series of saccadic eye movements prior to target detection. We considered in detail in Section 6.4.2 the possibility that covert attention scans several items during the course of each fixation in these cases. The evidence allowed us to reject this position in favour of a model in which overt scanning is accompanied by parallel processing within each fixation. Such models are more consistent with the neurophysiological data in which display items compete with each other and are differentiated over time.

CHAPTER 7

NATURAL SCENES AND ACTIVITIES

7.1 Introduction

In the preceding three chapters we have examined three situations in which active vision has been studied intensively. Orienting, reading and visual search are very different activities but progress has been possible in all three cases because of the constraints on the visual activity required. In the case of orienting, both visual material and task are extremely simple; in the case of reading, the text is ordered so that there is no choice to be made of saccade direction; in the case of visual search, the task is highly specified. In this chapter we consider active vision in less constrained situations.

In Chapter 1, we listed a set of investigative questions for active vision, suggesting, for example, that a full understanding of active vision would entail an ability to predict when and where the eyes moved for each gaze shift. We are far from a detailed understanding at this level of eye scanning and indeed it may be an unrealistic aim for the free viewing situation. However the gaze shifts that occur during picture and scene viewing have long proved a fascinating study area. In this chapter we review the work that has been carried out, showing that the principles emerging from studies of simpler areas can still operate. We have selected studies that have either historical or theoretical importance. We have had to exclude for reasons of space any detailed discussion of work in many important applications areas, e.g. radiology (Krupinski, 1996; Kundel *et al.*, 1978), driving (Chapman and Underwood, 1998; Land and Lee, 1994; Mourant and Rockwell, 1972) and sports (Williams and Davids, 1998; Williams *et al.* 1999).

In view of the wide prevalence of the moving image in contemporary life, it is remarkable that very little progress has been made in investigations of how people scan such images. An early finding by Guba *et al.* (1964) found that viewers had a strong tendency to look at the face of a narrator, even when a strong animated distractor was also present. More recently Tosi *et al.* (1997) have shown that rapid motion sequences in moving pictures or objects generate a strong tendency to fixate the screen centre. Yet, in general, this topic is ripe for future investigation.

7.1.1 Early studies of picture scanning

Two classic studies of eye scanning, one American and one Russian, devoted much time to analysing records of individuals looking at pictorial material. Guy Buswell used a photographic technique to record eye movements both of reading (Buswell, 1922, 1937) and of picture viewing (Buswell, 1935). In the study of pictures, he used artistic material from a variety of sources, such as the classical print 'The Wave' by Hokusai (Fig. 7.1). He noted wide individual differences in all his measures but also showed that eye fixations in general concentrated on particular areas of the picture. So, for example, in pictures containing human figures, these figures were disproportionately likely to receive fixations. He offered relatively little detailed interpretation of his results, suggesting indeed that such an issue might be of more interest to the art expert than the psychologist.

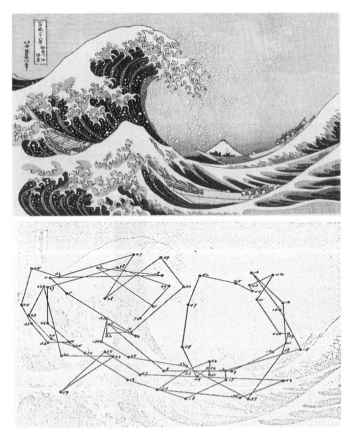

Figure 7.1 'The Wave' by Hokusai, and an eye scan of the same picture reported by Buswell in his early studies of eye scanning.

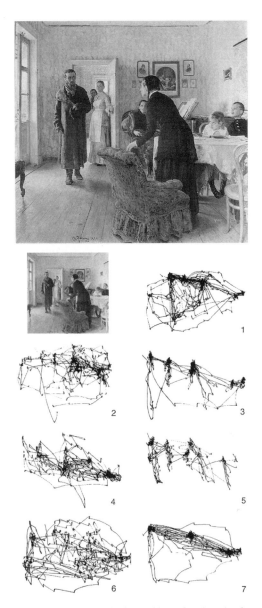

Figure 7.2 Examples of eye scanning records obtained by Yarbus (1967). Observers were given different instructions while viewing the picture 'They did not expect him' by Ilya Repin. Each of the traces shows a three minute record of eye scanning with the following instructions (1) Free examination, (2) following request to estimate the material circumstances of the family, (3) following request to give the ages of the people, (4) following request to surmise what the family were doing before the visitor's arrival, (5) remember the clothes worn by the people in the picture, (6) remember the position of the people and objects in the room, (7) estimate how long the 'unexpected visitor' had been away.

Nevertheless, some interesting generalisations emerge. Buswell made detailed measurements of fixation durations during picture scanning and noted a tendency for fixation duration to increase with increased viewing time. He suggested that a general survey, in which the viewer takes in the main areas of a picture, is followed by a more detailed study of localised regions. Buswell compared scans over coloured versus black/white versions of the same picture and reported that colour had surprisingly little effect on eye scanning. Finally he compared art students with others and found that art training resulted in a tendency to make shorter fixations.

Alfred Yarbus pursued a solitary line of investigation in Moscow at a time when the political vicissitudes of the Cold War prevented much East–West scientific interchange. His work was consequently little known in the West until an admirable translation was made by Lorrin Riggs, an American oculo-motor specialist (Yarbus, 1967). Yarbus used a 'suction cap', which fitted onto the eyeball and had a small mirror attached. A light beam reflected from a mirror attached to the cap was deviated as the eye rotated. This enabled a photographic record of the eye movements to be obtained (a similar technique was in use at the same time in the UK and the US for studying miniature eye movements (Section 2.3.2).

As well as studying basic aspects of eye movement control, Yarbus recorded the scanning eye movements of observers looking at pictures. He used a set of pictures, such as Fig. 7.2, from the Russian realist school and other sources. His fascinating records have become deservedly well known through frequent reproductions. Yarbus confirmed many of Buswell's findings; for example, the minimal influence of colour on eye scanning patterns (also reported by Tosi *et al.*, 1997). He appreciated that scanning patterns were very sensitive to the specific mental task of the observer, showing this clearly by comparing scans where observers viewed pictures after having been given very specific instructional questions (Fig. 7.2). In one aspect, a clear difference from Buswell's account appears. Yarbus, although at times suggesting that a scan is first used to form a 'general impression', used his data to draw the conclusion that 'additional time spent on perception is not used to examine the secondary elements, but to re-examine the most important elements' (Yarbus, 1967, p. 193). It is certainly the case that the records of Yarbus show this repetitive characteristic. This is quite surprising, given the records were often made over an abnormally long viewing period (many seconds).

7.1.2 Average characteristics of eye movement patterns during picture viewing

Buswell, Yarbus and a number of subsequent workers have accumulated much data on average parameters of the eye movements made during picture scanning. These measures have been reviewed in a number of places (Henderson and Hollingworth, 1998; Rayner and Pollatsek, 1992). Figures in the range 2°–4° are the most commonly reported estimates of average saccade amplitude during picture viewing. It should be noted that saccade size reports are generally given in degrees visual angle. In the study of saccades during reading (Section 5.2), absolute measures of saccade size vary with the size of the print and it is much more appropriate to use a measure in terms of number of characters of text. It is very likely that the same consideration should apply in the case of scenes or pictures, since it is evident that a pictorial representation can be scaled to a wide range of sizes.

Fixation durations when viewing pictures and scenes show a skewed distribution, with a mode at 230 ms, a mean of 330 ms and a range from less than 50 ms to more than 1000 ms (Henderson and Hollingworth, 1999a). The finding that the mean fixation duration increases as viewing continues was noted by Buswell (1935) and has been replicated several times (Viviani, 1990). For example, Antes (1974) reported that the mean duration of early fixation was 215 ms and that this increased progressively to 310 ms after a few seconds inspection.

Just as in the case of reading (Chapter 5), a variety of low level and high level factors affect fixation durations during picture viewing. Loftus (1985) showed that presenting a line drawing at a low contrast resulted in an increase in mean fixation duration in comparison with that found with a normal contrast presentation, from ca. 300 ms to ca. 400 ms with an even greater effect on the first fixation (200 ms to 500 ms). Low pass filtering has a similar effect (Mannan *et al.*, 1995). Low pass filtering is an operation carried out on a visual image which removes high spatial frequency, fine detail, information. The effect is similar to blurring. More cognitive factors likewise affect fixation duration. Fixation durations on objects that are implausible in the scene context are generally longer (Section 7.2.5).

7.1.3 Scanpaths

An idea that aroused considerable interest was the 'scanpath' (Noton and Stark, 1971a,b). Noton and Stark claimed that when a particular visual pattern is viewed, a particular sequence of eye movements is executed, and furthermore that this sequence is important in accessing the visual memory for the pattern. They obtained some experimental support for their first postulate by showing reproducible scanpaths, albeit in a situation with very large and very dim displays. However, there seems to be almost no evidence for the second postulate, and several findings are incompatible with it. Walker-Smith *et al.* (1977) recorded scanning patterns when observers carried out tasks involving facial recognition (faces were one type of item used by Noton and Stark). When an individual test face was examined to determine a match to a memorised face, some reproducible scanning sequences were observed. However when observers were asked to make a direct comparison between two simultaneously presented faces, there was no suggestion that a scanpath occurred on one face at a time. Rather, a repeated scanning between the two faces, resembling a feature-by-feature comparison, occurred. Parker (1978) carried out a task which involved memorising a scene containing about six objects, always in identical locations. Subjects generally fixated each object in the scene in a preferred viewing order although use of a different order was not disruptive. Other work (e.g. Mannan *et al.*, 1997; Hodgson *et al.*, 2000) has failed to find evidence for consistent replicable scanning sequences. In spite of occasional revivals of the idea (Stark and Ellis, 1981), it is now widely accepted that the scanpath suggestion in its original strong form was of little generality.

Arising, in part, from interest in scanpaths, a number of workers have developed techniques to capture statistical regularities in the pattern of eye scanning. One approach has considered statistical dependencies in parameters such as saccade direction or fixation location (Ellis and Stark, 1986; Ponsoda *et al.*, 1995). An example of their use has been discussed in connection with visual search in Chapter 6 (Gilchrist and Harvey, 2000). The simplest form of such a sequential dependence is the Markov process in which the properties of the immediately preceding saccade constrain the probabilities of the one currently programmed. Markov analyses have been used with human scanning data (Bozkov *et al.*, 1977) and have been proposed as a way of controlling robot vision scanners (Rimey and Brown, 1991). Several papers have explored the relationship between scanning statistical properties and image statistics (Krieger *et al.*, 2000; Mannan *et al.*, 1996, 1997). Relationships emerge, but the major component appears to relate to the simple generality described in the next section.

7.1.4 The gaze selects informative details

Buswell and Yarbus both reported that eye fixations tended to fall on the important details of pictures. Mackworth and Morandi (1967) elaborated this into the formal statement that forms the title of this section. Mackworth and Morandi generated an informativeness measure for different regions of a picture. This was achieved by cutting up the picture into 64 separate segments. A separate group of 20 observers were shown these segments individually and asked to rate how informative they appeared to be using a nine-point scale. The informativeness rating obtained for a region was highly predictive of the probability that the region would be fixated when an observer viewed the picture in a preference task.

Whilst useful as a general summary of observations, there are grave difficulties in using this statement in any more detailed way. It is tempting to believe that the idea of informativeness might be the key that allows cognitive activity to be revealed from patterns of eye scanning. However, as Viviani (1990) has argued with particular force, it is simply not possible to use eye scanning patterns in this way. Viviani makes a number of critical points. Scene information is generally available at a multiplicity of spatial scales and eye gaze measures cannot reveal whether a particular scale is selected. Thus 'what meets the fovea is only a part of what meets the (mind's) eye' (Viviani, 1990, p. 360). Indeed, the direction of eye gaze may not necessarily even correspond to the direction of attention (Chapter 3). Even more fundamental is the fact that informativeness depends on the cognitive task being undertaken (cf. Fig. 7.2). Although uniform or uniformly repetitive areas of a scene can never convey much information, in general there is little relationship between the purely visual properties of a scene and their information content. Finally, cognitive processes may often take place in parallel whereas eye scanning is necessarily a serial operation. Although this led Viviani to dismiss many attempts to use eye scan data, he expressed more optimism about situations in which eye scanning is properly matched to an articulated theory of cognitive activity for the task in question.

7.2 Analytic studies of scene and object perception

7.2.1 Scenes and objects

Historically, the mid-1970s represented something of a watershed in studies of active vision. At this point, the gaze-contingent methodology was introduced into studies of reading (Chapter 5) and analyses such as those of the amplitude transition function were developed in visual orienting (Chapter 4). Furthermore, considerable theoretical developments occurred in the areas of object perception and scene perception. In this section we summarise these developments.

The visual world presents a *scene*, which in general contains a number of well defined and often well located *objects*. It is usually accepted that scene perception involves more global properties of the visual world than simply the collection of objects. Thus a countryside scene might consist of objects such as a farmhouse, animals and hedges, but it is also clear that configurational coherence is an essential characteristic of a scene. Object perception can be studied in isolation from scene perception but it is less clear that the converse is true. It is not, in general, possible to envisage a scene devoid of objects, which creates a practical problem in disentangling scene perception from object perception. The scene provides context for the objects and one question that has received extensive investigation is whether objects are more readily perceived in an appropriate scene context (Section 7.2.5).

7.2.2 Theories of object perception and scene perception

Individual objects viewed foveally can be recognised rapidly and generally within a single fixation (Section 7.2.3). The process by which this occurs has been, and is still, a matter of active and fierce debate but all contenders accept that foveal recognition of single objects is an area where the passive vision approach, i.e. massive parallel processing of retinal information, is legitimate. Only a very brief sketch of the different theories of object perception can be given here. One early approach was to consider an object as made up of a distinctive collection of *features* and to postulate that object recognition was achieved through detection of features and feature combinations. The inadequacy of this view was argued, amongst others, by Marr (1982), whose view of vision was that a set of computational processes transformed the retinal image into a *three-dimensional representation*, which formed the basis for recognition. Biederman (1987) developed this idea into a more fully elaborated theory of object recognition. In his theory, objects are represented as an organised collection of *geon* primitives. Geons, or geometric icons, are elementary three-dimensional shapes that can be recognised on the basis of properties such as parallel sides that produce a viewpoint invariant two-dimensional projection.

An alternative to Biederman's theory suggests that three-dimensional representations are not primarily involved in object recognition (although they may be needed to support visual actions—Section 2.2.2). The alternative suggestion is that objects are recognised on the basis of their 2D properties with a small number of stored two-dimensional 'views' of an object operating in conjunction with interpolation processes (Poggio and Edelman, 1990; Tarr and Bülthoff, 1995). Current thinking suggests that the key biological importance of recognition may have resulted in a multiplicity of visual recognition systems (Logothetis and Sheinberg, 1996). An additional complication is that, for any particular experimental task, objects may be partially recognised on the basis of a few simple features. Such partial recognition may be adequate, for example, to allow an experimental subject to show object discrimination, particularly where the set of possible objects is small and is shown repeatedly.

Scene perception has been less investigated and no theoretical position has emerged of comparable strength to those in object perception. Biederman (1981; Biederman *et al.*, 1982) attempted to analyse what might be involved in the 'configurational coherence' concept which, as discussed above, differentiates a scene from a random collection of objects. He suggested, using an analogy with analyses of language material, that scenes could be regarded as *schemas*, providing a frame in which objects are viewed. He proposed several properties which an object present in a real world scene would normally satisfy. The object would have *support*; in general, objects are not free floating and thus part of the scene will be underneath the object. The object would occlude the scene background; *interposition* of background and object occurs only rarely with transparent materials. Support and interposition can be likened to the syntactic constraints in linguistic analyses. Corresponding to the semantics of language, the object would have a high *probability* of occurring within the scene frame. Cookers are unlikely to occur in a street scene. Objects would also be the appropriate *size* and have the appropriate *position* in the scene. Biederman and his group have carried out a number of experiments showing that these relationships affect the speed of perception when scenes are viewed. If scenes are presented, in which the relationships of support, interposition etc are violated, then recognition is slowed.

7.2.3 Are eye movements necessary for scene and object perception?

Studies on picture memory have demonstrated that picture memory is good, even with very brief exposures. For example, Intraub (1980), using a set of 250 pictures cut from magazines, compared recognition memory after a subset had been shown. With 6 seconds viewing time, recognition rates were 94 per cent. With tachistoscopic exposure durations, the rate fell to about 80 per cent (and the false positive rate rose from 8 per cent to 11 per cent). This confirms earlier findings (Loftus, 1972; Potter and Levy, 1969) that the opportunity to inspect a picture with eye movements is beneficial, but nevertheless the memory ability for material shown in a single glimpse is still impressive. However, it is probable that the majority of the pictures used contained prominent objects viewed foveally.

Object recognition deteriorates quite rapidly in the parafovea and periphery. Nelson and Loftus (1980) allowed subjects a limited amount of time to scan a picture and they then performed a recognition test, viewing a version of the picture in which one object had been changed. Their task was to detect the changed object. Detection rate for small objects (1°) was above 80 per cent for objects that had been directly fixated and higher if they received two fixations. However it fell to 70 per cent for objects where the closest original fixation had been at a distance from the object in the range 0.5°–2° and to a chance level (or in one case slightly above chance) for objects viewed more peripherally. This suggests that the gaze needs to be directed to within 2° of an object in a scene for it to be reliably encoded (see also Irwin and Zelinsky, 2002). As discussed in Chapters 2 and 5, the absolute eccentricity of a stimulus is likely to be less important than the eccentricity in relation to the object size and viewing distance. However, with rare exceptions (Saida and Ikeda, 1979), this relationship does not appear to have been investigated formally in studies of object perception. Work discussed in the next section suggests that information from objects seen in isolation can be obtained more peripherally but only when the object is a target for a forthcoming saccade. Other estimates of objects perceived in scenes (Rayner and Pollatsek, 1992) have emerged with broadly similar figures. One exceptional result (Loftus and Mackworth, 1978) suggesting that objects could be identified in more extreme peripheral locations is discussed in detail later (Section 7.2.5).

Some significant scene information that is not dependent on object identification can be acquired in a single glimpse. Schyns and Oliva (1994) presented subjects with 50 ms views of scenes that had been either high-pass or low-pass spatial-frequency filtered. The low-pass filtering prevented recognition of objects in the scene but nevertheless the scene could be 'recognised', although 'recognition' in this experiment implied merely discrimination from a small number of possibilities. Schyns and Oliva argue that scene recognition normally depends on the low spatial frequency configurational information, but the system is also flexible enough to allow recognition from high-pass filtered versions (Schyns and Oliva, 1997). Recent work has examined the possibility that the rapid recognition stage may be based on statistical properties, for example, related to the colour distribution (Oliva and Schyns, 2000)

Biederman (1981; Biederman et al., 1982) has also argued that scene information is captured within a single glimpse. He based this argument on experiments in which subjects are given a brief presentation (150 ms) of a scene and have to respond whether a prespecified object is present in the scene at a location specified by a flashed post-exposure marker. The scenes were line drawings containing 8–12 objects. Detection accuracy was about 70 per cent (with a 20 per cent false alarm rate) in scenes with normal structural relationships. However accuracy showed a substantial decline when the structural setting of the cued object violated the structural relationships specified in Section 7.2.2. No effect was found if the violations occurred in relation to an object other than the target object (an 'innocent bystander'). His conclusion, that scene properties are processed and can affect object recognition, seems justified. However, as in the case of visual search (Chapter 6), only a limited number of objects can be processed in parallel. Further discussion of the relationship between scene perception and object perception occurs subsequently (Section 7.2.5).

Another paradigm that has proved productive in examining the amount that can be taken in from a brief presentation is that of conceptual identification. Intraub (1981) presented pictures of objects at a rapid sequential rate (113 ms/picture). The task was to identify a picture that belonged to a specified category (e.g. food). Performance was high (60 per cent); good performance was also obtained in the converse task with negative instructions (identify a non-food item in a sequence of food items). More recently, a similar task has been employed with more complex material (Delorme et al., 2000; Fabre-Thorpe et al., 1998; Thorpe et al., 1996). Participants in these experiments are required, for example, to identify whether or not a briefly exposed scene contained an animal. Good identification is found with exposure durations as brief as 20 ms. Moreover, by recording brain (evoked response) activity in the paradigm, it has been shown that significant differences are found as early as 150 ms in the responses evoked on target trials, in comparison with those on non-target trials. A detailed analysis in relation to viewing position has not been made in these experiments, but in the example scenes shown, the target objects are in central or near central view.

The conclusions from this section are that objects viewed foveally or in the close parafovea can be identified and categorised very rapidly. However the evidence suggests that objects not fixated closer than 2° or 3° are not recognised and thus eye movements are in general necessary for the identification of objects within scenes. A certain amount of scene information (the *gist*) can be extracted from a single glimpse of a scene and this allows the scene schema to be evoked with very little delay. It is likely that eye movements over a scene will provide additional information, as well as information about specific objects. However, at present no metric exists for scene measurement and so this proposition has not been tested.

7.2.4 Object perception in peripheral vision

Systematic studies have investigated the extraction of information about objects seen in peripheral vision, using a *boundary technique* similar to that employed in the study of reading (Section 5.3.1). Recollect the logic of the technique is to display material to be identified in peripheral vision that may change as the subject's eyes make a saccadic movement to view it. The change occurs as the eye crosses an imaginary boundary and the aim of the approach is to investigate the extent to which peripheral preview assists the recognition process.

A series of studies at the University of Massachusetts, Amherst, used the boundary technique (Fig. 7.3) to explore the *preview benefit* of pre-saccadic material in peripheral vision. Pollatsek *et al.* (1984) measured the speed of object naming when various forms of preview occurred. They found that full peripheral preview produced a substantial benefit (120 ms). Benefits, albeit of a reduced magnitude, also occurred if the previewed picture came from the same category as the target picture. A small benefit, also occurred when the previewed picture had the same overall visual shape as the picture (e.g. carrot → baseball bat). This latter effect occurred only with tests at 10° eccentricity, and not at 5°.

Henderson *et al.* (1989) ran another gaze-contingent experiment to examine a further question—would preview information be taken in automatically from any location in the periphery, or would the information only be extracted from the location to which the saccade was directed. Displays of four objects were made, located at the corners of an imaginary square, and the subjects were asked to scan these in a fixed order. Processing speed increased if the object could be seen in the peripheral location about to be fixated, but not if it was located elsewhere although subsequent work (Pollatsek *et al.* 1990) showed preview benefit from objects in proximal locations. Peripheral information can be usefully extracted from pictorial material viewed in isolation, although only at the destination point of a planned saccade. Studies in visual search (Chapter 6) have also demonstrated, under some circumstances, that

Figure 7.3 Procedure used by Pollatsek *et al.* (1984) to demonstrate preview benefit in picture naming. The black triangle symbolises the eye location. The picture is altered during the saccadic movement to the object.

processing of pictorial material is possible in peripheral vision but once again with displays consisting of discrete elements.

The work discussed up to now has shown that peripheral preview benefits later foveal viewing. Henderson *et al.* (1997) demonstrated that objects can be recognised when only ever seen in peripheral vision. They used the foveal mask gaze-contingent technique to create a situation of an artificial foveal scotoma (Section 5.3.1). Subjects viewed a linear array of three pictorial line drawings of objects chosen from the Snodgrass and Vanderwart (1980) collection and were required to indicate whether a subsequently named item was part of the set. The objects were of overall size $1.5°$–$2.0°$ and were separated by $2.4°$. In the scotoma condition, the object to which the gaze was directed was obscured. Performance in the scotoma condition was high (85 per cent–93 per cent) and only slightly below that in the normal viewing condition (95 per cent). Henderson *et al.* contrast this result with the disastrous decline with a foveal scotoma when reading performance is assessed (Section 4.3.2).

Attempts have been made to describe the useful field of view for picture perception using a gaze-contingent window technique, in a similar manner to that used in studies of reading. Saida and Ikeda (1979) created a viewing situation with an electronic masking technique in which subjects saw only a central square region of an everyday picture. Viewing time and recognition scores were impaired unless the window was large enough for about half the display to be visible. This fraction applied both to $14° \times 18°$ displays and to $10° \times 10°$ ones. A follow up study by Shiori and Ikeda (1989) looked at the situation where the picture was seen normally inside the window but in reduced detail outside. Even very low-resolution detail (very well below the acuity limit at the peripheral location) aided performance considerably. Shiori and Ikeda used a pixel shifting technique to reduce resolution. Van Diepen *et al.* (1998) have developed a technique whereby a moving window can be combined with Fourier filtering. Somewhat surprisingly, performance is better when the degraded peripheral material is high-pass filtered than when it is low-pass filtered.

7.2.5 Scene context and object perception

A question that has provoked intense interest is whether scene context facilitates object recognition. An early piece of work on scene perception (Biederman, 1972) found this to be the case. Biederman carried out an experiment comparing recognition speed for detecting an object when it was present in a coherent scene with that when the same scene was jumbled by cutting it into pieces that were randomly rearranged. The object's contours were preserved during the jumbling operation but the time taken to detect its presence was significantly longer. Biederman interpreted this to indicate that scene context was important in facilitating object recognition although Henderson (1992) has pointed out an alternative possible interpretation of the results which is that the additional contours introduced by the jumbling operation added noise to the situation, thus slowing detection.

An important subsequent study that supported this position was reported in 1978 by Loftus and Mackworth. We shall describe this study in detail because of its significance for the general theme of the book and because it has considerably shaped subsequent thinking and experimentation. Loftus and Mackworth's result implied that objects were assessed in relation to the scene context and furthermore that this assessment was carried out over a substantial part of the visual field. It thus provided support for the passive vision approach which, as we outlined in Chapter 1, may be regarded as an implicit statement about scene perception. Passive vision claims that vision achieves a representation in which three-dimensional information, adequate to support object recognition, is present over the entire visual scene.

Loftus and Mackworth aimed to determine the relative significance of high-level and low-level properties in controlling fixations on a scene (Section 7.1.4). They carried out the following experiment. Line drawings of scenes were constructed, in which one object in the scene might be carefully replaced with a drawing of a different object, the replacement having broad visual similarity, but a very different contextual probability of appearing in the scene. Thus, in a farmyard picture, a tractor was replaced by an octopus of similar size and shape (Fig. 7.4), and in a stadium scene, a footballer was replaced by a ballet dancer. Control trials were used with the tractor in the farmyard and the octopus in an underwater scene. Observers were instructed to expect a recognition test and their eye movements were recorded as they viewed the scenes. Loftus and Mackworth were interested in how quickly the incongruous object was detected, and how far in the periphery the object was at the time of detection. The estimate of the latter measure came from the size of the saccade that immediately preceded the fixation on the incongruous object. Loftus and Mackworth found that incongruous objects were looked at more often and for longer durations, that fixations subsequent to the very first fixation on the scene were more likely to fall on the incongruous object than the control context appropriate object, and that the average saccade size prior to looking at the critical object was about 7°.

The last two of these results imply that the scene is analysed to a very high level using peripheral vision. In some way, it appears that objects in peripheral vision were identified as being improbable in the particular scene context. This suggests that the object is implicitly recognised and furthermore related to the scene properties. The peripheral recognition abilities found in the Loftus and Mackworth study are much greater than those found in visual search experiments discussed in Chapter 6. The visual search experiments used isolated objects, rather than contextualised objects. It is thus conceivable that superior perceptual abilities occur in scenes. However, as discussed below, and in detail by Henderson and Hollingworth (1998,1999a), attempts to replicate the results of Loftus and Mackworth have found much less evidence for such perceptual discriminations and have led to increasing concern over the result.

Figure 7.4 Example of pictures used in the study of Loftus and Mackworth (1978). Different individuals viewed each version of the picture with instructions to memorise. The measures of interest concerned the time at which the inconsistent object (in this case the octopus) affected the eye scanning pattern.

Friedman and Liebelt (1981) analysed data from subjects viewing scenes in which incongruous objects might be present. Incongruity affected the duration of fixations once the objects were fixated, but had no effect on the probability that an object would be fixated. This pattern of results has now been found in a number of other studies. De Graef *et al.* (1990) used a task in which subjects viewed drawings of scenes containing objects and also one or more constructed 'non-objects'; geometrically plausible sculpted constructions of similar size to real objects in the scene. The task was to report on the non-objects but the interest of the study was to compare fixations in a task where object-decisions (corresponding to the more familiar lexical decisions of Section 5.4) were important. De Graef *et al.* used the same manipulation as Loftus and Mackworth, to include objects that were both plausible and implausible in the scene context. De Graef *et al.* found *no* evidence that implausible objects were more likely than plausible ones to be fixated at any stage in the viewing period. They did, in part, replicate the first finding of Loftus and Mackworth. Implausible objects, once fixated, held the gaze for longer. However these longer fixation durations did not appear in the early fixations (at least the first eight) of the viewing sequence.

Other work does suggest that an immediate effect of scene context can be found when an object is first fixated. Boyce and Pollatsek (1992) took advantage of the very powerful potential of visual transients to attract the eyes (Chapter 4). Subjects were presented with a scene and shortly (75 ms) after, a target object was 'wiggled' (given a brief small displacement before returning to its original position). The task was to name the object. The wiggle ensured that the subjects' eyes are directed towards the object. Boyce and Pollatsek found that the naming latency of objects presented in context was substantially shorter than that of those violating the scene context.

Henderson and Hollingworth (1998), in a review of the area, report two further experiments of their own, attempting, and failing, to replicate the Loftus and Mackworth finding that contextually implausible objects attract fixations. They conclude that the weight of evidence is now against a position that suggests that detailed object analyses can be carried out over a wide region of peripheral vision during scene viewing. The alternative view is that our subjective impression of an immediate pictorial reality is illusory. This has received increasing support from recent studies, particularly of the phenomenon discussed in the next section.

7.2.6 Change blindness

Grimes (1996), working in the laboratory of George McConkie, reported some results where a saccade-contingent paradigm (Section 5.3.1) was employed to study picture perception. In the studies reported by Grimes, an observer views a picture and at some point whilst a saccade is in progress, aspects of the picture were changed. Participants viewed full colour pictures of scenes and were told to expect a memory test. They were also forewarned that something in the scene might occasionally change and were asked to report any such changes. Surprisingly large changes were often undetected. Thus, in a picture of two men wearing hats, swapping the hats was never detected. Movement of a child in playground scene, involving an image size change of 30 per cent showed a detection rate of under 20 per cent. Changing the colour of a parrot, occupying 25 per cent of the picture space, from brilliant green to brilliant red, was occasionally (18 per cent of occasions) not detected. Further important work with this paradigm (Currie *et al.* 2000; McConkie and Currie, 1996) will be discussed in Chapter 9.

One implication of the failure to detect changes in Grimes' experiment is that, contrary to expectation, the relevant information for detecting changes is just not available in any visual representation of the scene. If this were so, making the change simultaneous with a saccade would not be important. Of course if changes are made to a scene during a fixation, visual transients are introduced and these transients have the effect of directing attention to the area of the change (Chapters 3 and 4). Several slightly different ways have now been used to get around the problem that this introduces. One effective approach has been to mask a scene change by making several simultaneous conspicuous changes at different locations in the scene. This has been termed the 'mudsplash' technique because of the similarity to a familiar event on car windscreens. Investigations using this technique (O'Regan *et al.*, 1999; Rensink *et al.*, 1997) have shown that surprisingly large changes can fail to be detected.

The results have shown that, provided the attention capture introduced by visual transients is in some way masked, viewers frequently fail to detect substantial scene modifications. This striking phenomenon has been termed *change blindness.* Most people are somewhat amazed when first encountering the change blindness phenomenon. This was shown formally by Levin *et al.* (2000) who carried out a study in which individuals were asked to indicate how likely they would be to notice particular types of scene change in a test. There was a considerable discrepancy between the expected changes and the reported changes when the individuals were given the test. The participants had no formal training in vision. Change blindness is clearly incompatible with the 'picture in the head' account which we have termed passive vision. Levin's finding suggests that the passive vision assumptions are found widely in the population and do not depend on specific experience with passive vision theories.

Change blindness is of course less surprising if the active vision perspective is adopted. Objects that are not fixated in a scene are generally not remembered (Section 7.2.3) and thus a close correlation between fixation and the ability to detect change would be expected. This has been found. O'Regan *et al.* (2000) showed that, for objects directly fixated, change detection ability was high. Henderson and Hollingworth (1999*b*) showed in addition a greater capacity for detection of change at the location to which the saccade was directed than that at the saccade launch point. However, the correlation between fixation and change detection is not total. In the study by

O'Regan *et al.,* a considerable number of cases occured where change at a fixated location was not detected. Zelinsky (2001) has also reported results indicative that changes can be detected in peripheral vision.

7.3 Dynamic scenes and situations

The various situations discussed up to this point have had in common the fact the observer was simply taking in information from the visual environment. We have argued that eye scanning forms an active way of obtaining and selecting information in these situations. Although such observing occurs frequently in everyday life, a situation that is probably even more common is one in which the viewer is also engaged in carrying out some action. Under these circumstances, the pattern of eye scanning must be integrated into an overall action sequence. We turn now to examine some recent studies where this integration has been explored.

7.3.1 Deictic vision

Ballard *et al.* (1992, 1997, see also Hodgson *et al.,* 2000) devised an artificial manipulative task carried out by mouse-controlled manipulations of a computer screen display. The set up allowed a detailed record to be kept of both the manipulative actions and the eye scanning of the individual carrying out the action. The block assembly task that they used is shown in Fig. 7.5. Ballard *et al.* used this situation to illustrate the following theoretical account of active vision.

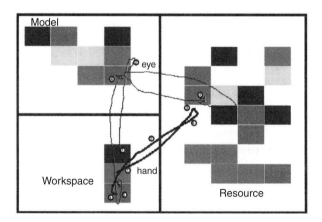

Figure 7.5 The 'blocks' task studied by Ballard *et al.* The subject operates on a computer display of coloured blocks (denoted here by grey levels) and has the task of assembling a copy of the Model (top left) in the Workspace (bottom left). To do this it is necessary to operate with the mouse, obtaining blocks from the Workspace (right) using a click and drag procedure. The traces show an episode of visual and motor activity. The heavy trace shows the mouse movement while the light trace shows the corresponding eye scan record.

The crux of the theory is that the eyes are used *deictically*. The term *deictic* refers to the intrinsic ability of a certain action to serve as a pointer to information. From general considerations of computational theory, Ballard *et al.* argue that the use of pointers is essential for a cognitive system to operate. Eye pointing is one of several ways in which the cognitive system operates using pointers. Eye pointing becomes particularly important when vision interfaces with cognitively controlled action (as discussed in Chapter 2, visual control of non-cognitive aspects of action does not necessarily need eye pointing).

Fixation on an object allows 'the brain's internal representations to be implicitly referred to an external point' (Ballard *et al.*, 1997, p. 72). The deictic strategy employs this pointer as part of a general 'do it where I'm looking' strategy to select objects for action. This is the crucial reason for directing the eyes to an object, and, of course, is supplemented by the enhanced visual resolution that occurs through foveal vision. The enhanced resolution and ready mobility of the eyes result in gaze shifts being the process of choice for this deictic activity, although covert attention may provide an alternative additional pointer (see Chapters 3 and 6). Further additional pointers relate to purely memory-based activity. However, a consistent finding that emerges in part from the experimental investigations presented in the paper is that use of memory pointers is avoided if an alternative is available.

The data collected from the block assembly task supported this characterisation of the underlying cognitive operations. Blocks were invariably fixated before they were operated on. Furthermore, there was clear evidence that the preferred strategy involved making minimal demands on any internalised memory. In the block assembly task, as has been found in other tasks, many more saccades were made than appear necessary on a logical basis. The most common sequence observed in the block assembly task was eye-to-model, eye-to-resource, pick-from-resource, eye-to-model, eye-to-construction, drop-at-construction. The first eye-to-model shift would appear to be to acquire the colour information of the next block to be assembled, a suitable block is then found in the resource space. The second look at the model establishes, or at least confirms, the location of this block in the pattern, which is then added to the construction. This second look could be avoided if the location information was also stored on the first look. On occasions, the second look was omitted, indicating that such use of memory was an option. However these sequences were much less common than the sequences in which a return was made to the model.

Ballard *et al.* conclude that memory minimisation is a significant feature of activity in the situation. Cognitive representations (in this case the position of the block in the model) are computed as late as possible before the necessary action. This *just-in-time* strategy, it is argued, minimises both memory and computational loads. This is in complete contrast with the traditional passive vision account involving intensive computation of an internalised representation. Detailed representations are computed only as they are needed. What is held in memory is the location in the display where the visual information can be obtained. Efficient use of serial procedures involving eye fixations in this way minimises both the computational load and the memory load.

7.3.2 Vision supporting everyday actions

An important series of ground-breaking studies has been carried out by a group led by Michael Land. Land has an established reputation as a biologist with an interest in invertebrate vision (e.g. Land, 1995) and his interest in dynamic patterns of human vision emerged from that background. He devised and built a light head-mounted video-based eye tracking system (Land and Lee, 1994), which enabled a record to be built up of the fixation positions adopted by an observer during a variety of active tasks (see Fig. 7.6). Tasks studied have ranged through driving (Land and Lee, 1994), table tennis (Land and Furneaux, 1997), piano playing (Land and Furneaux, 1997) and tea-making (Land *et al.*, 1999).

The results, obtained during active vision supporting action, all demonstrate the strength of the principle that the gaze is directed to the points of the scene where information is to be extracted. Exactly which regions of the visual scene are important for the task is often easy to define, such as when objects are being manipulated. However, in certain cases, the eye records have revealed, in an unexpected way, how vision is used. While driving around corners on a curving road, the eyes fixate the inside edge of the corner. While playing table tennis, the eyes are very active. Their activity takes roughly the same path as the ball. Contrary to popular belief, they do not *follow* the ball. The eye works in an anticipatory way. As the opponent makes the return shot, the player fixates the top of the net, using the clearance at this point to judge the ball's trajectory.

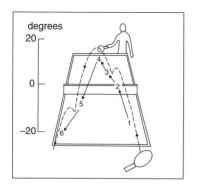
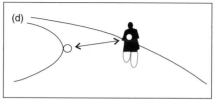

Figure 7.6 Two tasks studied by Land and Furneaux (1997). The left diagram shows a typical eye scan as an individual plays table tennis. The right hand diagram shows part of an eye scan of a driver negotiating a road curve in the presence of a cyclist.

Land's analysis of tea making (Land *et al.*, 1999) introduces the concept of *object-related action* units (ORAs) which he regards as the basic units of an action sequence (in the tea-making case, 'find the kettle' and 'transport to sink' are examples of such units). These units, with very rare exceptions, are carried out sequentially and involve engagement of all sensorimotor activity on the relevant object or objects. The eyes move to the object, or the point at which the object's activity is directed, *before* the manipulation starts. In general the eyes anticipate the action by about 0.6 sec. There may be action that precedes the eye movement. In cases where it is necessary to reposition the body, the movement of the trunk occurs first, in turn a further 0.6 sec before the eyes start to move. During a single ORA, saccades move the gaze around the object, but when shifting between one ORA and another, very large saccades can occur. Although most saccades had amplitudes between 2.5° and 10°, as a result of these large saccades, the mean saccade size over the whole action was thus 18°–20°. This is appreciably larger than previous estimates (Section 2.4).

The eye movements could, with only occasional exceptions, be placed into one of the following categories: *locate* – an object to be used; *direct* – fixate an object which is to be manipulated; *guide* – bring two objects (e.g. kettle and lid) into contact; *check* the state of an object (e.g. water level). The 'locate' part of the sequence frequently required a search process. Land *et al.* suggest that search patterns show that memory for object locations is not precisely coded. During the 'guide' process, the eyes frequently made a sequence of fixations from one object to the other. During the 'locate' and 'check' stages, quite long fixations occurred, as though the eyes were waiting for events to catch up. In a similar way to the case of saccade amplitudes, this led to a long tail on the distribution of fixation durations and a mean fixation duration of 0.42 sec, significantly longer than that found in picture scanning (Section 7.1.2).

Although Land is less concerned with the computational aspect of the brain activities involved in active vision, there are evident similarities between his analyses and those of Ballard's group presented in the previous section. In both cases, visual actions are based around objects in a deictic way. A highly important feature of these analyses is the potential for a long overdue integration of work in eye scanning with emerging theories of sequential action (Norman and Shallice, 1986; Schwartz *et al.*, 1995).

Recent studies of simple pointing and prehension movements have thrown further light on how these tasks are controlled through active vision. Neggers and Bekkering (2000, 2001) have demonstrated a powerful *gaze anchoring* phenomenon. They show that during a manual pointing task, the gaze is directed at the target movement and, until the hand reaches this target, it is immune to distraction from a peripheral stimulus which would normally be considered a powerful stimulus for orienting (Section 6.5). Johannson *et al.* (2001) studied a task where subjects reached to grasp an object and use it to operate a control target switch. They report that 'landmarks where contact events took place are obligatory gaze targets'. Gaze is also likely to be directed at obstacles in the path of the action, but this is less obligatory.

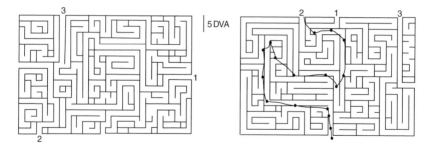

Figure 7.7 Maze task used by Crowe *et al.* (2000). Participants were presented with a maze (example in left diagram) and asked to find which exit (1, 2 or 3) corresponded with a path through the maze. An example of an eye scan while performing the task is shown on the right.

Another recent piece of work has also considered how eye movements might be involved in visual behaviour where the emphasis, rather than bringing a target object into foveal vision, concerns tasks of spatial routefinding. Crowe *et al.* (2000) looked at the microstructure of behaviour as participants worked out a route through a geometric maze (see Fig. 7.7). As participants worked out a route through a simple maze, their eye fixations fell at successive points on the route. However instances were observed where a large re-entrant section of the maze was not fixated. Crowe *et al.* suggested that the omitted part of the route was in fact scanned with covert attention. Such an appeal to covert attention might obtain support from work on a task of following a continuous line in the presence of a second, intersecting, line (Roelfsema, Lamme and Spekreijse 1998).

7.4 Summary

This chapter has given a brief review of studies aimed at developing under standing of how eye scanning operates in less constrained visual environ ments. Research in this area is very active, and the wide variety of approaches reflect the excitement felt by individuals who converge on a common problem from a variety of start points.

CHAPTER 8

HUMAN NEUROPSYCHOLOGY

One approach to investigating cognitive or perceptual systems is to test patients with damage to the brain. Traditionally the patients tested have anatomically localised damage that is accompanied by a deficit in a specific function. The pattern of impairments can be used to differentiate which behaviours share a common functional basis and those which have distinct functional bases. In turn, it is also possible to map these functions on to specific anatomical regions within the brain. This traditional approach is based on a number of key assumptions. The first of these assumptions is stability of function: little or no neural adaptation or plasticity occurs after the brain insult. Second, it is assumed that functions are, at least in part, modular: specific functions are encapsulated and operate independently from other functions (Fodor, 1983). At least on the face of it the occurrence of patients with a very specific deficit such as a deficit in colour vision without a deficit in motion, contrast, or depth processing supports these interrelated assumptions. A more detailed analysis of the foundation principles of human neuropsychology can be found in Shallice (1988).

The study of patients with disorders of eye movement control has a long history. Balint (1909) described 'psychic paralysis of gaze' as one of the defining characteristics of what later came to be known as Balint's syndrome (see also Holmes, 1919). Yarbus, one of the pioneers of detailed eye movement measurement, worked with Luria, the eminent Russian neuropsychologist, to study the eye movements of patients (Luria *et al.*, 1963). More recently, with more accurate brain imaging techniques, there has been an increasing focus on the exact location of the brain lesion and the pattern of eye movement disorders present. This move towards anatomical localisation of function is supported by the comparatively sophisticated understanding of the physiology of saccade control (Section 4.3) even for relatively high-level visual function such as visual search (Section 6.7).

It is not possible here to do full justice to the rich literature on the neuropsychology of eye movement control. Specifically, we make no reference to the extensive and detailed patient work in which non-saccadic eye movements have been studied. In addition, we have not reviewed studies that have been carried out on psychiatric disorders (e.g. Hutton and Kennard, 1998; Crawford, *et al.*, 1995*a,b*; Sereno and Holzman, 1993) or degenerative diseases such as Parkinson's disease (e.g. Crawford, *et al.*, 1989). Instead, this chapter provides a selective review of neuropsychological deficits which relate closely to the issues discussed elsewhere in this book. Specifically, we review deficits which we feel add to the main argument of the importance of an active vision approach. We hope that the examples we have selected will illustrate the utility of an active vision approach to understanding these deficits. Conversely, the deficits we describe also played an important part in the development of the active vision approach. We discuss the disorders of blindsight; Balint's syndrome and simultanagnosia; Neglect and Frontal lobe damage. We also discuss in some detail a case that we studied ourselves, in which the patient was unable to move her eyes as a result of paralysis of the eye muscles.

8.1 Blindsight

Loss or destruction of the striate cortex results in blindness in the contra-lateral half of the visual field, known as a hemianopia. Pöppel, *et al.* (1973) reported that some hemianopic patients were able to generate saccades to targets in the blind part of the visual field, even though they denied ever seeing the targets. In addition, the amplitudes of these saccades were sensitive to the eccentricity of the target (see also Barbur, *et al.* 1988). The term *blindsight* (coined by Weiskrantz, 1986) neatly captures this apparently contradictory behaviour. Even though these patients are functionally blind in part of their visual field and report no conscious awareness of stimuli, when appropriate testing procedures are employed, they do show some residual visual abilities.

This residual visual ability in the absence of visual awareness is not only restricted to the saccadic response. For example, when asked to point to a target presented in his blind field, one patient, DB, made a quite accurate pointing action to targets he was unaware of (Weiskrantz, *et al.* 1974). In the current chapter we will focus in more detail on the eye movement based performance of this type of patients. The amplitudes of saccades produced by DB are illustrated in Fig. 8.1. Although these showed some sensitivity to the target location, they were really quite inaccurate (see Fig. 8.1), particularly for large target eccentricities (see also Barbur *et al.*, 1988). This contrasted with manual pointing performance to a similarly sized target, which was more accurate. Subsequent work by Zihl (1980) demonstrated that saccade accuracy into the blind field could be substantially improved by training.

A number of authors have tested blindsight patients with some of the eye movement paradigms discussed in the previous chapters. These experiments investigate two interrelated questions. First, what components of saccadic behaviour are dependent on visual awareness, and second, what components of

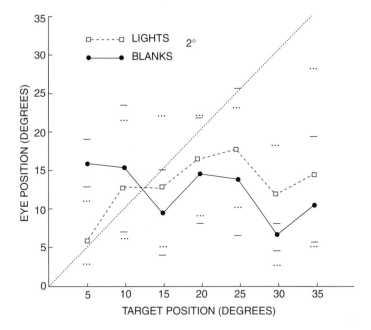

Figure 8.1 Saccade amplitude plotted against target position for a blindsight patient generating saccades to a single target at different eccentricities in the 'blind' field (dotted line). The saccades generated show some sensitivity to the eccentricity of the target. (from Weiskrantz *et al.*, 1974).

saccadic behaviour are dependent on striate cortex. For example, Barbur *et al.* (1988) showed that patient G produced a global effect for saccades made into the blind field. In that, when two targets were presented at the same time saccades were directed to the midpoint between the two targets, rather than to one target or the other. Interestingly, when two targets were presented in the good field, the global effect was not always found, possibly indicative of a learned orienting strategy to maintain viewing in the good field following orienting.

Rafal *et al.* (1990) investigated the remote distractor effect (Section 4.2.3) in hemianopia. They asked hemianopic subjects to make a saccade to a target in the unimpaired portion of the visual field and compared saccade latencies to this target either in the presence or in the absence of a distractor presented within the blind field. They found evidence of a remote distractor effect: there was an increase in saccade latency to a target when a distractor was presented in the blind field even though the distractor was not perceived. Testing was carried out monocularly and the effect was restricted to the conditions in which the distractor was presented in the temporal visual field. Rafal *et al.* (1990) proposed that the effect was mediated by subcortical pathways that did not pass through striate cortex. In addition, they argued that the asymmetry in the effect was a result of the difference in the strength of the direct retinal projections to the superior colliculus. However in contrast to this result,

Barbur *et al.* (1988) failed to find a remote distractor effect in there study of patient G, for whom there was clear evidence for both stimuli elicited saccades into the blind field and a range of other blindsight phenomena. More recently Walker *et al.* (2000) tested 6 patients with hemianopia and failed to find any evidence of the remote distractor effect. One possible explanation for this difference proposed by Walker *et al.* (2000) is that the remote distractor effect in hemianopia may only occur when blindsight is also present. As the incidence of blindsight in hemianopia may be as low as 20 per cent (Blythe *et al.*, 1987), whether such an effect is found will depend on whether a subgroup of the heminopic patients in the study have blindsight. However, even this explanation cannot give an account for the pattern of data across all patients; for example, patient G who clearly showed blindsight did not show a remote distractor effect (Barbur *et al.*, 1988). It would appear that further testing is required in which an assessment of blindsight along with testing for the remote distractor effect is carried out with the same patients.

There are three main explanations for blindsight behaviour. First, that vision is partially intact in the blind region of the visual field and that this residual vision supports some visual behaviour but is not sufficient to support awareness. The second explanation for blindsight (see for example Weiskrantz, 1986) is that the residual visual function is subserved by subcortical routes that carry visual information directly to motor control centres such as the superior colliculus. A third alternative, but related, account is that visual function is supported by direct neural routes to extra striate areas that do not pass through the damaged striate cortex.

In support of the first position, Fendrich and co-workers (Fendrich *et al.*, 1992; Wessinger *et al.*, 1997) demonstrated, using accurate eye movement monitoring equipment, that some patients who showed blindsight have isolated islands of spared vision within the hemianopic region. Although these data are compelling, there are a number of reasons to suspect that this may not provide an explanation for blindsight in all patients. First, Kentridge *et al.* (1997) report data from one blindsight patient who appears to have no such islands of spared vision. In addition, if blindsight was simply a result of residual vision, we might expect visual behaviour to stimuli in the blind field to be qualitatively similar to behaviour to visually degraded stimuli in the unimpaired field. Azzopardi and Cowey (1997) made a comparison between near threshold visual performance in the intact field and performance in the blind region of the visual field in blindsight. These results suggested that degraded vision might not be able to explain blindsight in all patients. In the same study, they used signal detection theory to demonstrate a genuine shift in sensitivity in the blind region of the visual field rather than a shift in bias associated with the change from a 2 alternative force choice, in which the patient has to guess if a stimulus is present, and a yes-no procedure, in which the patient has to report an awareness of the presence of a stimulus.

The second alternative explanation is that the residual visual function is subserved by subcortical visual routes that carry visual information directly to motor control centres such as the superior colliculus (see for example Weiskrantz, 1986). Rafal *et al.* (1990) invoke such an explanation for the presence of a remote distractor effect in hemianopia as discussed above. An alternative, but related, account is that direct neural routes to extra striate areas that do not pass through the damaged striate cortex may support visual function. This function could be supported by either direct connections from LGN, or by ascending projections from superior colliculus, via the pulvinar. For example, using magnetoencephalographic (MEG) brain image techniques, Holliday *et al.* (1997) showed that in one blindsight patient, motion processing in the blind field was served by a non-geniculostriate input to extrastriate motion areas.

It may not be appropriate to simply think of these explanations for blindsight as being in conflict. A single account of blindsight may not serve to explain the performances of all patients. Instead, blindsight in different patients may have a different underlying cause. However, the results from patients with blindsight suggest that saccade selection of a target, or overt attention, does not depend on awareness of the target. Recently, Kentridge *et al.* (1999*a,b*) reported evidence for the benefit of a covert attentional cue for the detection of items in the blind field. This suggests that covert attention, like overt attention or saccades, is not dependent on awareness. The relationship between attention and awareness is an important theoretical question (e.g. James, 1890) and these results suggest a surprising disassociation between attention and awareness. In addition, as both overt and covert attention dissociate from awareness in a similar manner these results provide some further support for a link between covert and overt attention.

8.2 Neglect

Patients who have visual neglect fail to respond to objects on one side of visual space. The side of space *neglected* is generally contralesional and classically results from damage to the parietal cortex. Although some neglect patients also have hemianopias, many do not (Walker *et al.*, 1991) and can respond to an item placed in the affected field when presented in isolation. In addition, the severity of neglect is affected by the nature of the task the patient is required to carry out; the structures of the display; the nature of the response required and the exact anatomical locus of the damage (e.g. Husain and Kennard, 1997). For a review of this rich and complex research area, see Robertson and Halligan (1999).

Neglect patients not only often fail to respond to items in the neglected field but also fail to make saccades into the affected field (see Fig. 8.2). In addition, even when tested in complete darkness some neglect patients spend less time fixating in the contralesional side of space (Hornak, 1992). Heide

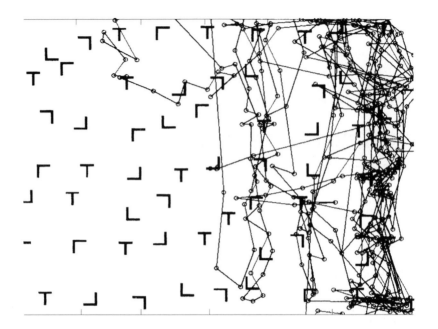

Figure 8.2 Fixations (circles) and saccades (black lines) in a neglect patient during a visual search task. (from Husain *et al.*, 2001).

and Kompf (1998) investigated performance on saccade tasks in neglect patients. Based on the locus of the lesion, they drew a distinction between different patient types. Amongst their patients, damage to posterior parietal cortex led to a deficit in stimulus driven saccades. Damage to the frontal eye fields in contrast left these saccades unimpaired but instead impaired intentional exploration of space. Finally, damage to supplementary motor areas impaired the timing of saccade sequences. This fractionation of function supports the idea, developed in the previous chapters, that saccades are controlled by a multi component system. Additional support for this idea comes from a rehabilitation study by Brown *et al.* (1999). Brown *et al.* investigated the effect of limb activation on performance in neglect patients, across a number of tasks. Limb activation improved performance in a reading task, but had no reliable effect on the leftward saccades made by the patients or on performance in a digit report task. In these patients, neglect affected both stimulus driven orienting and voluntary orienting. However only the voluntary orienting system was sensitive to the limb activation treatment. This disassociation provides additional support for the functional independence of stimulus driven orienting processes and the voluntary orienting processes. Support for a further fractionation of the saccadic deficit in neglect comes from recent work by Harvey *et al.* (2002). The results from this study are presented in Fig. 8.3. In this visual search study, the target item was either

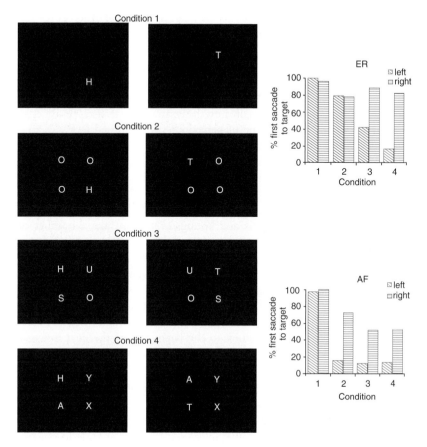

Figure 8.3 The performance of two neglect patients (ER and AF) in four simple search tasks. Example displays from the four tasks are reproduced on the left hand side. The task for the participant is to decide whether an H or a T is present in the display. On the right hand side are plots of first saccade to target for the two patients plotted for target on the left and on the right hand side respectively. AF shows a marked left-right asymmetry whenever distractor items are present; in contrast ER shows increasing evidence for asymmetry as search difficulty increases (conditions 2–4). (Adapted from Harvey *et al.*, 2002).

presented alone or along with distractor items. One patient (AF) showed stong neglect symptoms when additional distractors were present, regardless of the properties of the distractors. In contrast another patient (ER) only showed neglect-like symptoms when the distractors became more similar to the target.

Walker and Findlay (1996) investigated the gap effect (Section 4.2.2) and the remote distractor effect (Section 4.2.3) in neglect patients. In the gap condition, they found no improvements in the number of saccades into the affected field in three out of four of their patients, but did find reduced latencies. The latency for a saccade to a target in the good field was not altered when an item was presented in the neglected field, in other words the remote distractor effect was absent in the neglect patients studied for distractors on the affected side.

Behrmann *et al.* (1997) had patients with left neglect carry out a visual exploration task. The patients made fewer fixations and so spent less time inspecting the contralesional left side. The effect was continuous in that the number of fixations fell off gradually into the contralesional side. Husain *et al.* (2001) have argued that this type of behaviour (as illustrated in Fig. 8.2) is a result of a combination of failures to orient to the contralesional side, along with a deficit in working memory which results in a failure to mark items in the good field as previously fixated (Section 6.6). This would explain why neglect patients often make large number of refixations in the good field.

Neglect patients can also experience a range of difficulties with reading. These neglect dyslexias (see Ellis and Young, 1988) can take a number of forms and the combined features may occur within a single patient. Some patients simply read all the text on one side of the page while other patients will misread the end of each individual word. Karnath and Huber (1992) studied eye movements during reading in a patient who failed to read the words on one side of the page. They found a deficit in the size of the large leftward saccade that accompanied reading of the next line of text (see Chapter 5). This failure to look to the beginning of the next line was not a result of a basic ocular motor disorder, but reflected a breakdown of intentional scanning.

Neglect affects a number of orienting processes. Taken together, the results from these patients support the distinction between voluntary and stimulus-driven orienting systems. Neglect can also be object based. When presented with a task which contains multiple objects, these neglect patients will respond to each object present, but will systematically neglect one side of each object. Walker and colleagues (Walker *et al.*, 1996; Walker and Young, 1996) carried out a detailed study of the eye movements of one such patient, RR. RR showed left-sided neglect and when asked to copy a line drawing of a scene, he drew the right side of each individual object. Mirroring this drawing behaviour, RR made left saccades to objects to the left of the midline of the scene, but restricted his fixations to the right side of individual objects when they were fixated. This tendency was also present when RR viewed faces. However, when only the left half of the face was presented, RR scanned and recognised the face successfully. The patient did not have a deficit in generating left saccades between objects, but had a deficit when generating such saccades within objects. This suggests that these two types of saccade might be guided and generated by at least partially independent systems.

Visual neglect is a multi component disorder which affects in a systematic manner the exploration of space. The disorder can have an impact on orienting to objects on one side of space, reading ability, and orienting to one side of individual objects. Where studies have been carried out, it is clear that there is a close coupling between the nature of the disorder and the type of eye movement abnormalities detected. In addition the location of the lesion in the patient appears to alter the exact nature of the saccade deficit identified (see Heide and Kompf, 1998 as discussed above). This suggests two important things. First that the study of saccadic eye movements in such patients can reveal more about the neural substrate of saccade generation, and second that by studying the saccadic eye movements of neglect patients we can get a more detailed insight into the exact nature of the disorder and how it fractionates.

8.3 Balint's syndrome and dorsal simultanagnosia

Balint's syndrome (Balint, 1909) refers to a collection of related symptoms that result typically from bilateral damage to the parietal lobe. These symptoms are: (1) Gaze apraxia, also termed psychic paralysis of gaze or sticky fixation, which is an inability or severely impaired ability, to move the eyes on a voluntary basis to fixate a peripheral target. (2) Like overt shifts of attention, covert attention appears to be restricted. (3) An impairment in manual reaching to visual targets, often termed optic ataxia. As these patients do not have the same problems in the auditory domain, this rules out an explanation in terms of a primary motor deficit. Balint's syndrome is often characterised as attentional 'stickiness' or paralysis, echoing the 'stickiness' that appears in normal development (see Section 4.7). Dorsal simultanagnosia is a related disorder in which responses to single items are unimpaired but responses to multi element displays are impaired (see for example Warrington and Shallice, 1980). This may simply be a less severe manifestation of part of the cluster of symptoms of Balint's syndrome.

Robertson and co-workers have carried out an extensive study of a patient RM who shows Balint's syndrome as a result of bilateral parietal damage (Friedman-Hill, et al., 1995; Robertson, et al., 1997). When presented with a shape of one colour and a different shape of another colour, RM would often report the colour associated with the wrong object. Within Feature Integration Theory (Section 6.2.1), different features associated with the same object can only be combined when attention is allocated to that object. These illusory conjunctions suggest that attention is not available to bind the correct features together in this patient. Consistent with this, RM shows particular trouble with serial visual search (Section 6.1) during which attention is required for target detection.

Because such patients are relatively rare, there have been only a limited number of studies of the details of the eye movement disturbances in Balint's syndrome. Girotti et al. (1982) carried out a review of the eye movement characteristics of the patients reported in the literature. This review covers patients from the original report of Balint (1909) up to 1980. They noted that, of the cases where the relevant data was reported, all but one showed non-target elicited 'wandering saccades' which typically had very small amplitudes when attempting to voluntarily fixate a target. However, in general, the same patients were able to generate saccades on verbal command. Fixation spasm also appeared to be a defining characteristic of this group. Girotti *et al.* (1982) then reported a detailed single case study in which they made careful recording of the saccade parameters. Stimulus driven saccades had very long latencies, often over four times the latency of controls and it took as many as 5 saccades to reach a target presented in isolation. The saccades generated were erratic, and in only half the trials the target was finally fixated. In contrast, this patient could make saccades on verbal command. It should be noted, however, that the patient had bilateral occipital damage which may have resulted in a unilateral or even bilateral hemianopia. Such a deficit alone could not account for the extreme slowing and apraxic nature of the saccades this patient produced; however, it could have contributed to the disturbance of saccade control.

8.4 Frontal lobe damage

Damage to the frontal lobe of the human cortex leads to a range of disorders including poor organisation strategy, poor constructional ability, and problems of motor programming and sequencing in complex tasks (e.g. Stuss and Knight, 2002). Damage is often associated with perseveration, that is the tendency to repeat the same motor action a number of times under circumstances when it is inappropriate. Many of these problems may be associated with a working memory deficit (see Goldman-Rakic, 1992). The impact of this spectrum of symptoms on eye movements has been particularly studied in patients using the anti-saccade paradigm (Section 4.4.5).

In an anti-saccade task the subject is required to make a saccade in the opposite direction to the target (Hallett, 1978), so if the target is on the left hand side of fixation then the correct response is to make a rightward saccade. For the present purposes two main features of this behaviour are important. First, saccade latencies are longer than in a saccade to target condition, and second, even unimpaired subjects tend to make errors, with average error rates reported between 10 and 20 per cent (Guitton *et al.*, 1985; Everling and Fischer, 1998). This large variability is probably a result of the large variability between subjects in error rates as well as in age related effects, and a strategic trade off in some subjects between speed and accuracy.

Guitton *et al.* (1985) tested 10 patients with frontal lobe damage on an anti-saccade task and compared them with 7 temporal lobe damaged patients along with 9 intact controls. The results of there study are reproduced in Fig. 8.4. The frontal patients showed elevated error rates (50 per cent) when compared with the controls and temporal patients (20 per cent errors). The frontal patients clearly had difficulty making anti-saccades.

The anti-saccade task provides a sensitive marker for frontal lobe damage, but given the multi component nature of the task it is no surprise that

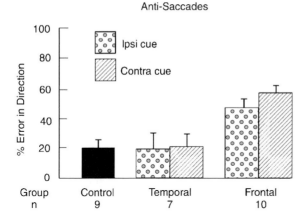

Figure 8.4 Anti-saccade performance in a control group, a group of patients with damage to the temporal lobe, and a group of patients with damage to the frontal lobe (from Guitton *et al.*, 1985).

damage to other neural areas can affect performance on this task. For example Pierrot-Deseilligny *et al.* (1991) reported a temporary impairment of anti-saccade generation following damage to the superior colliculus.

Given the strong relationship between the frontal lobes and working memory, one possible reason for the failure of these patients in an anti-saccade task is that they fail to retain in memory some part of the task instruction. However such an explanation seams unlikely. On error trials, Guitton *et al.*'s (1985) patients often successfully made a corrective second saccade to the anti location. In addition, the fast latencies of these second saccades suggested that some programming of the anti saccade has occurred concurrently with the erroneous pro-saccade. Walker *et al.* (1998) tested a patient with frontal damage who was found to be impaired on tests of spatial working memory and executive functioning and who also showed poor performance on the anti-saccade task. His performance was better in a task in which a pro-saccade was required but had to be delayed. His performance was also improved on a task where the target was presented and then removed and a saccade was required to the remembered target location. Finally the patient showed improved performance, when fixation had to be maintained while targets were presented. Errors that occurred across the conditions tended to be to contralesional stimuli rather than ipsilesional. These data suggest that it is unlikely that the deficit was simply in working memory, a conclusion supported by the evidence that the patient could successfully generate anti-pointing movements.

The various tasks that Walker *et al.* (1998) carried out with their patient suggest that the anti-saccade deficit was not simply a result of the demand to maintain fixation in the presence of a peripheral target onset. In addition it is clear from the memory guided saccade experiments that the patient was able to generate a saccade to a part of the display in which no item was displayed. It would appear then that poor performance at least in this patient might have resulted from an interactive combination of these and other task demands.

Everling and Fischer (1998) provide a more extensive review of clinical studies using the anti-saccade task. They suggest that poor performance on an anti-saccade task could be a result of failure of fixation maintenance or failure to produce the anti-saccade. However, it is difficult to classify the deficit of the patient studies by Walker *et al.* (1998) as being a deficit in one of these processes alone. What the study of anti-saccade performance in patients does reveal is the multi component nature of an apparently simple task.

Here we would want to emphasise that the proposed role of the frontal lobes in inhibiting the automatic response is borne out by studies of voluntary saccades as measured in the anti-saccade task. One role of the frontal lobes is to control behavioural responses. Frontal damage has an impact on active vision. Without this important control system the saccadic system may, in the most extreme case, become a slave to events in the world rather than the goal of the task.

8.5 Orienting without eye movements

In 1995, we had the opportunity to study a subject, AI, who, as a result of extra-ocular fibrosis (presumed congenital) could not move her eyes in her head (Gilchrist *et al.*, 1997, 1998; Land *et al.*, 2002). This subject came to us by chance, when she responded to an advertisement in the student newspaper for subjects with squints. AI replied to the advert saying she had a squint but added that she didn't think she would be of much use, as she couldn't move her eyes. It is difficult now to reconstruct our a-priori predictions about her visual performance or experience. What was clear was that we expected her to have quite a marked deficit. How, after all, could the visual system cope without its specialised ocular-motor apparatus which, according to our thinking, had co-evolved with the visual brain to allow for active vision? This individual would seem to offer a very strong test for the active vision thesis: if she was relatively unimpaired then saccades could be assigned to the class of peripheral mechanisms that played no real central role to vision. As it turned out this was the case, AI was remarkably unimpaired by her deficit; she took part in an ordinary student life, was reading for a degree in English with no extra assistance and was quite able to walk unaided. She had never learnt to drive and was not keen on sport, but was to all other extents remarkably unimpaired.

Nevertheless, when we studied in detail how AI achieved this without eye movements, we discovered that although her oculomotor system was defective, her saccadic system was very much intact. What emerged provided the strongest and most startling support for the active vision approach. In short AI made saccadic movements of her head. AI's head movements mirrored in a number of significant ways eye movements. We will turn to look in detail at these similarities in a moment, but first it is worth taking a moment to think about what this means. Every time AI wants, or needs, to move her fovea to look at something, whether it's a face in the crowd or words on a page, rather than the movement being made by moving the small, relatively light orbit of the eye, with its specialised set of eye muscles, AI moves her whole head.

8.5.1 Peripheral neuropsychology

As we saw at the beginning of this chapter human neuropsychology is based on a number of core assumptions. It is particularly important here to make these assumptions explicit, as AI is an example of a rather unusual type of neuropsychology. The architypical neuropsychological single case study is an adult who has localised brain damage. This damage leads to loss or impairment of a specific function or set of functions. By studying such patients, behaviours that have a common function basis can be identified. However, single cases are rarely that clear cut, a single brain lesion can lead to two deficits that have distinct underlying function but happen to be processed in an anatomically adjacent area. For example, visual agnosia, a deficit in recognising objects, often co-occurs with achromatopsia, a deficit in colour perception.

This approach of studying dysfunction to understand function has also been extended to the study of developmental disorders. Although successful, such an approach is not without problems, particularly given the potential for differential development in light of the disorder (see Bishop, 1997). AI has suffered from an inability to move her eyes apparently since birth. In addition she does not have damage to the central nervous system. Instead AI has a peripheral deficit, and so is an example of what we could call *peripheral neuropsychology*. Although the study of such patients with peripheral deficits to understand central neural functioning is unusual, there are a number of examples in the literature.

Nicholas *et al.* (1996) investigated visual performance in subjects who only had one functioning eye, having had the other eye removed at various ages. The central question addressed was: what is the visual capacity of the remaining eye? Nicholas *et al.* showed that the remaining eye had supernormal performance in a contrast sensitivity test in comparison with monocular sensitivity shown by normal observers. In addition they demonstrated a relationship between performance improvement and the age at which the eye was removed. The important point here is that this is a study of a peripheral deficit, the removal of the eye and its consequence on visual performance, which is a function of the central nervous system.

Ramachandran (1995) reports a number of studies of adult subjects who had limbs amputated. The patients described suffered from *phantom limbs*—they experienced sensory events that were associated with a limb that no longer existed. Some of these patients also showed systematic remapping of the phantom limb onto other parts of the body. So, for example, one subject when touched on the remaining part of the amputated arm reported the sensation of being touched on the thumb and when touched on an adjacent part of the arm reported being touched on the adjacent phantom finger.

These case studies and our own illustrate the central difference in flavour between traditional neuropsychology and what we have called peripheral neuropsychology. All three examples are interesting because they demonstrate adaptation of central processes: AI uses her head for saccades; Nicholas *et al*.'s subjects have supernormal acuity in their one remaining eye, and Ramachandran's patients have undergone quite radical reorganisation of the somatosensory maps. So in this sense peripheral neuropsychology is different from traditional neuropsychology in that it does not assume that once damaged, the brain is not the subject of neural adaptation or plasticity of function. Indeed studies in peripheral neuropsychology go in search of such adaptation.

8.5.2 Reading without eye movements

In our initial investigation of AI we looked at her reading ability. We did this in the main because we were most surprised by her ability to read so efficiently. As discussed in Chapter 5, the patterns of eye movements in reading are very well documented. Eye-saccades in reading can be usefully characterised by two parameters, whose distributions are shown in Fig. 5.1. The first is fixation time, which is the time for which the eyes are static between saccadic movements. The distribution of fixation durations has a peak between 200 and 250 ms and a positively skewed distribution. The other parameter that is useful in characterising saccades is the movement size. The sizes of the movements are dependent on the size of the characters and, when measured in relation to the character unit, tend to be relatively constant over a wide range of text sizes. The distribution of movement sizes is more complex than the distribution of fixation durations. For forward saccades along the text, the saccade size peaks at 7–8 characters and in addition there are a small number of saccades made back along the text.

We recorded AI's head movements while she read and divided the records into periods of fixation (when the eyes were relatively still) and periods when the eyes moved. For this analysis, we used a simple velocity criterion: a methodology that is often used to divide eye movements into saccades and fixations. The distributions of AI's fixation durations and saccade sizes are shown in Fig. 8.5. The similarity to the distributions shown in Fig. 5.1 is striking, for both fixation duration and movement size. AI's orienting while reading is quantitatively similar to the eye saccades of control subjects while reading. In one respect, this result, although striking, is perhaps not surprising. Reading provides one of the most *visually* challenging everyday tasks. One possible interpretation of these data is that, given the difficulty of the task, the visual system has no choice but to sample the visual input in such

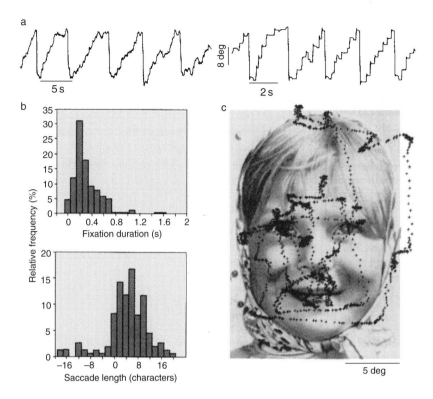

Figure 8.5 Head movement records from AI. The upper panel (a) shows head movements from AI while text reading (left hand side) compared with eye movements of a control participant. When the head movements from AI are divided into periods when the head is static and periods when the head is moving, very similar distributions of fixation duration and movement size are found to the eye movements of control participants (b, see also Fig. 5.1). Such fixate and saccade patterns are also present in picture scanning (c). (from Gilchrist *et al.*, 1997).

a stereotypical way. However, we also showed that saccade-like movements also occurred in other tasks such as picture scanning. Extensive scanning would not seem necessary to take in the face information of Fig. 8.5(c). Yet this is shown both by the eye scans of normal observers and by the head scans of AI. The conclusion must be that saccadic sampling is a preferred option for the visual system.

8.5.3 Saccadic head movements

If AI's head movements really were saccadic, the next question that we asked was the extent to which they were subject to the same experimental phenomena as eye-saccades (reported in Gilchrist *et al.*, 1998). We chose five classic saccade paradigms (see Chapter 4), the gap-effect, the remote distractor effect, the anti-saccade task and saccadic suppression. In all cases AI's head movements showed the effect that would be predicted from the eye movement literature. It would appear in this respect that AI's head movements were indeed saccade like.

In a further study, using a fully portable eye tracker, we studied AI's head movements while she performed the everyday task of making a cup of tea (Land *et al.*, 2002). Results from this study are shown in Fig. 8.6. AI was of course able to perform the task. However, we noted a number of differences between her behaviour and that of control participants. First, she made fewer orienting movements during the task, this is evident in Fig. 8.6. Second, we observed that AI made some slow drifting movements when the head was moved slowly across the scene at speeds below 30 deg/sec. We have argued that this additional orienting behaviour may be utilised for large orienting movements as an alternative to head saccades. Such drifting movements carry a cost: fine spatial scale visual information would not be available during such movements. However, these drift movements may well provide a benefit, given the long durations of the saccadic head movements when compared to saccadic eye movements. AI's orienting system may be sacrificing visual

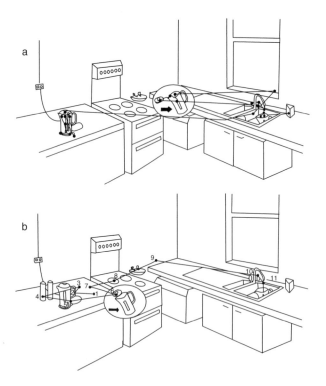

Figure 8.6 (a) Fixations and gaze shifts in a control participant while making a cup of tea in a kitchen. (b) Fixations and gaze shifts for AI (who is only able to move her head for orienting). (from Land *et al.*, 2002).

resolution in order to increase the amount of time for which some visual information is available.

AI's everyday life is relatively unimpaired by what at first sight would appear to be a catastrophic deficit. Where does this leave the role of saccades in vision? Saccades appear to be a ubiquitous part of everyday orienting. When the eyes are unable to make saccades than it would appear that the head is available to take over. Perhaps this allows information to be delivered to the visual system in the manner required by subsequent visual processing. A rather fundamental question then arises: Why then did eye movements evolve? After all, other species of animals evolved with either very restricted or no eye movements at all and AI is able to perform pretty well using her head for orienting. Walls (1962) argued that eye movements initially evolved to maintain a retina fixed with reference to the visual world and thus allow a stable representation of the world. This is reminiscent of the passive view of vision as outlined in Chapter 1. Within this view, vision consists of the analysis of a static spatially homogeneous input to form an internal representation of the external world although it is unclear how to map the results for AI on to such evolutionary questions. Here are two possible explanations. Firstly, it may be that the visual system evolved in a more visually challenging environment in which saccadic eye movements conferred an evolutionary advantage that is not clear in the context of a more slow-moving visual ecology. The second possibility is that saccadic eye movements do indeed confer additional advantages beyond the scope of the tests carried out by us. Thus it is clearly not possible to produce a vergence response with solely a head for orienting. In addition, the vestibulo-ocular reflex (VOR) delivers a stable visual platform that allows vision to be useful during observer locomotion, and the VOR depends on mobility of the eyes. Whether AI's lack of a VOR underlies the problems she reported with ball sports and driving remains unclear but it does seem likely.

8.6 Summary

The current chapter has reviewed a selected range of neuropsychological disorders in which eye movements have been monitored. It is clear from these examples that a rich understanding of these visual deficit has to include at its heart both a detailed account of the eye movement behaviour and a real integration of these behaviours into explanations of the clinical disorder.

Active vision accounts of visual behaviour have a great deal to contribute to neuropsychology and in turn neuropsychology has informed the development of the approach. For example, studies of blindsight demonstrate a clear disassociation between awareness and saccadic targeting; studies of neglect allow a fractionation of different kinds of orienting and studies of patients like AI lead us to ask fundamental questions about why we make saccades and what place they should have in a model of vision.

CHAPTER 9

SPACE CONSTANCY AND TRANS-SACCADIC INTEGRATION

In the preceding chapters, we have shown how the active vision approach may be developed in diverse areas of visual perception. We conclude our account by examining a question that has for many years taxed workers in vision. We suggest that recent developments show how a solution to this problem may be formulated in the framework of active vision.

The issue concerns trans-saccadic integration; how our appreciation of a coherent and stable visual world occurs when, as the remainder of the book has shown, our eyes are continually engaged in an irregular sequential sampling process. We shall first discuss briefly a traditional approach that appeared to offer a conceptually simple solution. Following a discussion of the inadequacies of this approach, we shall discuss recent work which both shows the vital necessity of addressing the problem of trans-saccadic integration and points to a solution to the problem in a novel and unexpected manner.

9.1 The traditional approach: 'compensatory taking into account'

When the eyes move, there is relative motion between retina and retinal image. The retinal signal clearly undergoes considerable change but this change is unperceived. In contrast, an image fixed on the retina, such as an afterimage, does appear to move when the eyes move. How can that be? It is clear that our perceptual experience cannot be entirely based on the 'raw' signal arising from the retina but must result from some combination of this signal with a signal carrying information about how the eyes have moved. Such a signal is referred to as an *extra-retinal signal*. Two further questions then follow. First, what is the origin of this extra-retinal signal? Second, how does it operate to achieve perceptual stability?

The first question is the one that has traditionally been the major focus. Many accounts have emphasized the distinction between *inflow* and *outflow* theories of the origin of the signal indicating that the eyes have moved. In inflow theory, the signal arises from sensors in the eye muscles whereas in outflow theory, the signal is assumed to come from the centres programming the eye movement. In this debate, outflow theory generally emerges victorious. Helmholtz (1866) considered the question and was influenced by the finding that passive movement of the eyes (for example by gently poking them with a finger) *does* result in the experience of an unstable, moving, world. A further important result appeared when Kornmüller (1931, cited in Carpenter, 1988) injected large quantities of anaesthetic into his eye cavity (the retrobulbar block) and reported that the resulting partial paralysis of the extraocular muscles leads to the perception of illusory motion when an eye movement is attempted. Subsequent work (e.g. Stevens *et al.*, 1976) has replicated this finding; although when the eyes are *totally* paralysed, this illusory motion is not present. Rather, the observer becomes aware that his attempts to move the eyes are unsuccessful. Another influential piece of work supporting outflow theory came from some elegant experiments on invertebrate vision by von Holst and Mittelstaedt (see von Holst, 1954). These workers found that when the head of a fly was surgically rotated, the insect engaged in compulsive rotatory motion. Their interpretation turned on an outflow-like signal arising from the fly's motor system, to which they gave the term *efference copy* (Efferenzkopie). They suggested that head rotation created a positive feedback loop in which the efference copy signal, rather than providing its normal compensation for head motion, acted to magnify the consequences.

How might the extra-retinal signal be used? One possibility is that visual information about change is suppressed, and so does not lead to awareness. Saccadic suppression is a well established phenomenon that has been extensively studied (Section 2.4.3) and may well account for certain aspects of the lack of perception during saccades (e.g. motion: Bridgeman *et al.*, 1994). The critical issue, however, concerns the unawareness of the displacement resulting from the eye movement. Saccades produce changes in an object's retinal co-ordinates and there seems no way in which a suppression account can accommodate such changes. A popular alternative suggestion is that the extra-retinal signal acts in a *compensatory* way to somehow *cancel out* the position changes produced by the eye movement. The result of von Holst, described above, implies that the extra-retinal signal operates in an active compensatory way rather than through suppression, at least in their invertebrate preparation. The passive vision approach to perception described in Chapter 1 relates perceptual experience to the retinal image and brain representations arising from retinotopic projections of this image. It has sometimes been suggested that trans-saccadic integration might occur at the level of an iconic signal. In other words, an iconic retinotopic representation somewhere in the brain is combined with an appropriate compensatory shift every time the eyes move, resulting in a representation which remains stable in head- or body-centred spatial co-ordinates. One apparent additional attraction of the 'compensatory' approach is the emergence of a spatiotopic representation, a representation of the visual world in a form that remains stable during eye movements. As well as being in concordance with visual experience, such a representation also seems essential to account for the obvious fact that visually controlled behaviour does not suffer major disruption when the eyes move.

In the next section we consider various experimental approaches that have looked for evidence for such a compensatory signal. The data are, at first sight, confusing and contradictory. Some approaches find clear evidence of compensation, and others little or no evidence. A possibility for the resolution of this apparently paradoxical situation has recently emerged and this is discussed in the final section.

9.2 Trans-saccadic integrations

If a compensatory mechanism were at work taking account of saccades, several outcomes would appear to be predicted.

9.2.1 Detection of displacement during saccades

A compensatory signal would maintain a record of a target's location in space. Hence, if the target moved, either individually or with the remainder of the

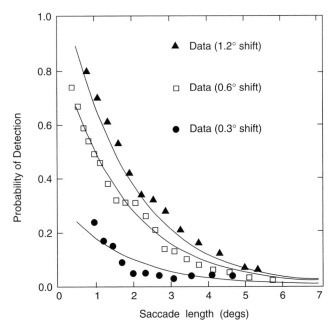

Figure 9.1 Results from the experiment of McConkie and Currie (1996). Participants viewed a picture on a display screen. Displacements of the display were occasionally triggered by a scanning saccade and the observer had to report when such changes were detected. The plots show the probability of detecting displacements of three different sizes as a function of the length of the saccade during which the displacement occurred. The lines represent best fitting exponential functions.

visual scene, such movements should be registered. Several studies have enquired whether the displacement of visual targets during saccades can be detected. The phenomenon of saccadic suppression (Section 2.4.3) allows changes to be made during saccades that are not immediately detectable through the alerting system for detecting transients (Section 3.1).

It has been found that quite large displacements can occur during saccades without the subject being aware that these have occurred. Bridgeman *et al.* (1975) reported that translations of up to one third of the saccade size were undetected. The viewed scene consisted of a simple linear array. More recently McConkie and Currie (1996) have measured the ability to detect displacement of a pictorial scene being viewed. Their results were consistent with those from the Bridgeman *et al.* experiment and they also found that the ability to detect a small displacement decreased in a very systematic way as saccade size increased (Fig. 9.1). Size changes of 10 per cent were only detected on about one quarter of occasions tested, and size changes of 20 per cent were not detected on almost half the trials. Shifts in the same direction as the saccade were detected somewhat more frequently than those in the opposite direction. The rather poor ability demonstrated by these results seems at variance with the idea that any precise map of space is maintained across eye movements.

9.2.2 Trans-saccadic fusion

Another prediction arises if a compensatory signal associated with saccades operates at the level of an image representation. The prediction is that pre-saccadic visual material occupying the same location in visual space could be integrated with post-saccadic material. The pre- and post-saccadic material would of course be presented at different locations on the retina. Although a number of experiments have searched for evidence of such a process, none has been found. One consequence that might be expected from such an integrative process is the successful integration of two fragmentary parts of a picture, one presented pre-saccadically and the other post-saccadically. Figure 9.2 demonstrates how the idea was tested in the experiments of O'Regan and Lévy-Schoen (1983). No evidence for integration was found in this experiment, or in subsequent carefully controlled ones (Irwin, 1991), although positive findings can occur if display persistence is not well controlled (Jonides *et al.* 1982, 1983). The peripheral preview phenomenon in conjunction with the perception of words was discussed earlier (Section 5.3.3), and it was noted that the representations involved in this form of trans-saccadic integration were more abstract than those of the iconic level.

9.2.3 Localisation of peri-saccadic probes

Another approach to the problem has been to require an observer to make a judgement about a visual probe signal, briefly presented at about the time the eyes move in an otherwise dark field. Early work required a perceptual

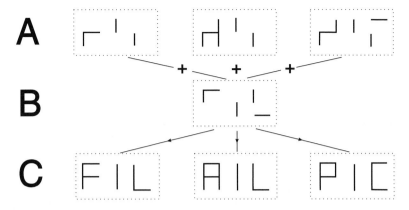

Figure 9.2 Experiment by O'Regan and Lévy-Schoen (1983) to test for iconic trans-saccadic fusion. On each trial, one of the fragments in row A was flashed briefly before a saccade with the fragment in Row B being presented briefly post-saccadically in the same spatial location. Iconic fusion would produce the character strings in Row C but observers showed no ability to report these strings although such integration could occur if the fragments were presented in a similar sequence at one retinal location without the eyes moving.

judgement about the probe location relative to a reference location such as the saccade goal. As summarised by Matin (1972), judgments showed high variability, but additionally some systematic trends. Targets flashed well before the initiation of the saccadic eye movement or well after the end of the saccade were accurately localised but targets flashed immediately before or after the saccade were mislocalised in a way consistent with that expected if an extra-retinal compensatory signal was involved, but one which operated over a considerably longer time course than the duration of the saccade. The pattern of errors is complex but is also consistent with the proposal that 'visual space is compressed' at the time of a saccadic movement (Ross *et al.*, 1997).

In Section 2.2.2 we introduced the important idea that perceptual experience and perception for action use different processing routes within the brain. Several investigators have enquired whether, if a requirement is made for visually controlled action, evidence of a more precise spatial signal might be obtained. Considerable interest was generated in a report by Hallett and Lightstone (1976) that much higher accuracy could be achieved if a modified probe procedure was used, in which the observer was required to indicate the localisation of the probe by making a subsequent movement of the eyes to it. However, the careful analyses by Honda (1989, 1990) have shown that alternative interpretations of the results can be given.

Other results have also been interpreted to suggest that an egocentric visual representation is continuously available to guide action. Thus Skavenski and Hansen (1978) required subjects to make a ballistic pointing response (using a pointed 'ballpeen' hammer) to a target that was flashed at some point during a saccadic movement of up to 15°. The responses were reported to strike the actual target location with an accuracy of 15 min arc. Skavenski and Hansen argued that an egocentric signal is available to control motor action but is not available for conscious perception. In a similar experiment in which participants were asked to control an unseen visual pointer, Bridgeman *et al.* (1979) also found accurate ability to direct pointing responses in contrast to degraded perceptions. More recent work has again supported this distinction (Burr *et al.*, 2001), although contrary claims have also been made (Dassonville *et al.*, 1995).

9.2.4 Memory guidance of saccades

A rather different approach to trans-saccadic integration comes from the familiar everyday observation that it is often possible to re-orient back to a remembered location of an object or event; indeed it can plausibly be claimed that spatial locations have a pre-eminent role in most forms of memory. Specific study of saccades to memorised locations has become of increasing interest to two somewhat different groups of workers; first, physiologists whose interest is to locate the memory mechanisms in the visual system that allow accurate saccades to be made to memorised targets, and second, cognitive scientists who study the phenomenon as part of the deictic approach to cognition (Section 7.3.1).

Saccades to remembered targets show considerable loss of accuracy, particularly in the vertical dimension (Gnadt *et al.*, 1991; White *et al.*, 1994). Both systematic and variable errors increase, and much of the increase occurs within the first second of the memorisation process. In a study of patients with brain damage, Ploner *et al.* (1999) have reported the interesting finding that damage to frontal eye fields is associated with increased systematic error, while damage to prefrontal cortex increases variable error. It seems likely that, at least in the short term, the necessary spatial representation for memorised saccades is coded in continuing activity of cells in areas such as the frontal eye fields (Umeno and Goldberg, 2001), dorso-lateral prefrontal cortex (Funahashi *et al.*, 1989) or area LIP of parietal cortex (Gnadt and Andersen, 1988). For area LIP, Xing and Andersen (2000) have recently proposed a way in which this neural activity could form a memory in a true spatiotopic reference frame. A pathway from the superior colliculus through the dorsomedial thalamus has also been identified as contributing the required oculomotor information to keep the spatial representation updated when intervening eye movements occur (Sommer and Wurtz, 2002).

From a more cognitive perspective, the existence of accurately directed regressive saccades in reading (Section 5.2) demonstrates the ability to remember locations. Kennedy and Murray (1989) showed that regressive saccades could be accurate although a more recent study (Fischer, 1999) suggests that only a few such locations are held in memory. Even when text disappears from a screen, readers will return their eyes to previously fixated locations in the same way (Kennedy, 1983). This phenomenon is observed also with pictorial material (Richardson and Spivey, 2000). Richardson and Spivey carried out experiments, where items were presented at one of several possible different locations on a display while some information about the item was presented auditorily. When asked to recall the information, subjects tended to look at the item location, but this looking did *not* assist the recall of the associated information. Richardson and Spivey propose that item—location associations are developed in implicit memory and thus dissociated from the other information about the item coded explicitly.

9.3 Resolution of the conflicting results

The results of the previous section show that an extra-retinal signal is operative, although results from situations which require an immediate perceptual judgement suggest that its accuracy is low. However, evidence for the existence of an *accurate* matching of pre and post saccadic position information comes from two phenomena discussed in Chapter 4. Both are dependent on an ability to make a comparison between an eye command signal and the target displacement. Both are affected if the target is displaced during a saccade. In Section 4.4.1, we noted that saccadic orienting is frequently accomplished by a primary saccade, followed by a second corrective movement. Such corrective movements are generally based on the displacement of the saccade target from the fovea. Thus, if the target is moved during the saccade, changes to the corrective saccades occur. These changes are not detected by the observer; indeed, observers are entirely unaware that they are making corrective saccades. A further important consequence of displacing a target during saccadic movements has been noted in Section 4.7. If a series of saccades are made where target displacement occurs in a systematic way, a compensatory adaptational process can be observed. This process occurs rapidly, being clearly manifest after only a few instances (Fig. 4.14, p. 81). The implication must be made that an adaptive recalibration takes place with each saccadic movement.

9.3.1 Target displacements during saccades can be detected under some circumstances

The results discussed so far are consistent with the position that an extra-retinal signal is used for some purposes but is not available to conscious awareness. However a major revision of this position was initiated following the findings of Deubel *et al.* (1996). These workers showed that a minor modification of the testing technique of the paradigm discussed in Section 9.2.1 could radically change the outcome. In the Deubel *et al.* experiment, subjects made a saccade to a target which might be displaced during the saccade. If the target was visible immediately after the saccade, large displacements were undetected, confirming previous results. However, if a brief delay intervened the end of the saccade and the reappearance of the target, then observers demonstrated a much greater ability to detect

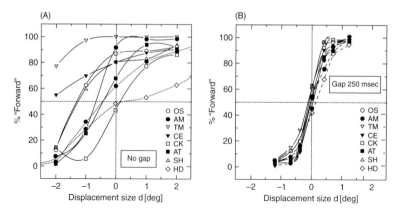

Figure 9.3 Psychometric functions for the detection of a target displacement during a saccade. Results from eight observers. Displacements of various sizes and directions occurred, always during the saccade. Observers were required to make a forced choice 'forward' or 'backward' response, indicating whether they believed the displacement of the target was in the same direction as their saccade, or opposite to that direction. Panel A shows results from the normal viewing situation with the target visible immediately after the saccade. In B, a blank period of 200 ms intervened following the end of the saccade. From Deubel *et al.* (1996).

displacement (see Fig. 9.3). Displacements of a few percent of the saccade size were readily detected.

Furthermore, as can be seen clearly from Fig. 9.3, two other differences occur. Figure 9.3 derives from an experiment in which observers were required to make a forced choice 'forward' or 'backward' response. The graphs show the percentage of forward responses for displacements of different types. Without the blank period, observers show considerable variability and often show a systematic bias towards giving a 'forward' response. With the blank interval, variability is greatly reduced and the biases are almost eliminated.

In a follow up study, Deubel *et al.* (1998) required participants to move their eyes to a target (a cross) in the presence of a distractor (a circle). A position displacement of either distractor or target occurred during the saccade, and the blanking procedure discussed above could be used for either target or distractor. The results were unequivocal. Whichever stimulus was visible immediately after the end of the saccade was perceived to be stable whereas displacement was attributed to the blanked stimulus.

9.3.2 A revised theory of space constancy and trans-saccadic integration

The results just discussed necessitate a radical new view about the events during and following each saccade. The failure to detect displacement of targets moved during saccades does not at all imply that the information is not available. The information is used to control the saccadic adaptation process: it is used to influence corrective saccades. By using the blanking manoeuvre of Deubel *et al.*, the information becomes available to consciousness. The result thus presents a paradox. In the highly artificial blanking situation, observers can judge accurately whether there has been a displacement. However this ability is almost entirely lacking in the situation of everyday perception.

The conclusion seems inescapable that the failure to detect trans-saccadic location changes is not any indication of system inadequacy, but rather demonstrates a very remarkable and important characteristic of active vision. Active vision operates on the basis of a sophisticated process that matches pre-saccadic and post-saccadic information about target location. There is generally a mismatch because the saccadic targeting system does not show perfect accuracy. This regularly occurring mismatch between saccade target and saccade landing position does, if substantial enough, lead to a corrective saccade and it does continually form part of the adaptive self-calibrating process of the saccadic system (Section 4.7). Yet this mismatch does *not* give rise to any conscious experience. Our conscious impression is of a stable visual world. Hence, *the failure to detect trans-saccadic changes must be an essential part of the way that this 'illusion' is maintained.* Although similar in some ways to a compensatory mechanism, we are actually postulating a very different set of processes. A new spatial map is created with every saccade, referenced to the saccade target. In this way corrections are made on-line for saccade variability.

Several theorists have reached similar conclusions. Bridgeman *et al.* (1994) made an insightful analysis of the issue of trans-saccadic visual stability. They pointed to the confusion that has arisen through the assumption that every retinotopic map in the brain codes visual position (essentially the passive vision assumption). The brain needs some way of representing spatial position in order to control action. Bridgeman *et al.* argued that, for these representations, the essential requirement is to recalibrate the retinotopic map for every new fixation. These unperceived recalibrations also keep the saccadic part of the oculomotor system in tune. However Bridgeman *et al.* proposed that the recalibration was based on an imprecise extraretinal signal, coupled with suppression of any displacement error signal. Experimental observations subsequent to this proposal have shown, on the contrary, that a very precise spatial signal is maintained across saccades. A rather similar position has been advocated by McConkie and Currie (1996) and Currie *et al.* (2000). They present a *saccade target theory* of the trans-saccadic process based on further analyses of their data discussed in Section 9.2.1. They suggest that changes are detected on the basis of *local information at the saccade goal location* rather than any more global pattern.

Overall, these results might be taken to show that the brain has developed a simple and elegant solution to the 'problem' of trans-saccadic integration. However, we emphasise once again that much of the perceived problem has only arisen because of the mistaken passive vision assumption of a global internal visual representation.

9.3.3 The neurophysiology of trans-saccadic processes

The way in which the brain deals with the problems of a mobile eye has become a challenging issue for neurophysiologists. Only a brief summary can be given here of recent work (see e.g. Snyder, 2000). As discussed in Section 4.5.1, the receptive fields of cells in the visual system remain fixed in retinocentric coordinates (exceptions to this general rule have been reported by Duhamel *et al.*, 1997). For visually elicited saccades, the proposal of Robinson (1975) involving a double remapping from retinocentric to head-centred to oculocentric coordinates seemed overelaborate and unsupported. Nonetheless, coordinate transformations are clearly necessary in the case of visually guided actions and for memorised saccade sequences. We are beginning to learn how these might be achieved.

A novel and highly significant observation was made by Andersen *et al.* (1985). They studied responses of cells in monkey posterior parietal cortex and confirmed that the cell's receptive field, i.e. the *location* at which a visual stimulus would activate the cell, remained at a constant retinal location wherever the monkey's eye was directed. However the monkey's eye position did affect the *magnitude* of the cell's response in a systematic way, with the response magnitude increasing progressively as the eye position changed in the head from one extreme to the other. The term *gain field* was employed to describe this relationship. Such modulation of firing with eye position has been found widely, both in parietal and in occipital cortex, and cells whose firing is modulated by head position have also been found (Snyder, 2000). The gain field phenomenon shows how extraretinal information may be combined with retinal information. Over an ensemble of neurons, this combination provides information for target location in space to be extracted and thus provides an implicit space-centred representation (Zipser and Andersen, 1988; Xing and Andersen, 2000)

9.4 Conclusion: The Active Vision Cycle

We conclude with a diagram summarising the conclusions from this chapter and elsewhere in the book (Fig. 9.4). It portrays the diverse processes occurring each time the eye makes a saccadic movement. Selection of the saccade target forms a convenient starting point to break into the cycle. It is the point at which top-down influences must obviously enter into the process. The selection process has been discussed at several points in the course of the book. In Chapter 4, we discussed visual orienting to well defined targets, often with sudden onset. Target selection is pre-empted but it was also noted (Section 4.4.3) that the presence of distractors may influence the saccade selection process. In Chapter 6, it was argued that targets for visual search can be conceptualised as the location of highest activity on a hypothesised salience map (Section 6.6). Physiological work (Section 4.3.2) suggests that a correlate

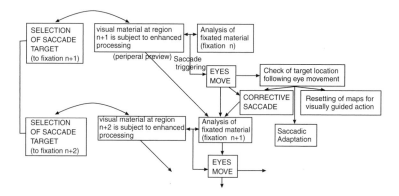

Figure 9.4 The Active Vision cycle.

of the selection process is found in the development of a pattern of activity in the build-up cells of the superior colliculus. As their name implies, these show a gradual, rather than sharply defined, selective process.

Chapter 5 concentrated on reading, the area where in many ways the active vision account is best developed. Theories of target selection in reading have often involved selection by an attentional mechanism (Section 5.7), which is given primacy in the process. As we have argued in Chapter 3, our preference is to avoid such terminology. We are concerned that statements like 'the target for the saccade is selected by an attentional pointer' introduce a number of problems. First, explanation is thrown back to a 'hidden homunculus' with a capacity for intelligent selection. Second, it implies that the selection is a discrete event in space and time, whereas it seems more probable that it involves a slow build up of activation over an extended region.

Target selection precedes the saccadic movement but its occurrence leads to enhanced processing at and around the selected location. This gives rise to the phenomenon of peripheral preview (Section 5.3.3, Section 7.2.3) as indicated in the adjacent box. The actual triggering of the eye movement takes place subsequently, at a time that we argue is determined by competition between processing at the fixated location and that at the selected target location (Section 4.6). We also note the possibility that a replica process may be operative whereby more than one target selection is made in parallel (as discussed in Section 4.4.4) to produce the phenomenon of pipelined saccades.

The eye movement itself is always accompanied by the processes that we have described in the current chapter. The processes operate to initiate a corrective saccade, if one is required, to reset and update the representations used for visually guided action, and to adaptively maintain the saccadic system in long term calibration with the visual environment. These processes operate below the level of consciousness but are absolutely vital in maintaining the usefulness of vision. The perceiver can be blissfully unaware of this activity, and, as we argued in Chapter 1, may even have the illusory belief that the visual system provides him/her with an immediate and fully articulated representation of the visual world.

9.5 Future directions

The Active Vision perspective we have presented in this book places eye movements, and particularly saccades, at the centre of a theory of vision. We hope that the individual chapters will have illustrated the value of such an approach in understanding the role of vision in such diverse areas as reading, searching and scene scanning. Underpinning this approach is a belief that visual perception and cognition is shaped by the manner in which the visual information is structured by the fixation-saccade sequences. It is only now at the end of this book, that we can suggest that the Active Vision account developed so far is only the first step towards a rich account of visual behaviour.

The first challenge for the future developments of these ideas is to continue research (Section 7.3.2) placing vision in a context. We move in the environment, the environment moves towards us and, importantly, we act on the environment. In Chapter 2, we highlighted the danger of studying vision without paying attention to some of the basic principles of the input to the visual system. It may also be critical to allow models of vision to be constrained by the nature of the output of these visual processes; this argument is made cogently by Milner and Goodale (1995). Ultimately, in order to have a rich model of vision we will need not only to embrace the active vision but also the active human.

The second related challenge is to accept the importance of emotional and social factors in affecting active visual behaviour. Vision is possibly the primary sense and as such provides us with the information that allows us to survive and thrive in not only a physical world but also a social world. Visual social cues convey important information that should never be underestimated. A momentary change in someone's facial expression can tell us if we are in imminent physical danger of attack or an amorous advance. Watching the visual behaviour when two other people interact can very quickly tell us a great deal about their relationship. A rich model of vision will also need to include social and emotional factors in ways that are only just starting to be considered (Eastwood *et al.*, 2001; Fox *et al.*, 2000; Hood *et al.*, 1998; Langton *et al.*, 2000)

We do not expect that it will be an easy task to integrate active vision into a human psychology involving interaction with a physical and social world. However, our belief is that an active vision perspective provides a scaffold on which we can begin to integrate theories of vision into an understanding of what it is to be human.

REFERENCES

Allport, A. (1993). Attention and control: have we been asking the wrong questions. A critical review of the last twenty five years. *Attention and Performance XIV* (ed. D. E. Meyer and S. Kornblum), pp. 183–218, MIT Press, Cambridge, MA.

Aloimonos, J., Bandopadhay, A. and Weiss, I. (1988). Active vision. *International Journal of Computer Vision*, **1**, 333–56.

Andersen, R. A., Essick, G. K. and Siegel, R. M. (1985). Encoding of spatial location by posterior parietal neurons. *Science*, **230**, 456–58.

Anstis, S. M. (1974). A chart demonstrating variations in acuity with retinal position. *Vision Research*, **14**, 589–92.

Antes, J. R. (1974). The time course of picture viewing. *Journal of Experimental Psychology*, **103**, 62–70.

Aslin, R. N. and Salapatek, P. (1975). Saccadic localization of targets by the very young human infant. *Perception and Psychophysics*, **17**, 293–302.

Aslin, R. N. and Shea, S. L. (1987). The amplitude and angle of saccades to double-step target displacements. *Vision Research*, **27**, 1925–42.

Azzopardi, P. and Cowey, A. (1993). Preferential representation of the fovea in primary visual cortex. *Nature*, **361**, 719–21.

Azzopardi, P. and Cowey, A. (1997). Is blindsight like normal, near-threshold vision? *Proceedings of the National Academy of Sciences, USA*, 94, 14190–94.

Bahill, A. T., Adler, D. and Stark, L. (1975a). Most naturally occurring saccades have magnitudes of 15 degrees or less. *Investigative Ophthalmology*, **14**, 468–9.

Bahill, A. T., Clark, M. R. and Stark, L. (1975b). The main sequence: a tool for studying eye movements. *Mathematical Biosciences*, **24**, 191–204.

Baker, C. L. and Braddick, O. J. (1985). Eccentricity-dependent scaling of the limits of short-range motion perception. *Vision Research*, **25**, 803–12.

Balint, R. (1909). Seelenlähmung des 'Schauens', optische Ataxie, räumliche Störung der Aufmerksamkeit. *Monatsschrift für Psychiatrie und Neurologie*, **25**, 51–81.

Ballard, D. H. (1991). Animate vision. *Artificial Intelligence*, **48**, 57–86.

Ballard, D. H., Hayhoe, M. M., Li, F. and Whitehead, S. D. (1992). Hand-eye coordination during sequential tasks. *Philosophical Transactions of the Royal Society, Series B*, **337**, 331–9.

Ballard, D. H., Hayhoe, M. M., Pook, P. K. and Rao, R. P. N. (1997). Deictic codes for the embodiment of cognition. *Behavioral and Brain Sciences*, **20**, 723–67.

Barbur, J. L., Forsyth, P. M. and Findlay, J. M. (1988). Human saccadic eye movements in the absence of the geniculo-calcarine projection. *Brain*, **111**, 63–82.

Baylis, G. C. and Driver, J. (1993). Visual-attention and objects—evidence for hierarchical coding of location. *Journal of Experimental Psychology: Human Perception and Performance*, **19**, 451–70.

Beauvillain, C. and Doré, K. (1998). Orthographic codes are used in integrating information from the parafovea by the saccadic computation system. *Vision Research*, **38**, 115–23.

Beauvillain, C., Doré, K. and Baudoin, V. (1996). The centre of gravity of words: evidence for an effect of the word initial letters. *Vision Research*, **36**, 589–603.

Becker, W. (1972). The control of eye movements in the saccadic system. *Bibliotheca Ophthalmologica*, **82**, 233–43.

Becker, W. (1989). Metrics. In *The neurobiology of saccadic eye movements* (ed. R. H. Wurtz and M. E. Goldberg), pp. 13–67, Elsevier, Amsterdam.

Becker, W. and Jürgens, R. (1979). An analysis of the saccadic system by means of double step stimuli. *Vision Research*, **19**, 967–83.

Behrmann, M., Watt, S., Black, S. E. and Barton, J. J. S. (1997). Impaired visual search in patients with unilateral neglect: an oculographic analysis. *Neuropsychologia*, **35**, 1445–58.

Biederman, I. (1972). Perceiving real world scenes. *Science*, **177**, 77–80.

Biederman, I. (1981). On the semantics of a glance at a scene. In *Perceptual organization*. (ed. M. Kubovy and J. R. Pomerantz), pp. 213–53, Lawrence Erlbaum, Hillsdale, NJ.

Biederman, I. (1987). Recognition by components: a theory of human image understanding. *Psychological Review*, **94**, 115–45.

Biederman, I., Mezzanotte, R. J. and Rabinowitz, J. C. (1982). Scene perception: detecting and judging objects undergoing relational violations. *Cognitive Psychology*, **14**, 143–77.

Binello, A., Mannan, S. and Ruddock, K. H. (1995). The characteristics of eye movements made during visual search with multi-element stimuli. *Spatial Vision*, **9**, 343–62.

Bishop, D. V. M. (1997). Cognitive neuropsychology and developmental disorders: uncomfortable bedfellows. *Quarterly Journal of Experimental Psychology*, **50A**, 899–923.

Blanchard, H. E., McConkie, G. W., Zola, D. and Wolverton, G. S. (1984). Time course of visual information utilization during fixations in reading. *Journal of Experimental Psychology, Human Perception and Performance*, **10**, 75–89.

Blythe, I. M., Kennard, C. and Ruddock, K. H. (1987). Residual vision in patients with retrogeniculate lesions of the visual pathways, *Brain*, **110**, 887–905.

Boman, D. K. and Hotson, J. R. (1992). Predictive smooth pursuit eye-movements near abrupt changes in motion detection. *Vision Research*, **32**, 675–89.

Bon, L. and Luchetti, C. (1992). The dorsomedial frontal cortex of the macaca monkey. Fixation and saccade-related activity. *Experimental Brain Research*, **89**, 571–80.

Bouma, H. (1970). Interaction effects in parafoveal letter recognition. *Nature*, **226**, 177–8.

Bouma, H. (1978). Visual search and reading: eye movements and functional visual field. A tutorial review. In *Attention and Performance, Vol. VII* (ed. J. Requin), pp. 115–47, Erlbaum Associates, Hillsdale, NJ.

Boyce, S. J. and Pollatsek, A. (1992). Identification of objects in scenes: the role of scene background in object naming. *Journal of Experimental Psychology: Learning, Memory and Cognition,* **18**, 531–43.

Bozkov, V., Bohdanecky, Z. and Radil-Weiss, T. (1977). Target point selection during scanning eye movements. *Biological Cybernetics,* **27**, 215–20.

Breitmeyer, B. (1980). Unmasking visual masking: a look at the 'why' behind the veil of the 'how'. *Psychological Review,* **83**, 1–36.

Bridgeman, B. (1983). Mechanisms of space constancy. In *Spatially oriented behaviour* (ed. A. Hein and M. Jeannerod), pp. 263–79, Springer-Verlag, New York.

Bridgeman, B., Hendry, D. P. and Stark, L. (1975). Failure to detect displacement of the visual world during saccadic eye movements. *Vision Research,* **15**, 719–22.

Bridgeman, B., Lewis, S., Heit, G. and Nagle, M. (1979). Relationship between cognitive and motor-oriented systems of visual position perception. *Journal of Experimental Psychology: Human Perception and Performance,* **6**, 692–700.

Bridgeman, B., van der Heijden, A. H. C. and Velichkovsky, B. M. (1994). A theory of visual stability across saccadic eye movements. *Behavioral and Brain Sciences,* **17**, 247–92.

Broadbent, D. E. (1958). *Perception and Communication.* Pergamon Press, London.

Brogan, D., Gale, A. G. and Carr, K. T. (1993). *Visual Search 2.* Taylor and Francis, London.

Bronson, G. W. (1974). The postnatal growth of visual capacity. *Child Development,* **45**, 873–90.

Brown, B., Haegerstrom-Portnoy, G., Yingling, C. D., Herron, J., Galin, D. and Marcus, M. (1983). Tracking eye movements are normal in dyslexic children. *American Journal of Optometry and Physiological Optics,* **60**, 376–83.

Brown, V., Huey, D. and Findlay J. M. (1997). Face detection in peripheral vision: do faces pop out? *Perception,* **26**, 1555–70.

Brown, V., Walker, R., Gray, C., Findlay, J. M. (1999). Limb activation and the rehabilitation of unilateral neglect: evidence of task-specific effects. *Neurocase,* **5**, 129–42.

Brysbaert, M. and Vitu, F. (1998). Word skipping: implications for theories of eye movement control. In *Eye guidance in reading and scene perception* (ed. G. Underwood), North-Holland, Amsterdam.

Burr, D. C. and Morrone, M. C. (1996). Temporal impulse response functions for luminance and colour during saccades. *Vision Research,* **36**, 2069–78.

Burr, D. C., Morrone, M. C. and Ross, J. (1994). Selective suppression of the magnocellular visual pathways during saccadic eye movements. *Nature,* **371**, 511–3.

Burr, D. C., Morrone, M. C. and Ross, J. (2001). Separate visual representations for perception and action revealed by saccadic eye movements. *Current Biology,* **11**, 798–802.

Bussetini, C., Miles, F. A. and Krauzlis, R. J. (1996). Short latency disparity vergence responses and their dependence on a prior saccadic eye movement. *Journal of Neurophysiology,* **75**, 1392–1410.

Buswell, G. T. (1922, 1937). Fundamental reading habits; a study of their development. *Supplementary Educational Monographs,* #21. *How adults read. Supplementary Educational Monographs,* #50. Cited in R. S. Woodworth and H. Schlosberg (1954). *Experimental Psychology*, Methuen, London.

Buswell, G. T. (1935). *How people look at pictures.* University of Chicago Press, Chicago.

Carpenter, R. H. S. (1981). Oculomotor procrastination. In *Eye movements, cognition and visual perception* (ed. D. F. Fisher, R. A. Monty and J. W. Senders) pp. 237–46, Lawrence Erlbaum, Hillsdale, NJ.

Carpenter, R. H. S. (1988). *Movements of the eyes* (2nd edn), Pion Press, London.

Carpenter, R. H. S. (1991). The visual origins of ocular motility. In Eye movements (ed. R. H. S. Carpenter), pp. 1–9, Volume 8 of *Vision and visual dysfunction* (ed. J. R. Cronly-Dillon), Macmillan, Basingstoke.

Carpenter, R. H. S. and Williams, M. L. L. (1995). Neural computation of log likelihood in control of saccadic eye movements. *Nature*, **377**, 59–62.

Carrasco, M. and Frieder, K. S. (1997). Cortical magnification neutralizes the eccentricity effect in visual search. *Vision Research*, **37**, 63–82.

Carrasco, M., Evert, D. L., Chang, I. and Katz, S. M. (1995). The eccentricity effect—target eccentricity affects performance on conjunction searches. *Perception and Psychophysics*, **57**, 1241–61.

Carrasco, M., Penpeci-Talgar, C. and Eckstein, M. (2000). Spatial covert attention increases contrast sensitivity across the CSF: support for signal enhancement. *Vision Research*, **40**, 1203–15.

Castiello, U. and Umiltà, C. (1990). Size of the attentional focus and efficiency of processing. *Acta Psychologica*, **73**, 1895–209.

Cattell, J. McK. (1885). Ueber die Zeit der Erkennung und Benennung von Schriftzeichen, Bilden und Farben. Philos. Stud. **2**, 635–650 (cited in R. S. Woodworth and H. Scholsberg, 1954. *Experimental Psychology*, New York, Holt, Reinhart and Winston).

Chapman, P. R. and Underwood, G. (1998). Visual search of dynamic scenes: event types and the role of experience in driving situations. In *Eye guidance in reading and scene perception* (ed. G. Underwood), pp. 369–93, Elsevier, Amsterdam.

Chelazzi, L., Duncan, J., Miller, E. K. and Desimone, R. (1998). Responses of neurons in inferior temporal cortexduring memory-guided visual search. *Journal of Neurophysiology*, **80**, 2918–40.

Chelazzi, L., Miller, E. K., Duncan, J. and Desimone, R. (1993). A neural basis for visual search in inferior temporal cortex. *Nature*, **363**, 345–7.

Cherry, E. C. (1953). Some experiments on the recognition of speech, with one or two ears. *Journal of the Acoustical Society of America*, **25**, 975–9.

Chou, I.-H., Sommer, M. A. and Schiller, P. H. (1999). Express averaging saccades in the monkey. *Vision Research*, **39**, 4200–16.

Churchland, P. S., Ramachandran, V. S. and Sejnowski, T. J. (1994). A critique of pure vision. In *Large scale neuronal theories of the brain* (ed. C. Koch and J. L. Davis), pp. 23–60. MIT Press, Cambridge, MA.

Clark, J. J. (1999). Spatial attention and latencies of saccadic eye movements. *Vision Research*, **39**, 585–602.

Colby, C. L. and Goldberg, M. E. (1999). Space and attention in parietal cortex. *Annual Review of Neuroscience*, **22**, 319–49.

Collewijn, H. J. (1998). Eye movement recording. In *Vision research: a practical guide to laboratory methods* (ed. R. H. S. Carpenter and J. G. Robson), pp. 245–85. Oxford University Press, Oxford.

Corbetta, M. (1998). Frontoparietal cortical networks for directing attention and the eye to visual locations: identical, independent, or overlapping neural systems. *Proceedings of the National Academy of Sciences, USA*, **95**, 831–8.

Corbetta, M., Miezin, F. M., Dobmeyer, S., Shulman, G. L. and Petersen, S. E. (1991). Selective and divided attention during visual discriminations of shape, color, and speed—functional anatomy by positron emission tomography. *Journal of Neuroscience*, **11**, 2383–2402.

Corbetta, M. and Shulman, G. L. (1998). Human cortical mechanisms of visual attention during orienting and search. *Philosophical Transactions of The Royal Society Series B*, **353**, 1353–62.

Courtney, A. J. and Chan, H. S. (1986). Visual lobe dimensions and search performance for targets on a competing homogeneous background. *Perception and Psychophysics*, **40**, 39–44.

Cowey, A., Small, M. and Ellis, S. (1994). Left visuospatial neglect can be worse in far than in near space. *Neuropsychologia*, **32**, 1059–1066.

Crawford, J. D. and Vilis, T. (1995). How do motor systems deal with the problems of controlling three-dimensional rotations. *Journal of Motor Behavior*, **27**, 89–99.

Crawford, T. J. (1991). Multisteppping saccade sequences. *Acta Psychologica*, **76**, 11–29.

Crawford, T. J., Haegar, B., Kennard, C., Reveley, M. A. and Henderson, L. (1995*a*). Saccadic abnormalities in psychotic patients. I. Neuroleptic-free psychotic patients. *Psychological Medicine*, **25**, 461–71.

Crawford, T. J., Haegar, B., Kennard, C., Reveley, M. A. and Henderson, L. (1995*b*). Saccadic abnormalities in psychotic patients. II. The role of neuroleptics treatment. *Psychological Medicine*, **25**, 473–83.

Crawford, T. J., Henderson, L. and Kennard, C. (1989). Abnormalities in non visually guided eye movements in Parkinson's disease. *Brain*, **112**, 1573–86.

Crawford, T. J. and Müller, H. J. (1992). Spatial and temporal effects of spatial attention on human saccadic eye-movements. *Vision Research*, **32**, 293–304.

Cronly-Dillon, J. (General Editor). (1991). *Vision and visual dysfunction*. Macmillan, Basingstoke. 16 volumes + index.

Crowe, D. A., Averbeck, B. B., Chafee, M. V., Anderson, J. H. and Georgopoulos, A. P. (2000). Mental maze solving. *Journal of Cognitive Neuroscience*, **12**, 813–27.

Currie, C. B., McConkie, G. W., Carlson-Radvansky, L. A and Irwin, D. E. (2000). The role of the saccade target object in the perception of a visually stable world. *Perception and Psychophysics*, **62**, 673–83.

Dassonville, P., Schlag, J. and Schlag-Rey, M. (1995). The use of egocentric and exocentric cues in saccadic programming. *Vision Research*, **35**, 2191–99.

De Bie, J. (1986). *The control properties of small eye movements*. Proefschrift. Technical University of Delft.

De Graef, P., Christiaens, D. and d'Ydewalle, G. (1990). Perceptual effects of scene context on object identification. *Psychological Research*, **52**, 317–29.

Delorme, A., Richard, G. and Fabre-Thorpe, M. (2000). Ultra-rapid categorisation of natural scenes does not rely on colour cues: a study in monkeys and humans. *Vision Research*, **40**, 2187–2200.

Desimone, R. and Duncan, J. (1995). Neural mechanisms of selective attention. *Annual Review of Neuroscience*, **18**, 193–222.

Deubel, H. (1987). Adaptivity of gain and direction in oblique saccades. In *Eye movements: from physiology to cognition* (ed. J. K. O'Regan and A. Lévy-Schoen), pp. 181–90, Elsevier, North Holland, Amsterdam.

Deubel, H. (1991). Plasticity of metrical and dynamical aspects of saccadic eye movements. In *Tutorials in Motor Neuroscience* (ed. J. Requin and G. E. Stelmach), pp. 563–79, Kluwer, Amsterdam.

Deubel, H. (1995). Separate adaptive mechanisms for the control of reactive and volitional eye movements. *Vision Research*, **35**, 3529–40.

Deubel, H. and Bridgeman, B. (1995). 4th Purkinje image signals reveal eye lens deviations and retinal image distortions during saccades. *Vision Research*, **35**, 529–38.

Deubel, H. and Schneider, W. X. (1996). Saccade target selection and object recognition: evidence for a common attentional mechanism. *Vision Research*, **36**, 1827–37.

Deubel, H., Schneider, W. X. and Bridgeman, B. (1996). Postsaccadic target blanking prevents saccadic suppression of image displacement. *Vision Research*, **36**, 985–96.

Deubel, H., Schneider, W. X. and Bridgeman, B. (1998). Immediate post-saccadic information mediates space constancy. *Vision Research*, **38**, 3147–59.

Deubel, H., Wolf, W. and Hauske, G. (1984). The evaluation of the oculomotor error signal. In *Theoretical and Applied Aspects of Eye Movement Research.* (ed. A. G. Gale and F. W. Johnson), pp. 55–62, North-Holland, Amsterdam.

DeYoe, E. A. and Van Essen, D. C. (1988). Concurrent processing streams in monkey visual cortex. *Trends in Neurosciences*, **11**, 219–26.

Ditchburn, R. W. (1973). *Eye movements and visual perception.* Oxford University Press, Oxford.

Ditchburn, R. W. and Ginsborg, B. L. (1952). Vision with a stabilised retinal image. *Nature*, **170**, 36–37.

Dodge, R. (1900). Visual perception during eye movements. *Psychological Review*, **7**, 454–65.

Dodge, R. and Cline, T. S. (1901). The angle velocity of eye movements. *Psychological Review*, **8**, 145–57.

Dorris, M. C., Paré, M. and Munoz, D. P. (1997). Neuronal activity in monkey superior colliculus related to the initiation of saccadic eye movements. *Journal of Neuroscience*, **17**, 8566–79.

Downing, C. J. (1988). Expectancy and visual spatial attention—effects on perceptual quality. *Journal of Experimental Psychology: Human Perception and Performance*, **14**, 188–202.

Downing, C. J. and Pinker, S. (1985). The spatial structure of visual attention. In *Attention and Performance XI* (ed. M. I. Posner and S. Marin), pp. 171–87, Lawrence Erlbaum, Hillsdale, NJ.

Drasdo, N. (1991). Neural substrates and threshold gradients of peripheral vision. In Limits of vision (ed. J. J. Kulikowski, V. Walsh and I. J. Murray), pp. 251–65, Volume 5 of *Vision and visual dysfunction* (ed. J. R. Cronly-Dillon), Macmillan, Basingstoke.

Droulez, J. and Berthoz, A. (1990). The concept of dynamic memory in sensorimotor control. In *Motor control: concepts and issues* (ed. D. R. Humphrey and H. J. Freund) Chichester, Wiley.

Droulez, J. and Berthoz, A. (1991). A neural network model of sensoritopic maps with predictive short-term memory properties. *Proceedings of the National Academy of Sciences*, USA, **88**, 9653–7.

Duhamel, J.-R., Bremmer, F., BenHamed, S. and Graf, W. (1997). Spatial invariance of visual receptive fields in parietal cortex neurons. *Nature*, **389**, 845–8.

Duncan, J. (1980). The locus of interference in the perception of simultaneous stimuli. *Psychological Review*, **87**, 272–300.

Duncan, J. (1984). Selective attention and the organization of visual information. *Journal of Experimental Psychology: General*, **113**, 501–17.

Duncan, J. and Humphreys, G. W. (1989). Visual-search and stimulus similarity. *Psychological Review*, **96**, 433–58.

Duncan, J. and Humphreys, G. W. (1992). Beyond the search surface—visual-search and attentional engagement. *Journal of Experimental Psychology: Human Perception and Performance*, **18**, 578–88.

Duncan, J., Ward, R. and Shapiro, K. (1994). Direct measurement of attentional dwell time in human vision. *Nature*, **369**, 313–5.

Dunn-Rankin, P. (1978). The visual characteristics of words. *Scientific American*, **238**(1), 122–30.

Eastwood, J. D., Smilek, D. and Merikle, P. M. (2001). Differential attentional guidance by unattended faces expressing positive and negative emotion. *Perception and Psychophysics*, **63**, 1004–13.

Eckstein, M. P. (1998). The lower visual search efficiency for conjunctions is due to noise and not serial attentional processing. *Psychological Science*, **9**, 111–18.

Eden, G. F., Stein, J. F., Wood, H. M. and Wood, F. B. (1994). Differences in eye movements and reading: problems in dyslexic and normal children, *Vision Research*, **34**, 1345–58.

Egeth, H. (1977). Attention and preattention. In *The Psychology of Learning and Motivation Vol. 11* (ed. G. H. Bower), pp. 277–320, Academic Press, New York.

Egeth, H. E. and Yantis, S. (1997). Visual attention: control, representation, and time course. *Annual Review of Psychology*, **48**, 269–97.

Egly, R., Driver, J. and Rafal, R. D. (1994). Shifting visual-attention between objects and locations: evidence from normal and parietal lesion subjects. *Journal of Experimental Psychology: General*, **123**, 161–77.

Ellis A. W. and Young A. W. (1988). *Human cognitive neuropsychology*. Hove: Erlbaum.

Ellis, S. R. and Stark, L. (1986). Statistical dependency in visual scanning. *Human Factors*, **28**, 421–38.

Engel, F. L. (1971). Visual conspicuity and the selective background interference in eccentric vision. *Vision Research*, **14**, 459–71.

Engel, F. L. (1977). Visual conspicuity, visual search and fixation tendencies of the eye. *Vision Research*, **17**, 95–108.

Engel, G. R. (1971). Visual conspicuity, directed attention and retinal locus. *Vision Research*, **11**, 563–76.

Enns, J. T. and Rensink, R. A. (1991). Preattentive recovery of 3-dimensional orientation from line drawings. *Psychological Review*, **98**, 335–51.

Enright, J. T. (1984). Changes in vergence mediated by saccades. *Journal of Physiology*, **350**, 9–31.

Enright, J. T. (1986). Facilitation of vergence changes by saccades: influences of misfocused images and of disparity stimuli in man. *Journal of Physiology*, **371**, 69–87.

Enroth-Cugell, C. and Robson, J. G. (1966). The contrast sensitivity of retinal ganglion cells in the cat. *Journal of Physiology*, **187**, 517–22.

Erdmann, D. and Dodge, R. (1898). *Psychologische Untersuchungen über das Lesen auf experimentelle Grundlage*. Max Niemeyer, Halle an der Saale.

Eriksen, C. W. and St James, J. D. (1986). Visual-attention within and around the field of focal attention—a zoom lens model. *Perception and Psychophysics*, **40**, 225–40.

Eriksen, C. W. and Yeh, Y. Y. (1985). Allocation of attention in the visual-field. *Journal of Experimental Psychology: Human Perception and Performance*, **11**, 583–97.

Erkelens, C. J., Steinman, R. M. and Collewijn, H. (1989). Ocular vergence under natural conditions. II Gaze shifts between real targets differing in distance and direction. *Proceedings of the Royal Society, Series B*, **236**, 441–65.

Everatt, J. (ed.) (1999). *Reading and dyslexia: visual and attentional processes*. Routledge, London.

Everling, S. and Fischer, B. (1998). The antisaccade: a review of basic research and clinical studies. *Neuropsychologia*, **36**, 885–99.

Evokimidis, I., Smyrnis, N., Constantinidis, T. S., Stefanis, N. C., Avramopoulos, D., Paximadis, C., Theleretis, C., Estrafatiadis, C., Kastinakis, G. and Stefanis, C. N. (2002). The antisaccade task in a sample of 2006 young men. 1 Normal population characteristics. *Experimental Brain Research*, **147**, 45–52.

Fabre-Thorpe, M., Richard, G. and Thorpe, S. J. (1998). On the speed of natural scene categorisation in human and non-human primates. *Cahiers de Psychologie Cognitive*, **17**, 791–805.

Feldman, J. (1985). Connectionist models and parallelism in high level vision. *Computer Vision, Graphics and Image Processing*, **31**, 178–200.

Felleman, D. J. and Van Essen, D. C. (1991). Distributed hierarchical processing in the primate cerebral cortex. *Cerebral Cortex*, **1**, 1–47.

Fendrich, R., Wessinger, C. M. and Gazzaniga, M. S. (1992). Residual vision in a scotoma—implications for blindsight. *Science*, **258**, 1489–91.

Ferrera, V. P., Nealy, T. A. and Maunsell, J. H. R. (1992). Mixed parvocellular and magnocellular geniculate signals in area V4. *Nature*, **358**, 756–8.

Findlay, J. M. (1982). Global processing for saccadic eye movements. *Vision Research*, **22**, 1033–45.

Findlay, J. M. (1983). Visual information for saccadic eye movements. In *Spatially oriented behavior* (ed. A. Hein and M. Jeannerod), pp. 281–303, Springer-Verlag, New York.

Findlay, J. M. (1995). Visual search: eye movements and peripheral vision. *Optometry and Vision Science*, **72**, 461–6.

Findlay, J. M. (1997). Saccade target selection during visual search. *Vision Research,* **37,** 617–31.

Findlay, J. M., Brogan, D. and Wenban-Smith, M. G. (1993). The visual signal for saccadic eye movements emphasizes visual boundaries. *Perception and Psychophysics,* **53,** 633–41.

Findlay, J. M., Brown, V. and Gilchrist I. D. (2001). Saccade target selection in visual search: the effect of information from the previous fixation. *Vision Research,* **41,** 87–95.

Findlay, J. M. and Crawford, T. J. (1986). Plasticity in the control of the spatial characteristic of saccadic eye movements. In *Sensorimotor plasticity: theoretical, experimental and clinical aspects* (ed. S. Ron, R. Schmid and M. Jeannerod), pp. 163–80, INSERM, Paris.

Findlay, J. M. and Gilchrist, I. D. (1998). Eye guidance and visual search. In *Eye guidance in reading and scene perception* (ed. G. Underwood), pp. 295–312, Elsevier Science, Amsterdam.

Findlay, J. M. and Gilchrist, I. D. (2001). Visual attention: the active vision perspective. In *Vision and Attention* (ed. M. Jenkin and L. R. Harris), pp. 83–103, Springer-Verlag, New York.

Findlay, J. M. and Harris, L. R. (1984). Small saccades to double stepped targets moving in two dimensions. In *Theoretical and applied aspects of oculomotor research* (ed. A. G. Gale and F. Johnson), pp. 71–7, Elsevier, Amsterdam.

Findlay, J. M. and Kapoula, Z. (1992). Scrutinization, spatial attention and the spatial properties of saccadic eye movements. *Quarterly Journal of Experimental Psychology,* **45A,** 633–47.

Findlay, J. M. and Walker, R. (1999). A model of saccadic eye movement generation based on parallel processing and competitive inhibition. *Behavioral and Brain Sciences,* **22,** 661–721.

Fischer, B., Biscaldi, M. and Otto, P. (1993). Saccadic eye movements of dyslexic adult subjects. *Neuropsychologia,* **31,** 887–906.

Fischer, B. and Boch, R. (1983). Saccadic eye movements after extremely short reaction times in the monkey. *Brain Research,* **260,** 21–6.

Fischer, B. and Ramsperger, E. (1984). Human express saccades: extremely short reaction times of goal directed eye movements. *Experimental Brain Research,* **57,** 191–5.

Fischer, B. and Weber, H. (1992). Characteristics of 'anti' saccades in man. *Experimental Brain Research,* **89,** 415–24.

Fischer, B. and Weber, H. (1993). Express saccades and visual attention. *Behavioral and Brain Sciences,* **16,** 553–610.

Fischer, B. and Weber, H. (1996). Effects of procues on errors rates and reaction times of antisaccades in human subjects. *Experimental Brain Research,* **109,** 507–12.

Fischer, M. H. (1999). Memory for word locations in reading. *Memory,* **7,** 79–116.

Fodor, J. A. (1983). *The Modularity of Mind.* MIT Press, Cambridge, MA.

Forbes, K. and Klein, R. (1996). The magnitude of the fixation offset effect with endogeneously and exogeneously controlled saccades. *Journal of Cognitive Neuroscience,* **8,** 344–52.

Fox, E., Lester, V., Russo, R., Bowles, R. J., Pichler, A. and Dutton, K. (2000). Facial expressions of emotion: are angry faces detected more efficiently? *Cognition and Emotion,* **14,** 61–92.

Frazier, L. and Rayner, K. (1982). Making and correcting errors during sentence comprehension: eye movements in the analysis of structurally ambiguous sentences. *Cognitive Psychology*, **14**, 178–210.

Friedman, A. and Liebelt, L. S. (1981). On the time course of viewing pictures with a view towards remembering. In *Eye movements: cognition and visual perception* (ed. D. F. Fisher, R. A. Monty and J. W. Senders), pp. 137–55, Lawrence Erlbaum, Hillsdale, NJ.

Friedman-Hill, S. R., Robertson, L. C. and Treisman, A. (1995). Parietal contributions to visual feature binding—evidence from a patient with bilateral lesions. *Science*, **269**, 853–5.

Fuchs, A. F., Kaneko, C. R. S. and Scudder, C. A. (1985). Brainstem control of saccadic eye movements. *Annual Review of Neuroscience*, **8**, 307–37.

Funahashi, S., Bruce, C. J. and Goldman-Rakic, P. S. (1989). Mnemonic coding of visual space in the monkey's dorsolateral prefrontal cortex. *Journal of Neurophysiology*, **61**, 331–49.

Gautier, V., O'Regan, J. K. and Le Gargasson, J. F. (2000) 'The-skipping' revisited in French: programming saccades to skip the article 'les'. *Vision Research*, **40**, 2517–31.

Gibson, J. J. (1966). *The senses considered as perceptual systems.* Houghton Mifflin, Boston.

Gibson, J. J. (1979). *The ecological approach to visual perception.* Houghton Mifflin, Boston.

Gilchrist, I. D., Brown, V. and Findlay, J. M. (1997). Saccades without eye movements. *Nature*, **390**, 130–1.

Gilchrist, I. D., Brown, V., Findlay, J. M. and Clarke, M. P. (1998). Using the eye movement system to control the head. *Proceedings of the Royal Society, Series B*, **265**, 1831–6.

Gilchrist, I. D. and Harvey, M. (2000). Refixation frequency and memory mechanisms in visual search. *Current Biology*, **10**, 1209–12.

Gilchrist, I. D., Heywood, C. A. and Findlay, J. M. (1999a). Saccade selection in visual search: evidence for spatial frequency specific between-item interactions. *Vision Research*, **39**, 1373–83.

Gilchrist, I. D., Heywood, C. A. and Findlay, J. M. (1999b). Surface and edge information for spatial integration: a saccadic-selection task. *Visual Cognition*, **6**, 363–84.

Gilchrist, I. D., Humphreys, G. W., Neumann, H. and Riddoch, M. J. (1997). Luminance and edge information in grouping: a study using visual search. *Journal of Experimental Psychology: Human Perception and Performance*, **23**, 464–80.

Girotti, F., Milanese, C., Casazza, M., Allegranza, A., Corridori, F., Avanzini, G. (1982). Oculomotor disturbances in Balints syndrome—an anatomoclinical findings and electrooculographic analysis in a case. *Cortex*, **18**, 603–14.

Glimcher, P. W. and Sparks, D. L. (1992). Movement selection in advance of action in the superior colliculus. *Nature*, **355**, 542–5.

Glimcher, P. W. and Sparks, D. L. (1993). Representation of averaging saccades in the superior colliculus of the monkey. *Experimental Brain Research*, **95**, 429–35.

Glue, P. (1991). The pharmacology of saccadic eye movements. *Journal of Psychopharmacology*, **5**, 377–87.

Gnadt, J. W. and Andersen, R. A. (1988). Memory related motor planning activity in posterior parietal cortex. *Experimental Brain Research*, **70**, 216–20.

Gnadt, J. W., Bracewell, M. and Andersen, R. A. (1991). Sensorimotor transformation during eye movements to remembered visual targets, *Vision Research*, **31**, 693–715.

Goldberg, M. E. and Segraves, M. A. (1987). The function of the projection from the frontal eye fields to the superior colliculus in the monkey. *Archives of Neurology*, **44**, 1209.

Goldberg, M. E. and Wurtz, R. H. (1972). Activity of superior colliculus cells in behaving monkey I. Visual receptive fields of single neurons. *Journal of Neurophysiology*, **35**, 542–59.

Goldman-Rakic, P. S. (1992). Working memory and the mind. *Scientific American*, 267(3), 111–17.

Goodale, M. A. and Milner, A. D. (1992). Separate visual pathways for perception and action. *Trends in Neurosciences*, **15**, 20–5.

Gouras, P. (1985). The oculomotor system. In *Principles of neural science (2nd edition)* (ed. E. R. Kandel and J. H. Schwartz) Chapter 43. Amsterdam, Elsevier.

Grimes, J. (1996). On the failure to detect changes in scenes across saccades. In *Perception*, Volume 5 of the Vancouver Studies in Cognitive Science (ed. K. Akins), pp. 89–110, Oxford University Press, New York.

Guba, E., Wolf, W., De Groot, S., Knemeyer, M., Van Atta, R. and Light, L. (1964). Eye movements and TV viewing in children. *Audio–Visual Communication Review*, **12**, 386–401.

Guitton, D., Buchtel, H. A. and Douglas, R. M. (1985). Frontal-lobe lesions in man cause difficulties in suppressing reflexive glances and in generating goal-directed saccades. *Experimental Brain Research*, **58**, 455–72.

Hainline, L. (1998). The development of basic visual abilities. In *Perceptual development: visual, auditory and speech perception in infancy* (ed. A. Slater), pp. 5–50. Psychology Press, Hove.

Hallett, P. E. (1978). Primary and secondary saccades to goals defined by instructions. *Vision Research*, **18**, 1279–96.

Hallett, P. E. (1986). Eye movements. In *Handbook of Perception and Human Performance*. Volume 1. Chapter 10 (ed. K. Boff, L. Kaufman and J. P. Thomas), Wiley, New York.

Hallett, P. E. and Adams, B. D. (1980). The predictability of saccadic latency in a novel voluntary oculomotor task. *Vision Research*, **20**, 329–39.

Hallet, P. E. and Lightstone, A. D. (1976). Saccadic eye movements to flashed targets. *Vision Research*, **16**, 107–14.

Halligan, P. W. and Marshall, J. C. (1991). Left neglect for near but not far space in man. *Nature*, **350**, 498–500.

Hanes, D. P. and Schall, J. D. (1996). Neural control of voluntary movement initiation. *Science*, **274**, 427–30.

Hanes, D. P. and Wurtz, R. H. (2001). Interaction of frontal eye field and superior colliculus for saccade generation. *Journal of Neurophysiology*, **85**, 804–15.

Harvey, M., Olk, B., Muir K. and Gilchrist, I. D. (2002). Manual responses and saccades in chronic and recovered hemispatial neglect: a study using visual search. *Neuropsychologia*, **40**, 705–17.

Hayhoe, M. M. (2000). Vision using routines: a functional account of vision. *Visual Cognition*, **7**, 43–64.

He, P. and Kowler, E. (1989). The role of location probability in the programming of saccades: implications for 'center-of-gravity' tendencies. *Vision Research*, **29**, 1165–81.

Heide, W. and Kompf, D. (1998). Combined deficits of saccades and visuo-spatial orientation after cortical lesions. *Experimental Brain Research*, **123**, 164–71.

Heller, D. and Radach, R. A. (1998). Eye movements in reading: are two eyes better than one? In *Current oculometer research* (ed. W. Becker, H. Deubel and T. Mergner), Plenum, New York.

Helmholtz, H. von (1866). *Treatise on physiological optics Volume III* (trans. 1925 from the third German edition), ed. J. P. C. Southall, New York: Dover, 1962.

Henderson, J. M. (1992). Object identification in context: the visual processing of natural scenes. *Canadian Journal of Psychology*, **46**, 319–41.

Henderson, J. M. (1992). Visual attention and eye movement control during reading and picture viewing. In *Eye movements and visual cognition* (ed. K. Rayner), pp. 260–83, Springer-Verlag, Berlin.

Henderson, J. M. and Ferreira, F. (1990). Effects of foveal processing difficulty on the perceptual span in reading: implications for attention and eye movement control. *Journal of Experimental Psychology: Learning, Memory and Cognition*, **16**, 417–29.

Henderson, J. M. and Hollingworth, A. (1998). Eye movements during scene viewing: an overview. In *Eye guidance in reading and scene perception* (ed. G. Underwood,), pp. 269–93, Elsevier, Amsterdam.

Henderson, J. M. and Hollingworth, A. (1999a). High-level scene perception. *Annual Review of Psychology*, **50**, 243–71.

Henderson, J. M. and Hollingworth, A. (1999b). The role of fixation position in detecting scene changes across saccades. *Psychological Science*, **10**, 438–43.

Henderson, J. M., McClure, K. K., Pierce, S. and Schrock, G. (1997). Object identification without foveal vision: evidence from an artificial scotoma paradigm. *Perception and Psychophysics*, **59**, 323–46.

Henderson, J. M., Pollatsek, A. and Rayner, K. (1989). Covert visual attention and extrafoveal information use during object identification. *Perception and Psychophysics*, **45**, 196–208.

Hendriks, A. W. (1996). Vergence eye movements during fixation in reading. *Acta Psychologica*, **92**, 131–51.

Henn, V., Büttner-Ennever, J. A. and Hepp, K. (1982). The primate oculomotor system I Motorneurons: a synthesis of anatomical, physiological, and clinical data. *Human Neurobiology*, **1**, 77–85.

Henson, D. B. (1993). *Visual fields.* Oxford University Press, Oxford.

Hikosaka, O., Takikawa, Y. and Kawagoe, R. (2000). Role of the basal ganglia in the control of purposive saccadic eye movements. *Physiological Reviews*, **80**, 954–78.

Hikosaka, O. and Wurtz, R. H. (1983). Visual and oculomotor functions of monkey substantia nigra pars reticulata. *Journal of Neurophysiology*, **49**, 1230–1301.

Hikosaka, O. and Wurtz, R. H. (1989). The basal ganglia. In *The neurobiology of saccadic eye movements* (ed. R. H. Wurtz and M. E. Goldberg), pp. 257–81, Elsevier, Amsterdam.

Hirsch, J. and Curcio, C. A. (1989). The spatial resolution capacity of human foveal retina. *Vision Research*, **29**, 1095–1101.

Hodgson, T. L. (2002). The location marker effect: saccade latency increases with target eccentricity. *Experimental Brain Research*, **145**, 539–42.

Hodgson, T. L., Bajwa, A., Owen, A. M. and Kennard, C. (2000). The strategic control of gaze direction in the tower of London task. *Journal of Cognitive Neuroscience*, **12**, 894–907.

Hoffman, J. E. and Subramaniam, B. (1995). The role of visual-attention in saccadic eye-movements. *Perception and Psychophysics*, **57**, 787–95.

Holliday, I. E., Anderson, S. J. and Harding, G. F. A. (1997). Magnetoencephalographic evidence for non-geniculostriate visual input to human cortical area V5 *Neuropsychologia*, **35**, 1139–46.

Holmes G. (1919). Disturbances of visual space perception. *British Medical Journal*, **2**, 230–3.

Honda, H. (1989). Perceptual localization of stimuli flashed during saccades. *Perception and Psychophysics*, **45**, 162–74.

Honda, H. (1990). Eye movements to a visual stimulus flashed before, during, or after a saccade. In *Attention and Performance XIII.* (ed M. Jeannerod), pp. 567–82. Erlbaum, Hillsdale NJ.

Hood, B. M. and Atkinson, J. (1993). Disengaging visual attention in the infant and adult. *Infant Behaviour and Development*, **16**, 405–22.

Hood, B. M., Atkinson, J. and Braddick, O. J. (1998). Selection for action and the development of orienting and visual attention. In *Cognitive neurosience of attention: a developmental perspective* (ed. J. E. Richards), pp. 219–50, Lawrence Erlbaum, Mahwah NJ.

Hood, B. M., Willen, J. D. and Driver, J. (1998). Adult's eyes trigger shifts of visual attention in human infants. *Psychological Science*, **9**, 131–4.

Hooge, I. T. C. and Erkelens, C. J. (1996). Control of fixation duration in a simple search task. *Perception and Psychophysics*, **58**, 969–76.

Hooge, I. T. C. and Erkelens, C. J. (1998). Adjustment of fixation duration in visual search. *Vision Research*, **38**, 1295–1302.

Hooge, I. T. C. and Erkelens, C. J. (1999). Peripheral vision and oculomotor control during visual search. *Vision Research*, **39**, 1567–75.

Hornak, J. (1992). Ocular exploration in the dark by patients with visual neglect. *Neuropsychologia*, **30**, 547–52.

Howard, I. P. (1982). *Human visual orientation.* Wiley, Chichester.

Howard, I. P. and Rogers, B. J. (1995). *Binocular vision and stereopsis.* Oxford University Press, New York.

Huey, E. B. (1908, 1968). *The psychology and pedagogy of reading.* Macmillan, New York, 1908 reprinted by MIT Press, Cambridge, MA, 1968.

Humphreys, G. W. and Müller, H. J. (1993). Search via recursive rejection (SERR)—a connectionist model of visual search. *Cognitive Psychology*, **25**, 43–110.

Humphreys, G. W. and Riddoch, M. J. (1993). Interactions between object and space systems revealed through neuropsychology. In *Attention and Performance XIV* (ed. D. E. Meyer and S. Kornblum), pp. 143–62, Cambridge MA, MIT Press.

Husain, M. and Kennard, C. (1997). Distractor-dependent frontal neglect *Neuropsychologia*, **35**, 829–41.

Husain, M., Mannan, S., Hodgson, T., Wojciulik, E., Driver, J. and Kennard, C. (2001). Impaired spatial working memory across saccades contributes to abnormal search in parietal neglect. *Brain*, **124**, 941–52.

Hutton, S. and Kennard, C. (1998). Oculomotor abnormalities in schizophrenia—a critical review. *Neurology*, **50**, 604–9.

Hyönä, J. (1995). Do irregular letter combinations attract readers' attention: evidence from fixation locations in words. *Journal of Experimental Psychology: Human Perception and Performance*, **21**, 61–81.

Hyönä, J., Niemi, P. and Underwood, G. (1989). Reading long words embedded in sentences: Informativeness of word parts affects eye movements. *Journal of Experimental Psychology: Human Perception and Performance*, **15**, 142–52.

Ikeda, M. and Takeuchi, R. (1975). Influence of foveal load on the functional visual field. *Perception and Psychophysics*, **18**, 255–60.

Inhoff, A. W. and Rayner, K. (1986). Parafoveal word processing during eye fixations in reading: effect of word frequency. *Perception and Psychophysics*, **40**, 431–9.

Intraub, H. (1980). Presentation rate and the representation of briefly glimpsed pictures in memory. *Journal of Experimental Psychology: Human Learning and Memory*, **6**, 1–12.

Intraub, H. (1981). Rapid conceptual identification of sequentially presented pictures. *Journal of Experimental Psychology: Human Perception and Performance*, **7**, 604–10.

Irwin, D. and Zelinsky, G. J. (2002). Eye movements and scene perception: memory for things observed. *Perception and Psychophysics*, **64**, 882–95.

Irwin, D. E. (1991). Information integration across saccadic eye movements. *Cognitive Psychology*, **23**, 420–56.

Irwin, D. E., Colcombe, A. M., Kramer, A. F. and Hahn, S. (2000). Attentional and oculomotor capture by onset, luminance and color singletons. *Vision Research*, **40**, 1443–58.

James, W. (1890). *The Principles of psychology.* Holt, New York.

Javal, E. (1878, 1879). Essai sur la physiologie de la lecture (in several parts). *Annales d'Oculistique* **79**, 97, 240; **80**, 135; **81**, 61; **82**, 72, 159, 242.

Jay, M. F. and Sparks, D. L. (1987). Sensorimotor integration in the primate superior colliculus. II Co-ordinates of auditory signals. *Journal of Neurophysiology*, **57**, 35–54.

Jeannerod, M. (1988). *The neural and behavioural organization of goal-directed movements.* Oxford University Press, Oxford.

Johansson, R. S., Westling, G., Bäckström, A. and Flanagan, J. R. (2001). Eye hand coordination in object manipulation. *Journal of Neuroscience*, **21**, 6917–32.

Johnson, M. H. (1997). *Developmental cognitive neuroscience.* Blackwell, Oxford.

Jonides, J., Irwin, D. E. and Yantis, S. (1982). Integrating information from successive fixations. *Science*, **215**, 192–4.

Jonides, J., Irwin, D. E. and Yantis, S. (1983). Failure to integrate information from successive fixations. *Science*, **222**, 188.

Just, M. A. and Carpenter, P. A. (1980). A theory of reading; from eye fixations to comprehension. *Psychological Review*, **87**, 329–54.

Jüttner, M. and Wolf, W. (1992). Occurrence of human express saccades depends on stimulus uncertainty and stimulus sequence. *Experimental Brain Research*, **68**, 115–21.

Kalesnykas, R. P. and Hallett, P. E. (1994). Retinal eccentricity and the latency of eye saccades. *Vision Research*, **34**, 517–31.

Kaplan, E., Lee, B. B. and Shapley, R. M. (1990). New views of primate retinal function. *Progress in Retinal Research*, **9**, 273–336.

Kapoula, Z. (1985). Evidence for a range effect in the saccadic system. *Vision Research*, **25**, 1155–57.

Kapoula, Z., Optican, L. M. and Robinson, D. A. (1989). Visually induced plasticity of postsaccadic ocular drift in normal humans. *Journal of Neurophysiology*, **61**, 879–91.

Kapoula, Z. and Robinson, D. A. (1986). Saccadic undershoot is not inevitable: saccades can be accurate. *Vision Research*, **26**, 735–43.

Karnath, H-O. and Huber, W. (1992). Abnormal eye-movement behavior during text reading in neglect syndrome—a case-study. *Neuropsychologia*, **30**, 593–8.

Kennedy, A. (1983). On looking into space. In *Eye movements in reading: perceptual and language processes.* (ed. K. Rayner), pp. 237–51, Academic Press, New York.

Kennedy, A. (2000). Parafoveal processing in word recognition. *Quarterly Journal of Experimental Psychology*, **53A**, 429–55.

Kennedy, A. and Murray, W. S. (1989). Spatial coordinates and reading: comments on Monk. *Quarterly Journal of Experimental Psychology*, **39A**, 649–56.

Kennedy, A., Radach, R., Heller, D. and Pynte, J. (2000). *Reading as a perceptual process.* Elsevier, Amsterdam.

Kentridge, R. W., Heywood, C. A. and Weiskrantz, L. (1997). Residual vision in multiple retinal locations within a scotoma: implications for blindsight. *Journal of Cognitive Neuroscience*, **9**, 191–202.

Kentridge, R. W., Heywood, C. A. and Weiskrantz, L. (1999*a*). Effects of temporal cueing on residual visual discrimination in blindsight. *Neuropsychologia*, **37**, 479–83.

Kentridge, R. W., Heywood, C. A. and Weiskrantz, L. (1999*b*). Attention without awareness in blindsight. *Proceedings of the Royal Society of London, Series B*, **266**, 1805–11.

Kingstone, A. and Klein, R. M. (1993). Visual offset facilitates saccade latency: does pre-disengagement of attention mediate this gap effect? *Journal of Experimental Psychology: Human Perception and Performance*, **19**, 251–65.

Klein, R. (1980). Does oculomotor readiness mediate cognitive control of visual attention? In *Attention and Performance* VIII (ed. R. S. Nickerson), pp. 259–76, Lawrence Erlbaum Associates, Hillsdale NJ.

Klein, R. M. (1988). Inhibitory tagging facilitates visual search. *Nature*, **324**, 430–1.

Klein, R. M. (2000). Inhibition of return. *Trends in Cognitive Science*, **4**, 138–47.

Klein, R. M. and Farrell, M. (1989). Search performance without eye-movements. *Perception and Psychophysics*, **46**, 476–82.

Klein, R. M. and MacInnes, W. J. (1999). Inhibition of return is a foraging facilitator in visual search. *Psychological Science*, **10**, 346–52.

Klein, R. M. and Pontefract, A. (1994). Does oculomotor readiness mediate cognitive control of visual-attention—revisited! In *Attention and Performance XV* (ed. C. Umiltà and M. Moscovitch), pp. 333–50, MIT Press, Cambridge, MA.

Koch, C. and Ullman, S. (1985). Shifts in visual attention: towards the underlying circuitry. *Human Neurobiology*, **4**, 219–22.

Kommerell, G., Olivier, D. and Theopold, H. (1976). Adaptive programming of phasic and tonic components in saccadic eye movements: investigations in patients with abducens palsy. *Investigative Ophthalmology*, **15**, 657–60.

Komoda, M. K., Festinger, L., Phillips, L. T., Duckman, R. H. and Young, R. A. (1973). Some observations concerning saccadic eye movements. *Vision Research*, **13**, 1009–20.

Kornmüller, A. E. (1931). Eine experimentelle Anästhesie der äusseren Augenmuskeln am Menschen und ihre Auswirkungen. *Journal für Psychologie und Neurologie*, **41**, 354–66. (cited in Carpenter, 1988)

Kowler, E., Anderson, E., Dosher, B. and Blaser, E. (1995). The role of attention in the programming of saccades. *Vision Research*, **35**, 1897–1916.

Kowler, E. and Blaser, E. (1995). The accuracy and precision of saccades to small and large targets. *Vision Research*, **35**, 1741–54.

Kowler, E. and Steinman, R. M. (1979). The effect of expectations on slow oculomotor control. I Periodic target steps. *Vision Research*, **19**, 619–32.

Krappman, P. (1998). Accuracy of visually and memory guided antisaccades in man. *Vision Research*, **38**, 2979–85.

Krauzlis, R. J., Basso, M. A. and Wurtz, R. H. (1997). Shared motor error for multiple eye movements. *Science*, **276**, 1693–5.

Krieger, G., Rentschler, I., Hauske, G., Schill, K. and Zetsche, C. (2000). Object and scene analysis by saccadic eye-movements: an investigation with higher-order statistics. *Spatial Vision*, **13**, 201–14.

Krupinski, E. A. (1996). Visual scanning patterns of radiologists searching mammograms. *Acta Radiologica*, **3**, 137–44.

Kundel, H. L., Nodine, C. F. and Carmody, D. (1978). Visual scanning, pattern recognition and decision making in pulmonary nodule detection. *Investigative Radiology*, **13**, 175–81.

Kustov, A. A. and Robinson, D. L. (1996). Shared neural control of attentional shifts and eye movements. *Nature*, **384**, 74–77.

Kusunoki, M., Gottlieb, J. and Goldberg, M. E. (2000). The lateral intraparietal area as a salience map: the representation of abrupt onset, stimulus motion, and task relevance. *Vision Research*, **40**, 1459–68.

LaBerge, D. (1983). Spatial extent of attention to letters and words. *Journal of Experimental Psychology: Human Perception and Performance*, **9**, 371–9.

Land, M. F. (1995). The functions of eye movements in animals remote from man. In *Eye movement research: mechanisms, processes and applications* (ed. J. M. Findlay, R. Walker and R. W. Kentridge), pp. 63–76. Elsevier, Amsterdam.

Land, M. F. and Furneaux, S. (1997). The knowledge base of the oculomotor system. *Philosophical Transaction of the Royal Society Series*, **352B**, 1231–39.

Land, M. F., Furneaux, S. M. and Gilchrist, I. D. (2002). The organisation of visually mediated actions in a subject without eye movements. *Neurocase*, **8**, 80–7.

Land, M. F. and Lee, D. (1994). Where we look when we steer. *Nature*, **369**, 742–3.

Land, M. F., Mennie, N. and Rusted, J. (1999). The roles of vision and eye movements in the control of activities of everyday living. *Perception*, **28**, 1311–28.

Land, M. F. and Nilsson, D.-E. (2002). *Animal Eyes*. Oxford University Press, Oxford.

Langton, S. R. H., Watt, R. J. and Bruce, V. (2000). Do the eyes have it? Cues to the direction of social attention. *Trends in Cognitive Sciences*, **4**, 50–9.

Latour, P. (1962). Visual thresholds during eye movements. *Vision Research*, **2**, 261–2.

Lee, C., Rohrer, W. H. and Sparks, D. L. (1988). Population coding of saccadic eye movements by neurons in the superior colliculus. *Nature*, **332**, 357–60.

Lee, D. K., Koch, C. and Braun, J. (1997). Spatial vision thresholds in the near absence of attention. *Vision Research*, **37**, 2409–18.

Leigh, R. J. and Zee, D. S. (1983). *The neurology of eye movements*. E. A. Davis, Philadelphia.

Lennie, P. (1993). Roles of M and P pathways. In *Contrast Sensitivity* (ed. R. M. Shapley and D. K. L. Lam), pp. 201–213, MIT Press. Cambridge, MA.

Levin, D. T., Momen, N., Drivdahl, S. B. and Simons, D. J. (2000). Change blindness: the metacognitive error of overestimating change-detection ability. *Visual Cognition*, **7**, 397–412.

Lisberger, S. G. (1990). Visual tracking in monkeys: evidence for short-latency suppression of the vestibulo-ocular reflex. *Journal of Neurophysiology*, **63**, 676–88.

Liversedge, S. P. and Findlay, J. M. (2000). Saccadic eye movements and cognitive sciences. *Trends in Cognitive Sciences*, **4**, 6–14.

Livingstone, M. S. and Hubel, D. H. (1987). Psychophysical evidence for separate channels for the processing of form, color, movement and depth. *Journal of Neuroscience*, **7**, 3416–68.

Loftus, G. R. (1972). Eye fixations and recognition memory for pictures. *Cognitive Psychology*, **3**, 525–51.

Loftus, G. R. (1985). Picture perception: effect of luminance level on available information and information extraction rate. *Journal of Experimental Psychology: Human Perception and Performance*, **114**, 342–56.

Loftus, G. R. and Mackworth, N. H. (1978). Cognitive determinants of fixation location during picture viewing. *Journal of Experimental Psychology: Human Perception and Performance*, **4**, 565–72.

Logothetis, N. K. and Sheinberg, D. L. (1996). Visual object recognition. *Annual Review of Neuroscience*, **19**, 577–621.

Luck, S. J., Chelazzi, L., Hillyard, S. A. and Desimone, R. (1997). Neural mechanisms of spatial selective attention in areas V1, V2, and V4 of macaque visual cortex. *Journal of Neurophysiology*, **77**, 24–42.

Ludwig, C. J. H. and Gilchrist, I. D. (2002). Stimulus-driven and goal-driven control over visual selection. *Journal of Experimental Psychology: Human Perception and Performance*, **28**, 902–12.

Luria, A. R., Pravdina-Vinarskaya, E. M. and Yarbus, A. L. (1963). Disorders of ocular movements in a case of simultanagnosia. *Brain*, **86**, 219–28.

Lynch, J. C., Mountcastle, V. B., Talbot, W. H. and Yin, T. C. T. (1977). Parietal lobe mechanisms for directed visual attention. *Journal of Neurophysiology*, **40**, 362–89.

Mackeben, M. and Nakayama, K. (1993). Express attentional shifts. *Vision Research*, **33**, 85–90.

Mackworth, N. H. and Morandi, A. J. (1967). The gaze selects informative detail within pictures. *Perception and Psychophysics*, **2**, 547–52.

Mannan, S. K., Ruddock, K. H. and Wooding, D. S. (1995). Automatic control of saccadic eye movements made in visual inspection of briefly presented 2-D images. *Spatial Vision*, **9**, 363–86.

Mannan, S. K., Ruddock, K. H. and Wooding, D. S. (1996). The relationship between the locations of spatial features and those of fixations made during visual examination of briefly presented images. *Spatial Vision*, **10**, 165–88.

Mannan, S. K., Ruddock, K. H. and Wooding, D. S. (1997). Fixation sequences during visual examination of briefly presented 2D images. *Spatial Vision*, **11**, 157–78.

Marr, D. (1982). *Vision*. W. H. Freeman, San Francisco.

Matin, E. (1974). Saccadic suppression: a review and an analysis. *Psychological Bulletin*, **81**, 899–917.

Matin, L. (1972). Eye movements and perceived visual direction. In *Handbook of sensory physiology. Volume 7/4 Visual Psychophysics* (ed. D. Jameson and L. M. Hurvich) pp. 331–80, Springer-Verlag, Berlin.

Maunsell, J. H. R. and Newsome, W. T. (1987). Visual processing in monkey extrastriate cortex. *Annual Review of Neuroscience*, **10**, 363–401.

Maunsell, J. H. R., Nealy, T. A. and DePriest, D. D. (1990). Magnocellular and parvocellular contributions to responses in the middle temporal area (MT) of the macaque monkey. *Journal of Neuroscience*, **10**, 3323–34.

Maurer, D. and Lewis, T. L. (1998). Overt orienting toward peripheral stimuli: normal development and underlying mechanisms. In *Cognitive neuroscience of attention: a developmental perspective* (ed. J. E. Richards), pp. 51–102, Lawrence Erlbaum, Mahwah NJ.

Mays, L. E. (1998). Has Hering been hooked? *Nature Medicine*, **4**, 889–90.

Mays, L. E. and Sparks, D. L. (1980). Saccades are spatially, not retinotopically, coded. *Science*, **208**, 1163–5.

McConkie, G. W. and Currie, C. B. (1996). Visual stability across saccades while viewing complex pictures. *Journal of Experimental Psychology: Human Perception and Performance*, **22**, 563–81.

McConkie, G. W., Kerr, P. W., Reddix, M. D. and Zola, D. (1988). Eye movement control during reading: I The location of initial eye fixations on words. *Vision Research*, **28**, 1107–18.

McConkie, G. W., Kerr, P. W., Reddix, M. D., Zola, D. and Jacobs, A. M. (1989). Eye movement control during reading: II Frequency of refixating a word. *Perception and Psychophysics*, **46**, 245–53.

McConkie, G. W. and Rayner, K. (1975). The span of the effective stimulus during a fixation in reading. *Perception and Psychophysics*, **17**, 578–86.

McConkie, G. W. and Zola, D. (1979). Is visual information integrated across successive fixations in reading? *Perception and Psychophysics*, **25**, 221–4.

McIlwain, J. T. (1976). Large receptive fields and spatial transformations in the visual system. In *Neurophysiology. International Review of Physiology*, Volume 10 II. (ed. R. Porter), pp. 223–48.

McIlwain, J. T. (1991). Distributed coding in the superior colliculus: a review. *Visual Neuroscience*, **6**, 3–13.

McLoughlin, S. (1967). Parametric adjustment in saccadic eye movements. *Perception and Psychophysics*, **2**, 359–62.

McPeek, R. M. and Keller, E. L. (2001). Short-term priming, concurrent processing, and saccade curvature during a target selection task in the monkey. *Vision Research*, **41**, 785–800.

McPeek, R. M. and Keller, E. L. (2002). Superior colliculus activity related to concurrent processing of saccade goals in a visual search task. *Journal of Neurophysiology*, **87**, 1805–15.

McPeek, R.M., Maljkovic, V. and Nakayama, K. (1999). Saccades require focal attention and are facilitated by a short-term memory system. *Vision Research*, **39**, 1555–66.

McPeek, R. M., Skavenski, A. A. and Nakayama, K. (2000). Concurrent processing of saccades in visual search. *Vision Research*, **40**, 2499–2516.

McSorley, E. and Findlay, J. M. (2001). Visual search in depth. *Vision Research*, **41**, 3487–96.

Merigan, W. H. and Maunsell, J. H. R. (1993). How parallel are the primate visual pathways? *Annual Review of Neuroscience*, **16**, 369–402.

Miles, F. A. (1995). The sensing of optic flow by the primate optokinetic system. In *Eye movement research: mechanisms, processes and applications* (ed. J. M. Findlay, R. Walker and R. W. Kentridge), pp. 47–62, Amsterdam, North-Holland.

Miles, F. A. (1998). The neural processing of 3-D information: evidence from eye movements. *European Journal of Neuroscience*, **10**, 811–22.

Milner, A. D. and Goodale, M. A. (1995). The *visual brain in action*. Oxford University Press, Oxford.

Mohler, C. W. and Wurtz, R. H. (1976). Organization of monkey superior colliculus: intermediate layer cells discharging before eye movements. *Journal of Neurophysiology*, **39**, 722–44.

Mohler, C. W. and Wurtz, R. H. (1977). Role of striate cortex and superior colliculus in visual guidance of saccadic eye movements in monkeys. *Journal of Neurophysiology*, **40**, 74–94.

Mokler, A. and Fischer, B. (1999). The recognition and correction of involuntary prosaccades in an antisaccade task. *Experimental Brain Research*, **125**, 511–16.

Moore, T. and Fallah, M. (2001). Control of eye movements and spatial attention. *Proceedings of the National Academy of Sciences USA*, **98**, 1273–6.

Moran, J. and Desimone, R. (1985). Selective attention gates visual processing in the extrastriate cortex. *Science*, **229**, 782–4.

Morrison, R. E. (1983). Retinal image size and the perceptual span in reading. In *Eye movements in reading: perceptual and language processes* (ed. K. Rayner), pp. 31–40. Academic Press, New York.

Morrison, R. E. (1984). Manipulation of stimulus onset delay in reading: evidence for parallel programming of saccades. *Journal of Experimental Psychology: Human Perception and Performance*, **5**, 667–82.

Morrison, R. E. and Rayner, K. (1981). Saccade size in reading depends on character spaces and not visual angle. *Perception and Psychophysics*, **30**, 395–6.

Morton, J. (1969). Interaction of information in word recognition. *Psychological Review*, **76**, 165–78.

Moschovakis, A. and Highstein, S. M. (1994). The anatomy and physiology of primate neurons the control rapid eye movements. *Annual Review of Neuroscience*, **17**, 465–88.

Motter, B. C. and Belky, E. J. (1998a). The zone of focal attention during active visual search. *Vision Research*, **38**, 1007–22.

Motter, B. C. and Belky, E. J. (1998b). The guidance of eye movements during active visual search. *Vision Research*, **38**, 1805–15.

Mourant, R. R. and Rockwell, T. H. (1972). Strategies of visual search by novice and experienced drivers. *Human Factors*, **14**, 325–35.

Müller, H. J. and Findlay, J. M. (1987). Sensitivity and criterion effects in the spatial cueing of visual attention. *Perception and Psychophysics*, **42**, 383–99.

Müller, H. J. and Rabbitt, P. M. A. (1989). Reflexive and voluntary orienting of visual attention: time course of activation and resistance to interruption. *Journal of Experimental Psychology: Human Perception and Performance*, **15**, 315–30.

Müller, H. J., Humphreys, G. W. and Donnelly, N. (1994). Search via recursive rejection (SERR)—visual-search for single and dual form-conjunction targets. *Journal of Experimental Psychology: Human Perception and Performance*, **20**, 23558.

Munoz, D. P. and Wurtz, R. H. (1993a). Fixation cells in monkey superior colliculus. I. Characteristics of cell discharge. *Journal of Neurophysiology*, **70**, 559–75.

Munoz, D. P. and Wurtz, R. H. (1993b). Fixation cells in monkey supeior colliculus II. Reversible activation and deactivation. *Journal of Neurophysiology*, **70**, 576–89.

Nakayama, K. (1992). The iconic bottleneck and the tenuous link between early visual processing and perception. In *Vision: coding and efficiency* (ed. C. Blakemore). Cambridge University Press, Cambridge.

Nakayama, K. and Silverman, G. H. (1986). Serial and parallel processing of visual feature conjunctions. *Nature*, **320**, 264–5.

Neggers, S. F. W. and Bekkering, H. (2000). Ocular gaze is anchored to the target of an ongoing pointing movement. *Journal of Neurophysiology*, **83**, 639–51.

Neggers, S. F. W. and Bekkering, H. (2001). Gaze anchoring to a pointing target is present during the entire pointing movement and is driven by a non-visual signal. *Journal of Neurophysiology*, **86**, 961–70.

Neisser, U. (1976). *Cognition and reality.* W. H. Freeman, San Francisco.

Nelson, W. W. and Loftus, G. R. (1980). The functional visual field during picture viewing. *Journal of Experimental Psychology: Human Learning and Memory*, **6**, 391–9.

Newsome, W. T., Wurtz, R. H., Dürsteler, M. R. and Mikami, A. (1985). Deficits in visual motion processing following ibotenic acid lesions of the middle temporal visual area of the macaque monkey. *Journal of Neuroscience*, **5**, 825–40.

Nicholas, J. J., Heywood, C. A. and Cowey, A. (1996). Contrast sensitivity in one-eyed subjects. *Vision Research*, **36**, 175–80.

Norman, D. A. and Shallice, T. (1986). Attention to action: willed and automatic control of behaviour. In *Consciousness and self-regulation: advances in research and theory*, Volume 4 (ed. R. J. Davidson, G. E. Schwartz and D. Shapiro), pp. 1–18, Plenum, New York.

Noton, D. and Stark, L. (1971*a*). Scanpaths in saccadic eye movements while viewing and recognising patterns. *Vision Research*, **11**, 929–42.

Noton, D. and Stark, L. (1971*b*). Scanpaths in eye movements during pattern perception. *Science*, **171**, 308–11.

O'Regan, J. K. (1980). The control of saccade size and fixation duration in reading: the limits of the linguistic control hypothesis. *Perception and Psychophysics*, **28**, 112–7.

O'Regan, J. K. (1992). Optimal viewing position in words and the strategy-tactics theory of eye movements in reading. In *Eye movements and visual cognition: scene perception and reading* (ed. K. Rayner), pp. 333–54, Springer-Verlag, New York.

O'Regan, J. K. (1992). Solving the 'real' mysteries of visual perception: the world as outside memory. *Canadian Journal of Psychology*, **46**, 461–88.

O'Regan, J. K., Deubel, H., Clark, J. J. and Rensink, R. (2000). Picture changes during blinks: looking without seeing and seeing without looking. *Visual Cognition*, **7**, 191–211.

O'Regan, J. K. and Jacobs, A. M. (1992). The optimal viewing position effect in word recognition: a challenge to current theory. *Journal of Experimental Psychology: Human Perception and Performance*, **18**, 185–97.

O'Regan, J. K. and Lévy-Schoen, A. (1983). Integrating information from successive fixations: does trans-saccadic fusion exist? *Vision Research*, **23**, 765–9.

O'Regan, J. K., Lévy-Schoen, A., Pynte, J. and Brugallière, B. (1984). Convenient fixation location within isolated words of different length and structure. *Journal of Experimental Psychology: Human Perception and Performance*, **10**, 250–7.

O'Regan, J. K., Rensink, R. and Clark, J. J. (1999). Change-blindness as a result of mudsplashes. *Nature*, **398**, 34.

Oliva, A. and Schyns, P. G. (2000). Diagnostic colors mediate scene recognition. *Cognitive Psychology*, **41**, 176–210.

Ottes, F. P., Van Gisbergen, J. A. M. and Eggermont, J. J. (1984). Metrics of saccade responses to visual double stimuli: two different modes. *Vision Research*, **24**, 1169–79.

Ottes, F. P., Van Gisbergen, J. A. M. and Eggermont, J. J. (1985). Latency dependence of colour-based target vs nontarget discrimination by the saccadic system. *Vision Research*, **25**, 849–62.

Paré, M. and Guitton, D. (1994). The fixation area of cat superior colliculus: effects of electrical stimulation and direct connection with brainstem omnipause neurons. *Experimental Brain Research*, **101**, 109–22.

Paré, M. and Munoz, D. (2001). Expression of a re-centring bias in saccade regulation by superior colliculus neurons. *Experimental Brain Research*, **137**, 354–68.

Parker, R. E. (1978). Picture processing during recognition. *Journal of Experimental Psychology: Human Perception and Performance*, **4**, 284–93.

Pashler, H. (1987). Detecting conjunction of color and form: re-assessing the serial search hypothesis. *Perception and Psychophysics*, **41**, 191–201.

Pashler, H. (ed.) (1998). *Attention*. Psychology Press, Hove.

Paterson, D. G. and Tinker, M. A. (1940). *How to make type readable*. Harper and Row, New York.

Pierrot-Deseilligny, C. P., Rivaud, S., Gaymard, B. and Agid, Y. (1991). Cortical control of reflexive visually-guided saccades. *Brain*, **114**, 1473–85.

Ploner, C. J., Rivaud-Péchoux, S., Gaymard, B., Agid, Y. and Pierrot-Deseilligny, C. (1999). Errors of memory-guided saccades in humans with lesions of the frontal eye field and the dorsolateral prefrontal cortex. *Journal of Neurophysiology*, **82**, 1086–90.

Poggio, T. and Edelman, S. (1990). A network that learns to recognise three dimensional objects. *Nature*, **343**, 263–6.

Pollatsek, A., Bolozky, S., Well, A. D. and Rayner, K. (1981). Asymmetries in perceptual span for Israeli readers. *Brain and Language*, **14**, 171–80.

Pollatsek, A., Rayner, K. and Collins, W. E. (1984). Integrating pictorial information across saccadic eye movements. *Journal of Experimental Psychology: General*, **113**, 426–42.

Pollatsek, A., Rayner, K., Fischer, M. H. and Reichle, E. D. (1999). Attention and eye movements in reading. In *Reading and dyslexia: visual and attentional processes* (ed. J. Everatt), pp. 179–209, Routledge, London.

Pollatsek, A., Rayner, K. and Henderson, J. M. (1990). Role of spatial location in integration of pictorial information across saccades. *Journal of Experimental Psychology: Human Perception and Performance*, **16**, 199–230.

Polyak, S. L. (1957). *The vertebrate visual system.* University of Chicago Press, Chicago.

Pomplun, M., Reingold, E. M. and Shen, J. Y. (2001a). Peripheral and parafoveal cueing and masking effects on saccadic selectivity in a gaze-contingent window paradigm. *Vision Research*, **41**, 2757–69.

Pomplun, M., Reingold, E. M. and Shen, J. Y. (2001b). Investigating the visual span in comparative search: the effects of task difficulty and divided attention. *Cognition*, **81**, B57-B67.

Ponsoda, V., Scott, D. and Findlay, J. M. (1995). A probability vector and transition matrix analysis of eye movements during visual search. *Acta Psychologica*, **88**, 167–85.

Pöppel, E., Held, R. and Frost, D. (1973). Residual visual function after brain wounds involving central visual pathways in man. *Nature*, **243**, 295–6.

Posner, M. I. (1978). *Chronometric explorations of mind.* Lawrence Erlbaum Associates Inc., Hillsdale, NJ.

Posner, M. I. (1980). Orienting of attention. *Quarterly Journal of Experimental Psychology*, **32A**, 3–25.

Posner, M. I. and Cohen, Y. (1984). Components of visual orienting. In *Attention and Performance X* (ed. H. Bouma and D. G. Bouwhuis), pp. 531–56, Lawrence Erlbaum, Hillsdale, NJ.

Posner, M. I., Nissen, M. J. and Ogden, M. C. (1978). Attended and unattended processing modes: the role of set for spatial location. In *Modes of perceiving and processing information* (ed. H. L. Pick and I. J. Saltzman), pp. 137–157, Lawrence Erlbaum, Hillsdale, NJ.

Posner, M. I., Rafal, R. D., Choate, L. S. and Vaughan, J. (1985). Inhibition of return—neural basis and function. *Cognitive Neuropsychology*, **2**, 211–28.

Posner, M. I., Snyder C. R. R. and Davidson, B. J. (1980). Attention and the detection of stimuli. *Journal of Experimental Psychology: General*, **109**, 160–74.

Posner, M. I., Walker, J. A., Friedrich, F. J. and Rafal, R. D. (1984). Effects of parietal, lobe injury on covert orienting of visual attention. *Journal of Neuroscience*, **4**, 1863–74.

Potter, M. C. and Levy, E. I. (1969). Recognition memory for a rapid sequence of pictures. *Journal of Experimental Psychology*, **81**, 10–15.

Radach, R., Heller, D. and Inhoff, A. W. (1998). Occurrence and function of very short fixation durations in reading. In *Current Oculomotor Research* (ed. W. Becker, H. Deubel and T. Mergner), Plenum, New York.

Radach, R. and McConkie, G. W. (1998). Determinants of fixation positions within words during reading. In *Eye guidance in reading and scene perception* (ed. G. Underwood), pp. 77–100, North-Holland. Amsterdam.

Rafal, R. D. and Posner, M. I. (1987). Deficits in human visual spatial attention following thalamic lesions. *Proceedings of the National Academy of Sciences USA*, **84**, 7349–53.

Rafal, R. D., Smith, J., Kranty, J., Cohen, A. and Brennan, C. (1990). Extrageniculate vision in the hemianopic human: saccade inhibition by signals in the blind fields. *Science*, **250**, 118–20.

Ramachandran, V. S. (1995). Perceptual correlates of neural plasticity in the adult human brain. In *Early vision and beyond* (ed. T. V. Papathomas, C. Chubb, A. Gorea, and E. Kowler), MIT Press, Cambridge, MA.

Rashbass, C. (1961). The relationship between saccadic and smooth tracking movements. *Journal of Physiology*, **159**, 326–38.

Rashbass, C. and Westheimer, G. (1961). Disjunctive eye movements. *Journal of Physiology*, **159**, 339–60.

Rayner, K. (1975). The perceptual span and peripheral cues in reading. *Cognitive Psychology*, **7**, 65–81.

Rayner, K. (1978). Eye movements in reading and information processing. *Psychological Bulletin*, **85**, 618–60.

Rayner, K. (1979). Eye guidance in reading : fixation locations in words. *Perception*, **8**, 21–30.

Rayner, K. (1986). Eye movements and perceptual span in beginning and skilled readers. *Journal of Experimental Child Psychology*, **41**, 211–36.

Rayner, K. (1995). Eye movements and cognitive processes in reading, visual search, and scene perception. In *Eye movement research: mechanisms, processes and applications* (ed. J. M. Findlay, R. Walker and R. W. Kentridge), pp. 3–22, North Holland, Amsterdam.

Rayner, K. (1998). Eye movements in reading and information processing. 20 years of research. *Psychological Bulletin*, **124**, 372–422.

Rayner, K., Balota, D. A. and Pollatsek, A. (1986). Against parafoveal semantic processing during eye fixations in reading. *Canadian Journal of Psychology*, **40**, 473–83.

Rayner, K. and Beretra, J. H. (1979). Reading without a fovea. *Science*, **206**, 468–89.

Rayner, K. and Fischer, M. H. (1996). Mindless reading revisited: eye movements during reading and scanning are different. *Perception and Psychophysics*, **58**, 734–47.

Rayner, K. and Fisher, D. L. (1987). Letter processing during eye fixations in visual search. *Perception and Psychophysics*, **42**, 87–100.

Rayner, K., Inhoff, A. W., Morrison, R., Slowiaczek, M. L. and Beretra, J. H. (1981). Masking of foveal and parafoveal vision during eye fixations in reading. *Journal of Experimental Psychology: Human Perception and Performance*, **4**, 529–44.

Rayner, K. and McConkie, G. W. (1976). What guides a reader's eye movements. *Vision Research*, **16**, 829–37.

Rayner, K., McConkie, G. W. and Zola, D. (1980). Integrating information across eye movements. *Cognitive Psychology*, **12**, 206–26.

Rayner, K. and Morris, R. (1992). Eye movement control in reading: evidence against semantic preprocessing. *Journal of Experimental Psychology: Human Perception and Performance*, **18**, 163–72.

Rayner, K., Murphy, L. A., Henderson, J. M. and Pollatsek, A. (1989). Selective attentional dyslexia. *Cognitive Neuropsychology*, **6**, 357–78.

Rayner, K. and Pollatsek, A. (1989). *The psychology of reading.* Prentice-Hall, Englewood Cliffs, NJ.

Rayner, K. and Pollatsek, A. (1992). Eye movements and scene perception. *Canadian Journal of Psychology*, **46**, 342–76.

Rayner, K., Sereno, S. C. and Raney, G. E. (1996). Eye movement control in reading: a comparison of two types of models. *Journal of Experimental Psychology: Human Perception and Performance*, **22**, 1188–1200.

Recihle, E. D., Rayner, K. and Pollatsek, A. (1999). Eye movement control in reading: accounting for the initial fixation locations and refixations within the E-Z reader model. *Vision Research*, **39**, 4403–11.

Reddi, B. A. J. and Carpenter, R. H. S. (2000). The influence of urgency on decision time. *Nature Neuroscience*, **3**, 827–30.

Regan, D. and Beverley, K. I. (1982). How do we avoid confounding the direction we are looking with the direction we are moving? *Science*, **213**, 194–6.

Reichle, E. D., Pollatsek, A., Fisher, D. F. and Rayner, K. (1998). Toward a model of eye movement control in reading. *Psychological Review*, **105**, 125–47.

Reilly, R. G. and O'Regan, J. K. (1998). Eye movement control during reading: a simulation of some word-targeting strategies. *Vision Research*, **38**, 303–17.

Remington, R. W. (1980). Attention and saccadic eye movements. *Journal of Experimental Psychology: Human Perception and Performance*, **6**, 726–44.

Rensink, R., O'Regan, J. K. and Clark, J. J. (1997). To see or not to see: the need for attention to perceive changes in scenes. *Psychological Science*, **8**, 368–73.

Reuter-Lorenz, P. A. and Fendrich, R. (1992). Oculomotor readiness and covert orienting—differences between central and peripheral precues. *Perception and Psychophysics*, **52**, 336–44.

Reuter-Lorenz, P. A., Hughes, H. C. and Fendrich, R. (1991). The reduction of saccadic latency by prior offset of the fixation point: an analysis of the gap effect. *Perception and Psychophysics*, **49**, 167–75.

Reuter-Lorenz, P. A., Oonk, H. M., Barnes, L. L. and Hughes, H. C. (1995). Effects of warning signals and fixation point offsets on the latencies of pro-versus antisaccades: implications for an interpretation of the gap effect. *Experimental Brain Research*, **103**, 287–93.

Richardson, D. C. and Spivey, M. (2000). Representation, space and Hollywood squares: looking for things that aren't there anyone. *Cognition*, **76**, 269–95.

Riggs, L. A. and Ratliff, F. (1952). The effects of counteracting the normal movements of the eye. *Journal of the Optical Society of America*, **42**, 872–3.

Riggs, L. A., Merton, P. A. and Morton, H. B. (1974). Suppression of visual phosphenes during saccadic eye movements. *Vision Research*, **14**, 997–1011.

Rimey, R. D. and Brown, C. M. (1991). Controlling eye movements with hidden Markov models. *International Journal of Computer Vision*, **7**, 47–65.

Rizzolatti, G., Riggio, L. and Sheliga, B. M. (1994). Space and selective attention. In *Attention and Performance XV* (ed. C. Umiltà and M. Moscovitch), pp. 231–65, MIT Press, Cambridge, MA.

Rizzolatti, G., Riggio, L., Dascola, I. and Umiltà, C. (1987). Reorienting attention across the horizontal and vertical meridians—evidence in favor of a premotor theory of attention. *Neuropsychologia*, **25**, 31–40.

Robertson, I. H. and Halligan, P. W. (1999). *Spatial Neglect.* Psychology Press, Hove.

Robertson, L., Treisman, A., Friedman-Hill, S. and Grabowecky, M. (1997). The interaction of spatial and object pathways: evidence from Balint's syndrome. *Journal of Cognitive Neuroscience*, **9**, 295–317.

Robinson, D. A. (1964). The mechanics of human saccadic eye movements. *Journal of Physiology*, **174**, 245–64.

Robinson, D. A. (1968). The oculomotor control system: a review. *Proceedings of the Institute of Electrical Engineers*, **56**, 1032–48.

Robinson, D. A. (1972). Eye movements evoked by collicular stimulation in the alert monkey. *Vision Research*, **12**, 1795–1808.

Robinson, D. A. (1975). Oculomotor control signals. In *Basic mechanisms of ocular motility and their clinical applications* (ed. P. Bach-y-Rita and G. Lennestrand), pp. 337–74, Pergamon, Oxford.

Robinson, F. R. and Fuchs, A. F. (2001). The role of the cerebellum in voluntary eye movements. *Annual Review of Neurosciences*, **24**, 981–1004.

Roelfsema, P. R., Lamme, V. A. F. and Spekreijse, H. (1998). Object-based attention in the primary visual cortex of the macaque. *Nature*, **395**, 276–381.

Ross, J., Morrone, M. C. and Burr, D. (1997). Compression of visual space before saccades. *Nature*, **386**, 598–601.

Ross, J., Morrone, M. C., Goldberg, M. E. and Burr, D. C. (2000). Changes in visual perception at the time of saccades. *Trends in Neurosciences*, **24**, 112–21.

Ross, L. E. and Ross, S. M. (1980). Saccade latency and warning signals: stimulus onset, offset and change as warning events. *Perception and Psychophysics*, **27**, 251–7.

Rubin, G. S. and Turano, K. (1992). Reading without saccadic eye-movements. *Vision Research*, **32**, 895–902.

Rumelhart, D. E., McClelland, J. L. (1982). An interactive activation model of context effects in letter perception. Part 2. *Psychological Review*, **89**, 60–94.

Rushton, S. K., Harris, J. M., Lloyd, M. R. and Wann, J. P. (1998). Guidance of locomotion on foot uses perceived target location rather than optic flow. *Current Biology*, **8**, 1191–94.

Saarinen, J. and Julesz, B. (1991). The speed of attentional shifts in the visual field. *Proceedings of the National Academy of Sciences*, **88**, 1812–14.

Saida, S. and Ikeda, M. (1979). Useful visual field size for pattern perception. *Perception and Psychophysics*, **25**, 119–25.

Sakata, H., Taira, M., Kusuonki, M., Murata, A. and Tanaka, Y. (1997). The parietal association cortex in depth perception and visual control of hand action. *Trends in Neurosciences*, **20**, 350–7.

Sanders, A. F. (1963). The selective process in the functional visual field. Report IZF22, Institute for Perception RVO-TNO, Soesterberg.

Saslow, M. G. (1967). Effects of components of displacement-step stimuli upon latency for saccadic eye movement. *Journal of the Optical Society of America*, **57**, 1030–1033.

Schall, J. D. (1991). Neural basis of saccadic eye movements in primates. In *The neural basis of visual function* Volume 4 of Vision and Visual Dysfunction (ed. A. G. Leventhal), pp. 338–442, Macmillan, Basingstoke.

Schall, J. D. (1995). Neural basis of saccade target selection. *Reviews in the Neurosciences*, **6**, 63–85.

Schall, J. D. and Hanes, D. P. (1993). Neural basis of target selection in frontal eye field during visual search. *Nature*, **366**, 467–9.

Schall, J. D. and Hanes, D. P. (1998). Neural mechanisms of selection and control of visually guided eye movements. *Neural Networks*, **11**, 1241–51.

Schall, J. D., Hanes, D. P., Thompson, K. G. and King, D. J. (1995). Saccade target selection in frontal eye field of macaque. 1. Visual and premovement activation. *Journal of Neuroscience*, **15**, 6905–18.

Schiller, P. H. (1998). The neural control of visually guided eye movements. In *Cognitive neuroscience of attention: a developmental perspective* (ed. J. E. Richards), pp. 3–50, Lawrence Erlbaum Associates, Malwah, NJ.

Schiller, P. H. and Koerner, F. (1971). Discharge characteristics of single units in superior colliculus of alert rhesus monkeys. *Journal of Neurophysiology*, **34**, 920–36.

Schiller, P. H. and Logothetis, N. K. (1990). The color-opponent and broad band channels of the visual system. *Trends in Neurosciences*, **13**, 392–98.

Schiller, P. H., True, S. D. and Conway, J. L. (1980). Deficits in eye movements following frontal eye field and superior colliculus ablations. *Journal of Neurophysiology*, **44**, 1175–89.

Schmolesky, M. T., Wang, Y. C., Hanes, D. P., Thompson, K. G., Leutgeb, S., Schall, J. D. and Leventhal, A. G. (1998). Signal timing across the macaque visual system. *Journal of Neurophysiology*, **79**, 3272–78.

Schroyens, W., Vitu, F., Brysbaert, M. and d'Ydewalle, G. (1999). Eye movement control during reading: foveal load and parafoveal processing. *Quarterly Journal of Experimental Psychology*, **52A**, 1021–46.

Schwartz, E. L. (1980). Computational anatomy and functional architecture of striate cortex: a spatial mapping approach to perceptual coding. *Vision Research*, **20**, 645–69.

Schwartz, M. F., Montgomery, M. W., Fitzpatrick-DeSalme, E. J., Ochiopa, C., Coslett, H. B. and Mayer, N. H. (1995). Analysis of a disorder of everyday action. *Cognitive Neuropsychology*, **12**, 863–92.

Schyns, P. G. and Oliva, A. (1994). From blobs to boundary edges: evidence for time and spatial scale dependent scene recognition. *Psychological Science*, **5**, 195–200.

Schyns, P.G. and Oliva, A. (1997). Flexible, diagnosticity-driven, rather than fixed, perceptually determined scale selection in scene and face recognition. *Perception*, **26**, 1027–38.

Scialfa, C. T. and Joffe, K. M. (1998). Response times and eye movements in feature and conjunction search as a function of target eccentricity. *Perception and Psychophysics*, **60**, 1067–82.

Scudder, C. A., Kaneko, C. R. S. and Fuchs, A. F. (2002). The brainstem burst generator for saccadic eye movements: a modern synthesis. *Experimental Brain Research*, **142**, 439–62.

Segraves, M. A. (1992). Activity of monkey frontal eye field neurons projecting to oculomotor regions of the pons. *Journal of Neurophysiology*, **68**, 1967–85.

Segraves, M. A. and Goldberg, M. E. (1987). Functional properties of corticotecal neurons in the money's frontal eye field. *Journal of Neurophysiology*, **58**, 1387–1419.

Semmlow, J. L., Hung, G. K., Horng, J. L. and Ciuffreda, K. J. (1994). Disparity vergence eye movements exhibit pre-programmed motor control. *Vision Research*, **34**, 1335–43.

Sereno, A. B. and Holzman, P. S. (1993). Express saccades and smooth-pursuit eye movement function. In Schizophrenic, affective-disorder, and normal subjects. *Journal of Cognitive Neuroscience*, **5**, 303–16.

Shallice, T. (1988). *From Neuropsychology to mental structure.* Cambridge University Press, Cambridge.

Sheliga, B. M., Craighero, L., Riggio, L. and Rizzolatti, G. (1997). Effects of spatial attention on directional manual and ocular responses. *Experimental Brain Research* **114**, 339–51.

Sheliga, B. M., Riggio, L., Craighero, L. and Rizzolatti, G. (1995). Spatial attention-determined modifications in saccade trajectories. *Neuroreport*, **6**, 585–88.

Shepherd, M., Findlay, J. M. and Hockey, R. J. (1986). The relationship between eye movements and spatial attention. *Quarterly Journal of Experimental Psychology*, **38A**, 475–91.

Shiori, S. and Ikeda, M. (1989). Useful resolution for picture perception as a function of eccentricity. *Perception*, **18**, 347–61.

Skavenski, A. A. and Hansen, R. M. (1978). Role of eye position information in visual space perception. In *Eye movements and the higher psychological functions* (ed. J. W. Senders, D. F. Fisher and R. A. Monty), pp. 15–34, Lawrence Erlbaum, Hillsdale, NJ.

Slater, A. M., Morison, V. and Rose, D. (1982). Perception of shape by the newborn baby. *British Journal of Developmental Psychology*, **1**, 135–42.

Snodgrass, J. G. and Vanderwart, M. (1980). A standardized set of 260 pictures: norms for name agreement, image agreement, familiarity and visual complexity. *Journal of Experimental Psychology: Human Learning and Memory*, **6**, 174–215.

Snyder, L. H. (2000). Coordinate transformations for eye and arm movements in the brain. *Current Opinion in Neurobiology*, **10**, 747–54.

Sommer, M. A. (1994). Express saccades elicited during visual scan in the monkey. *Vision Research*, **34**, 2023–38.

Sommer, M. A. and Wurtz, R. H. (2002). A pathway in primate brain for internal monitoring of movements. *Science*, **296**, 1480–82.

Stanovich, K. E. (1994). Does dyslexia exist? *Journal of Child Psychology and Psychiatry*, **35**, 579–95.

Stark, L. and Ellis, S. R. (1981). Scanpaths revisited: cognitive models direct active looking. In *Eye movements: cognition and visual perception* (ed. D. F. Fisher, R. A. Monty and J. W. Senders), pp. 193–226, Lawrence Erlbaum Associates, New Jersey.

Starr, M. S. and Rayner, K. (2001). Eye movements during reading: some current controversies. *Trends in Cognitive Sciences*, **5**, 156–63.

Stein, J. F. and Fowler, S. (1982). Ocular motor dyslexia. *Dyslexia Review*, **5**, 25–28.

Stein, J. F. and Walsh, V. (1997). To see but not to read: the magnocellular theory of dyslexia. *Trends in Neurosciences*, **20**, 147–52.

Steinman, R. M., Cunitz, R. J., Timberlake, G. T. and Herman, M. (1967). Voluntary control of microsaccades during maintained monocular fixation. *Science*, **155**, 1577–79.

Steinman, R. M., Cushman, W. B. and Martins, A. J. (1982). The precision of gaze. *Human Neurobiology*, **1**, 97–109.

Stevens, J. K., Emerson, R. C., Gerstein, R. L., Kallos, T., Neufeld, G. R., Nicholls, C. W. and Rosenquist, A. C. (1976). Paralysis of the awake human: visual perceptions. *Vision Research*, **16**, 93–98.

Stuss, D. T. and Knight, R. (2002). *Principles of frontal lobe function.* Oxford University Press, USA.

Styles, E. A. (1997). *The psychology of attention.* Psychology Press, Hove.

Takeda, M. and Findlay, J. M. (1993). Saccadic latency under numerical, verbal and spatial tasks. In *Visual and oculomotor functions: advances in eye movement research* (ed. G. d'Ydewalle and J. Van Rensbergen), pp. 55–60, North-Holland, Amsterdam.

Tam, W. J. and Stelmach, L. B. (1993). Viewing behavior: ocular and attentional disengagement. *Perception and Psychophysics*, **54**, 211–22.

Tarr, M. J. and Bülthoff, H. (1995). Is human object recognition better described by geon structural descriptions or by multiple views? *Journal of Experimental Psychology: Human Perception and Performance*, **21**, 1494–1505.

Tatler, B. W. and Wade, N. J. (2003). On nystagmus, saccades and fixations. *Perception*, **32**, 167–84.

Theeuwes, J. (1993). Visual selective attention—a theoretical-analysis. *Acta Psychologica*, **83**, 93–154.

Theeuwes, J., Kramer, A. F., Hahn, S. and Irwin, D. E. (1998). Our eyes do not always go where we want them to go: capture of the eyes by new objects. *Psychological Science*, **9**, 379–85.

Theeuwes, J., Kramer, A. F., Hahn, S., Irwin, D. E. and Zelinsky, G. J. (1999). Influence of attentional capture on oculomotor control. *Journal of Experimental Psychology: Human Perception and Performance*, **25**, 1595–1608.

Thorpe, S. J., Fize, D. and Marlot, C. (1996). Speed of processing in the human visual system. *Nature*, **381**, 520–2.

Tinker, M. A. (1946). The study of eye movements in reading. *Psychological Bulletin*, **43**, 93–120.

Tinker, M. A. (1958). Recent studies of eye movements in reading. *Psychological Bulletin*, **54**, 215–31.

Tinker, M. A. (1965). *Bases for effective reading.* University of Minnesota Press, Minneapolis.

Toet, A. and Levi, D. M. (1992). Spatial interaction zones in the parafovea. *Vision Research*, **32**, 1349–57.

Tosi, V., Mecacci, L. and Pasquali. E. (1997). Scanning eye movements made when viewing film: preliminary observations. *International Journal of Neuroscience*, **92**, 47–52.

Townsend, J. T. (1971). A note on the identifiability of parallel and serial processes. *Perception and Psychophysics*, **10**, 161–3.

Townsend, J. T. (1972). Some results on the identification of parallel and serial processes. *British Journal of Mathematical and Statistical Psychology*, **25**, 168–99.

Trappenberg, T. P., Dorris, M. C., Munoz, D. P. and Klein, R. M. (2001). A model of saccade initiation based on the competitive integration of exogenous and endogenous signals in the superior colliculus. *Journal of Cognitive Neuroscience*, **13**, 256–71.

Treisman, A. (1988). Features and objects: the 14th Bartlett memorial lecture. *Quarterly Journal of Experimental Psychology*, **40A**, 201–37.

Treisman, A. (1993). The perception of features and objects. In *Attention, selection, awareness and control* (ed. A. Baddeley and L. Weiskrantz), pp. 5–35, Clarendon Press, Oxford.

Treisman, A. (1996). The binding problem. *Current Opinion in Neurobiology*, **6**, 171–78.

Treisman, A. and Gormican, S. (1988). Feature analysis in early vision—evidence from search asymmetries. *Psychological Review*, **95**, 15–48.

Treisman, A. and Souther, J. (1985). Search asymmetry—a diagnostic for preattentive processing of separable features. *Journal of Experimental Psychology: General*, **114**, 285–310.

Treisman, A. M. and Gelade, G. (1980). A feature integration theory of attention. *Cognitive Psychology*, **12**, 97–136.

Umeno, M. M. and Goldberg, M. E. (2001). Spatial processing in the monkey frontal eye field. II. Memory responses. *Journal of Neurophysiology*, **86**, 2344–52.

Umiltà, C., Riggio, L., Dascola, I. and Rizzolatti, G. (1991). Differential effects of central and peripheral cues on the reorienting of spatial attention. *European Journal of Cognitive Psychology*, **3**, 247–67.

Underwood, G. (ed.). (1998). *Eye guidance in reading and scene perception*. North-Holland, Amsterdam.

Underwood, G., Clews, S. and Everatt, J. (1990). How do readers know where to look next? Local information distributions influence eye fixations. *Quarterly Journal of Experimental Psychology*, **42A**, 39–65.

Ungerleider, L. G. and Mishkin, M. (1982). Two cortical visual systems. In *Analysis of visual behavior* (ed. D. Ingle, M. A. Goodale and R. J. W. Mansfield), pp. 549–86, MIT Press, Cambridge, MA.

Van Diepen, P. M. J., Wampers, M. and d'Ydewalle, G. (1998). Functional division of the visual field: moving masks and moving windows. In *Eye guidance in reading and scene perception* (ed. G. Underwood), pp. 337–55, Elsevier, Amsterdam.

Van Gisbergen, J. A. M., Gielen, S., Cox, H., Bruijns, J. and Kleine Schaars, H. (1981). Relation between metrics of saccades and stimulus trajectory in visual target tracking;

implications for models of the saccadic system. In *Progress in Oculomotor Research* (ed. A. F. Fuchs and W. Becker), pp. 17–27, Elsevier, North Holland, Amsterdam.

Van Gisbergen, J. A. M., Van Opstal, A. J. and Roerbroek, J. G. H. (1987). Stimulus induced midflight modification of saccade trajectories. In *Eye movements: from physiology to cognition* (ed. J. K. O'Regan and A. Lévy-Schoen), pp. 27–36, North-Holland, Amsterdam.

Van Gisbergen, J. A. M., Van Opstal, A. J. and Schoenmakers, J. J. M. (1985). Experimental test of two models for the generation of oblique saccades. *Experimental Brain Research*, **57**, 321–36.

Van Gisbergen, J. A. M., Van Opstal, J. J. and Tax, A. A. M. (1987). Collicular ensemble coding of saccades based on vector stimulation. *Neuroscience*, **21**, 541–55.

Vecera, S. P. and Farah, M. J. (1994). Does visual attention select objects or locations? *Journal of Experimental Psychology: General*, **123**, 146–60.

Vergilino, D. and Beauvillain, C. (2000). The planning of refixation saccades in reading. *Vision Research*, **40**, 3527–38.

Virsu, V. and Rovama, J. (1979). Visual resolution, contrast sensitivity, and the cortical magnification factor. *Experimental Brain Research*, **37**, 475–94.

Vitu, F. (1991*a*). The existence of a centre of gravity effect during reading. *Vision Research*, **31**, 1289–1313.

Vitu, F. (1991*b*). Against the existence of a range effect during reading. *Vision Research*, **31**, 2009–15.

Vitu, F. (1991*c*). The influence of parafoveal preprocessing and linguistic context on the optimal landing position effect. *Perception and Psychophysics*, **50**, 58–75.

Vitu, F., McConkie, G. W. and O'Regan, J. K. (2001). Fixation location effects on fixation durations during reading: an inverted optimal viewing position effect. *Vision Research*, **41**, 3513–33.

Vitu, F., McConkie, G. W. and Zola, D. (1998). About regressive saccades in reading and their relation to word identification. In *Eye guidance in reading and scene perception* (ed G. Underwood), pp. 101–24, North-Holland, Amsterdam.

Vitu, F., O'Regan, J. K., Inhoff, A. W. and Topolski, R. B. (1995). Mindless reading: eye-movement characteristics are similar in scanning letter strings and reading texts. *Perception and Psychophysics*, **57**, 352–64.

Vitu, F., O'Regan, J. K. and Mittau, M. (1990). Optimal landing position in reading isolated words and continuous text. *Perception and Psychophysics*, **47**, 583–600.

Viviani, P. (1990). Eye movements in visual search. Cognitive, perceptual and motor control aspects. In *Eye movements and their role in visual and cognitive processes* (ed. E. Kowler), pp. 353–93, Elsevier, Amsterdam.

Viviani, P., Berthoz, A. and Tracey, D. (1977). The curvature of oblique saccades. *Vision Research*, **17**, 661–64.

Viviani P. and Swensson, R. G. (1982). Saccadic eye movements to peripherally discriminated visual targets. *Journal of Experimental Psychology: Human Perception and Performance*, **8**, 113–26.

Von Holst, E. (1954). Relations between the central nervous system and the peripheral organs. *Animal Behaviour*, **2**, 89–94.

Walker, R., Deubel, H., Schneider, W. X. and Findlay, J. M. (1997). The effect of remote distractors on saccade programming: evidence for an extended fixation zone. *Journal of Neurophysiology*, **78**, 1108–19.

Walker, R. and Findlay, J. M. (1996). Saccadic eye movement programming in unilateral neglect. *Neuropsychologia*, **34**, 493–508.

Walker R., Findlay J. M., Young, A. W. and Lincoln, N. B. (1996). Saccadic eye movements in object-based neglect. *Cognitive Neuropsychology*, **13**, 569–615.

Walker, R., Findlay, J. M., Young, A. W. and Welsh, J. (1991). Disentangling neglect and hemianopia. *Neuropsychologia*, **29**, 1019–27.

Walker, R., Husain, M., Hodgson, T. L., Harrison, J. and Kennard, C. (1998). Saccadic eye movement and working memory deficits following damage to human prefrontal cortex. *Neuropsychologia*, **36**, 1141–59.

Walker, R., Kentridge, R. W. and Findlay, J. M. (1995). Independent contributions of the orienting of attention, fixation offset and bilateral stimulation on human saccadic latencies. *Experimental Brain Research*, **103**, 294–310.

Walker, R., Mannan, S., Maurer, D., Pambakian, A. L. M. and Kennard, C. (2000). The oculomotor distractor effect in normal and hemianopic vision. *Proceedings of the Royal Society of London, Series B*, **267**, 431–8.

Walker, R. and Young A. W. (1996). Object-based neglect: an investigation of the contributions of eye-movements and perceptual completion. *Cortex*, **32**, 279–95.

Walker-Smith, G. J., Gale, A. G. and Findlay, J. M. (1977). Eye movement strategies involved in face perception. *Perception*, **6**, 313–26.

Walls, G. (1962). The evolutionary history of eye movements. *Vision Research*, **2**, 69–80.

Wann, J. P. (1996). Anticipating arrival: is the tau margin a specious theory. *Journal of Experimental Psychology, Human Perception and Performance*, **22**, 1031–48.

Wann, J. P. and Land, M. (2000). Steering with or without the flow: is the retrieval of heading necessary? *Trends in Cognitive Sciences*, **4**, 319–24.

Ward, R., Duncan, J. and Shapiro, K. (1996). The slow time-course of visual attention. *Cognitive Psychology*, **30**, 79–109.

Warrington, E. K. and Shallice, T. (1980). Word-form dyslexia. *Brain*, **107**, 829–53.

Weber, H., Aiple, F., Fischer, B. and Latanov, A. (1992). Dead zone for express saccades. *Experimental Brain Research*, **89**, 214–22.

Weiskrantz, L. (1986). *Blindsight: a case study and implications.* Oxford University Press.

Weiskrantz, L. Warrington, E. K., Saunders, M. D. and Marshall, J. (1974). Visual capacity of the hemianopic field following a restricted occipital ablation. *Brain*, **97**, 709–28.

Wenban-Smith, M. G. and Findlay, J. M. (1991). Express saccades: is there a separate population in humans? *Experimental Brain Research*, **87**, 218–22.

Wertheim, T. (1894). Über die indirekte Sehschärfe. *Z Psychol, Physiol, Sinnesorg*, **7**, 121–87.

Wessinger, C. M., Fendrich, R., Gazzaniga, M. S. (1997). Islands of residual vision in hemianopic patients. *Journal of Cognitive Neuroscience*, **9**, 203–21.

Westheimer, G. (1954). Eye movement responses to a horizontally moving stimulus. *Archives of Ophthalmology*, **52**, 932–41.

White, J. M., Sparks, D. L. and Stanford, T. R. (1994). Saccades to remembered target locations: an analysis of systematic and variable errors. *Vision Research*, **34**, 79–92.

White, S. J., and Liversedge, S. P. (2003, in press). Orthographic familiarity influences initial eye fixation positions in reading. *European Journal of Cognitive Psychology*.

Williams, A. M. and Davids, K. (1998). Visual search strategy, selective attention and expertise in soccer. *Research Quarterly for Exercise and Sport*, **69**, 111–28.

Williams, A. M., Davids, K. and Williams, J. G. (1999). *Visual perception and action in sport*. Taylor & Francis, London.

Williams, D. E., Reingold, E. M., Moscovitch, M. and Behrmann, M. (1997). Patterns of eye-movements during parallel and serial visual search tasks. *Canadian Journal of Experimental Psychology—Revue Canadienne de Psychologie Experimentale*, **51**, 151–64.

Williams, L. G. (1966). The effect of target specification on objects fixated during visual search. *Perception and Psychophysics*, **1**, 315–18.

Wilson, H. R., Levi, D., Maffei, L., Rovamo, J. and Devalois, R. (1990). The perception of form: retina to striate cortex. In *visual perception: the neurophysiological foundations* (ed L. Spillman and J. S. Werner), pp. 231–72, Academic Press, San Deigo.

Wolfe, J. M. (1994). Guided search 2.0—a revised model of visual search. *Psychonomic Bulletin and Review*, **1**, 202–38.

Wolfe, J. M. (1998). What can 1 million trials tell us about visual search? *Psychological Science*, **9**, 33–40.

Wolfe, J. M., Cave, K. R. and Franzel, S. L. (1989). Guided search—an alternative to the feature integration model for visual-search. *Journal of Experimental Psychology: Human Perception and Performance*, **15**, 419–33.

Woodworth, R. S. and Schlosberg, H. (1954). *Experimental Psychology*. Methuen, London.

Wright, R. D. (ed.) (1998). *Visual attention*. Oxford University Press, New York.

Wurtz, R. H. (1996). Vision for the control of movement. The Friedenwald Lecture. *Investigative Ophthalmology and Visual Science*, **37**, 2131–45.

Wurtz, R. H. and Goldberg, M. E. (ed.) (1989). *The neurobiology of saccadic eye movements*. Reviews of Oculomotor Research, Volume 3. Elsevier, Amsterdam.

Wurtz, R. H., Goldberg, M. E. and Robinson, D. L. (1982). Brain mechanisms of visual attention. *Scientific American*, **246**(6), 124–35.

Wyatt, H. J. and Pola, J. (1981). Slow eye movements to eccentric targets. *Investigative Ophthalmology and Visual Science*, **21**, 477–83.

Wyman, D. and Steinman, R. M. (1973). Latency characteristics of small saccades. *Vision Research*, **13**, 2173–75.

Xing, J. and Andersen, R. A. (2000). Memory activity of LIP neurons for sequential eye movements simulated with neural networks. *Journal of Neurophysiology*, **84**, 651–65.

Yarbus, A. L. (1967). *Eye movements and vision* (English trans. by L. A. Riggs), Plenum Press, New York.

Zahn, J. R., Abel, L. A. and Dell'Osso, L. F. (1978). The audio-ocular response characteristics. *Sensory Processes*, **2**, 32–7.

Zambarbieri, D., Schmid, R., Magenes, C. and Prablanc, C. (1982). Saccadic responses evoked by presentation of visual and auditory targets. *Experimental Brain Research*, **47**, 417–427.

Zangwill, O. L. and Blakemore, C. (1972). Dyslexia: reversal of eye movements. *Neuropsychologia,* **10**, 371–3.

Zee, D. S., Cook, J. D., Optican, L. M., Ross, D. A. and King Engel, W. (1976). Slow saccades in spinocerebellar degeneration. *Archives of Neurology,* **33**, 243–51.

Zee, D. S., Fitzgibbon, L. J. and Optican, L. M. (1992) Saccade-vergence interaction in humans. *Journal of Neurophysiology,* **68**, 1624–41.

Zeki, S. (1993). *A vision of the brain.* Blackwell, Oxford.

Zeki, S. M. (1976). The functional organization of projections from the striate to pre-striate visual cortex in the rhesus monkey. *Cold Spring Harbor Symposia on Quantitative Biology,* **15**, 591–600.

Zelinsky, G. J. (1996). Using eye saccades to assess the selectivity of search movements. *Vision Research,* **36**, 2177–87.

Zelinsky, G. J. (2001). Eye movements during change detection: implications for search constraints, memory limitations and scanning strategies. *Perception and Psychophysics,* **63**, 209–25.

Zelinsky, G. J., Rao, R. P. N., Hayhoe, M. M. and Ballard, D. H. (1997). Eye movements reveal the spatiotemporal dynamics of visual search. *Psychological Science,* **8**, 448–53.

Zelinsky, G. J. and Sheinberg, D. L. (1997). Eye movements during parallel-serial visual search. *Journal of Experimental Psychology: Human Perception and Performance,* **23**, 244–62.

Zhang, M. and Barash, S. (2000). Neuronal switching of sensorimotor transformations for antisaccades. *Nature,* **408**, 971–75.

Zhou, W. and King, W. M. (1998). Premotor commands encode monocular eye movements. *Nature,* **393**, 692–95.

Zihl, J. (1980). 'Blindsight': improvement of visually guided eye movements by systematic practice in patients with cerebral blindness. *Neuropsychologia,* **18**, 71–7.

Zingale, C. M. and Kowler, E. (1987). Planning sequences of saccades. *Vision Research,* **27**, 1327–41.

Zipser, D. and Andersen, R. A. (1988). A back-propagation programmed network that simulates response patterns of a subset of posterior parietal neurons. *Nature,* **331**, 679–84.

Zuber, B. L., Stark, L. and Cook, G. (1965). Microsaccades and the velocity-amplitude relationship for saccadic eye movements. *Science,* **150**, 1459–60.

INDEX